# CURRENT CONTINENTAL RESEARCH 003

**Stanley Deetz**

# Phenomenology
# In
# Rhetoric and Communication

# 1981

**Center for Advanced Research in Phenomenology
& University Press of America, Washington, D.C.**

University Press of America, Inc.
P.O. Box 19101, Washington, D.C. 20036

ISBN: 0-8191-2087-1 (Case)
0-8191-2088-X (Perfect)

Library of Congress Catalog Card Number: 81-43514

# Phenomenology
# in
# Rhetoric and Communication

**Current Continental Research
is co-published by
The Center For Advanced Research
In Phenomenology
and
University Press of America, Inc.**

### Editorial Board

**For
Each New Generation
of
Scholars**

# CONTENTS

# PREFACE

The papers included in this volume were presented at a Speech Communication Association sponsored Doctoral Honors Seminar held at Southern Illinois University at Carbondale in April, 1979. All are written by individuals pursuing advanced degrees in speech communication. The summary discussions were written by the senior critics for the seminar to reflect a few of the issues discussed. Practical limitations made it impossible to produce here any of the actual seminar discussion.

Several individuals and groups actively contributed to making the seminar both possible and a stimulating, beneficial experience. Only a few can be recognized here. Valuable financial assistance for the seminar came from the Graduate School and the College of Communication and Fine Arts at Southern Illinois University and from a grant by the Research Board of the Speech Communication Association. Len Hawes, Richard Lanigan, Michael McGuire, Joe Pilotta, and Larry Rosenfield all gave generously of their time and energy in serving as senior critics. Professor Lanigan further helped in the selection process and in innumerable other ways.

I wish to add a personal thanks to Gordon Nakagawa for compiling the index, Dennis Mumby for help in preparing the bibliography, and Ed McGlone and Sue Koch for help and support during various phases of the project.

The unspoken debt remains to a tradition which keeps the human conversation going and all those who struggle to speak carefully during their turn.

Stanley Deetz

6 September 1981

# INTRODUCTION / PHENOMENOLOGY AND SPEECH COMMUNICATION

## STANLEY DEETZ
## SOUTHERN ILLINOIS UNIVERSITY

The interest in research approaches grounded in phenomenology has increased in nearly every academic discipline during the last decade. While some of this interest is faddish and excessively negative in its criticism of competing research, much of it comes from a genuine concern with new questions--questions often overlooked in a technological society and by traditional research programs. Many of these questions are unaskable, let alone answerable, using the usual research methods. The papers here, each in their own way, attempt to get at a few of these questions. The breadth of subject matter and applied orientation of many papers attests to the potential these authors see in phenomenologically based work.

To the uninitiated phenomenology remains a mystery and its language a barrier. Even in the papers here the question: "What is phenomenology?" appears frequently and the authors struggle to use and/or avoid using Husserlian, Heideggerian, and so forth language. In most cases the difficult/ awkward language usage comes from the attempt to say something essentially new and to avoid traditional linguistic prejudices rather than from a desire to ossify or dress up common ideas. While several of the papers are as much practice exercises--trying phenomenology out--as original research, most make a clear attempt to de-mystify phenomenology and bring it to bear on questions of interest to speech communication researchers.

The task these authors took on is not an easy one. Modern phenomenology (beginning with Husserl) is not just another new method or school of thought but represents a radical shift in western thought--a shift so fundamental that the assumed relations between man and world and man and man are put into question for re-thinking. A phenomenological stance situates and makes possible a clarification of traditional scientific concepts and methods as well as opens the possibility for new ones. It is this productive power of phenomenology rather than its critique of naive philosophies of science that forms the basis for the papers in this volume.

While this is not the place for another introduction to phenomenology, a few words about this shift in thinking might clarify the unifying interest in the papers. As is well known, Husserlian phenomenology is intended as a science of experience. Conscious experience here is not intended as a psychological phenomenon which takes place in the head but the structured world which comes to meet us as we live, work, and play. Conscious experience serves as the ground for all knowledge and understanding including that of itself. Ultimately all begins and ends in experience. In that sense all that is human in everyday life and even the natural sciences arises out of experience. There can be no point outside of experience and no route to the world or to the person except through the experience of them.

Typically the scientist as well as the everyday actor assumes the "natural attitude" and accepts the objects of experience as they appear as "real" and does not reflect on their constitution in experience. In spite of their claim modern empirical sciences are not based on that which is given as concrete and first hand, i.e., experience, but on implicit theories and assumptions which are directed toward that which is presumed beyond experience.  While this is fine for certain purposes, researchers are often unaware of the construction of that which they define as real.

Phenomenology in its radical departure from this abstract tendency in Western thinking, returns to describe that which is concrete and certain--the experience itself.  Phenomenology is, thus, a kind of radical empiricism.  The obscurity of phenomenological language reflects the difficulty of this return and the extent to which we are accustomed to living through clear abstractions which we have come to accept as real.  The greatest task of phenomenology-- and the reason for its rigorous method--is to get beyond the abstractions, the psychological theories and contingent conditions, and return to the "things themselves."

In phenomenology conscious experience is described as composed of two absolutely correlated "movements:" 1) a non-psychological intending act (noesis, the consciousness of) and 2) object (noema, that which the consciousness is of).  Neither "movement" can stand alone.  It makes little sense to talk of an empty "intention" or an "object" not intended.  The constructed experience stands in back of "subjectivity" and "objectivity"--the focus on the intending act and the focus on the object intended.

The critique of the so-called "objective" sciences is not aimed at their presumed objectivity but their inability/lack of desire to examine their own subjectivity carried in their methods and concepts and to be aware of the social/ political consequences of their peculiar subjective stance.  While different, the phenomenological critique of subjective/naturalistic studies is as strong. In these, the research focus on the personal experiences/feelings/attitudes fails to account for the objective conditions in which they arise as well as the social/historical context in which these personal experiences/feelings/ attitudes are possible.  While both "objective" and "subjective" research productively answer certain types of questions, both are one-sided and become, at times, blind to their limits.  As in many American phenomenological writings, the papers here tend to guard more carefully against objectivism (being forgetful of noesis) than subjectivism (being forgetful of noema).

While all the included papers demonstrate some debt to Husserl's work, most have followed new schools of thought which have rejected Husserl's transcendental phenomenology in favor of various types of "social" phenomenology. Essentially the social orientations place phenomenology itself in the social/ historical world.  They share a view which makes the theories and assumptions which Husserl held as a kind of fog which had to be cut through, put out of play, to get at experience as the very stuff of experience in need of description. In these views "language" (the possibility of expression) replaces consciousness as the structuring, "intentional," movement in experience.

While structuralism, hermeneutics, semiotics, critical theory, and existentialism differ greatly from each other and from Husserlian phenomenology, they share a common legacy.  Key to this is a return to experience as primary data, the conception of experience in non-psychological terms, and the placement of inquiry in the ongoing social/historical situation.

Striking in the seminar discussion, as well as in the papers, is the variety of ways phenomenology itself is treated and the ambivalence expressed toward this common legacy.  Much discussion time was spent trying to reach a common understanding of basic phenomenological works and the significance of the phenomenological change in thinking.  In particular, there was evidence of great reliance on Husserl's work and yet much effort was expended trying to keep the present work distant from his.  Perhaps this is the adolescence of American phenomenological work with the excesses and identity confusion, yet, vigor and daringness associated with it.  I think all participants left with a better understanding of phenomenology and its applications and with a clearer notion of the place of their work in it.

The papers here are, of course, only a shadow of the discussion which took place in the seminar.  Certainly the vitality as well as flaws of the papers were clearer in the discussion context.  As early, preliminary papers they should be seen as part of a continuing dialogue.

This dialogue should continue to focus on the type of questions which dominated the seminar discussion:  What kind of knowledge/understanding is generated by phenomenological research?  What is the status of this knowledge/ understanding and how does it compare to that generated out of more traditional research orientations, particularly in terms of social relevance?  Does phenomenological research compete with other types of research or does it deal with essentially different questions?  Are we able to "think" phenomenologically and ask phenomenological questions or is phenomenology to be one more tool to be placed in the researcher's bag?  Can theory be built from phenomenologically based research?  Is theory necessary or are there other ways to build cumulative knowledge?  Can phenomenological research be replicated?  Is replication the appropriate way to assure that research is productive--that is, not merely a reflection of the researcher's subjectivity?  Is intersubjectivity an answer to subjectivity or does it merely support the type of collective systematic distortion characteristic of many "objective" sciences?  Can traditional research methods and concepts, properly understood, be used in doing phenomenological research or does phenomenology lead to a preference for particular methods?

The lists of questions could continue indefinitely or well into the night as they did at the seminar.  They will be more raised than answered in this volume.  The papers do, however, provide a healthy start toward establishing an appropriate role for phenomenology in the study of human communication.  Reading through the papers and talking to the seminar participants, I sense that the research of the next decade will struggle with more significant social questions than that of the last and that phenomenology will contribute greatly to the sense of this work.

# 1 / TALKING ABOUT FILMS:
## A PHENOMENOLOGICAL STUDY OF FILM SIGNIFICATION

BRYAN CROW
UNIVERSITY OF IOWA

Film viewing is a common experience in our society. Talking about films we have seen is also a common occurrence. By talking with others about a film, we often solidify and clarify our own reactions to the film. Depending on the extent of the shared reactions, much of the meaning of a film may be constructed through this kind of intersubjective process, which allows for the testing and refinement of each individual's original perceptions.

As anyone who often discusses films knows, people who have seen the same film sometimes have not "seen" the same film at all. That is, the meaning of a film or of any part of it is a function of the perceiver. Two people may share the same perceptual experience of watching a film, but their significations, or attributions of meaning to that experience, may be quite divergent. A striking example of this phenomenon is evident in a comparison of the following two student reactions to the film Face to Face:

a. Although Bergman probably offers the most critically in-depth journey into a woman's mind in Face to Face, he explicitly projects the psychological effects of a fatherless--or father-repressed--childhood on a woman. This exploration into the female psychiatrist's repressed feelings had a probing influence on me as I had experienced almost the same kind of fatherless childhood and have found myself reacting towards men in a defensive manner which relates directly to my relationship (or non-relationship) with my father. Watching Liv Ullmann release her repression was an explosive means for me to understand some of my attitudes.

b. Somewhere I think I missed something here. This was probably the strangest movie I have ever seen. For years I have heard people and critics rave about Ingmar Bergman's films and Liv Ullmann. If this is any example of what they are like, I pass on seeing any more in the future. About the only thing impressive was the independence portrayed by Ullmann. But, somehow I think even that was supposed to be a farce. Possibly it was too deep for me to understand but I felt I'd wasted two and a half hours.

The two statements obviously reflect different backgrounds and sets of assumptions, but the differences are more than just matters of taste. The perceptions of the film's meaning indicated by the two statements are entirely different. But even with such polarized reactions, it is not unreasonable to assume that, in a discussion, these two students could reach a consensus on at least some of the film's intended meanings, and that their interaction might uncover some meanings which neither of them had recognized before.

Phenomenology in Rhetoric and Communication, ed. Stanley Deetz. Copyright, 1981, The Center for Advanced Research in Phenomenology and the University Press of America.

The treatment of film as a medium of <u>communication</u>--one that does not mean until an audience interacts with it--raises some important questions about the very way in which filmic meaning is possible: How do people <u>do</u> film viewing? In other words, how do we experience a film in order to know something of its meanings, and how is it that we are able to express our own experience of a film to others in order to reach some consensus on meanings? Film theorists and researchers have traditionally addressed the problem of filmic meaning by studying the film or the perceptual apparatus rather than the intersubjective contribution to signification. Since we normally perceive a film as part of an audience and may subsequently extend our experience of a film through interaction with other people, a theory of signification in cinema should take as its starting point the audience's experience of a film rather than the individual's internal perceptions or the film itself.

This study is an initial attempt to explain an experience that we usually take for granted. We have somehow come to know how to make sense out of films, with varying degrees of sophistication, even without having been taught how to do so. But we seldom reflect on the process by which we come to know the meaning of a film. A phenomenological analysis is an appropriate approach to this problem because phenomenology "brackets" the naive experience of a phenomenon, in order to reveal the essential structure of the experience. Filmic meaning, we may assume, is constructed partly during the film-viewing experience, partly before and after the film in the individual's own reflection and reading, and partly in talking with other people about the film. Of these three settings for signification, the first two are only indirectly available to empirical observation, through individual self-reports or physical manifestations. But the third setting is directly available to phenomenological study, because meanings are being constructed in that intersubjective process.

Film-viewing is done in the natural attitude. In watching a film, we often become so caught up in its "reality" that it becomes in some respects indistinguishable from our experience of the everyday life-world. Talking about a film is a bracketing of and a reflection upon the naive experience of the film. A phenomenological bracketing of such talk can provide some understanding of an important way in which films mean.

Empirical research related to film has been conducted ever since the medium started to develop a distinct form. Early filmmakers and film theorists experimented with variables like the effects of editing on perception of meaning, in trying to determine the basic building blocks of the medium. This early research remains among the most significant about the nature of film and film-viewing. However, much of contemporary film theory has neither been based on nor tested by empirical research. And a survey of empirical investigations of film will show that these studies are more concerned with how films work on people than with how people work to understand and appreciate films. Many of the major concerns of film theory--such as the relationships between the structure of film and the structure of consciousness, the similarities and differences between film and other media, and the linguistic nature of film--have not been adequately investigated by actual empirical study of people <u>doing</u> film-viewing and film-discussing. Phenomenological analysis may be a way of bridging this gap between film theory and film research.

There are some serious shortcomings in much of the existing body of film research, if this research is to have any relevance in explaining film signification as it occurs in everyday life. Aside from some fascinating anthropological field studies of the uses of film,[1] most film research has consisted of laboratory experiments in which hypotheses were tested by manipulating such variables as length and sequencing of shots,[2] close-up vs. long shot,[3] type of cutting,[4] and interaction of audio and visual elements.[5] While such studies may be fruitful for explaining the perceptual processes of film viewing, the generalization of their findings to film signification as a complex whole experience is limited, because these studies (1) set up laboratory film-viewing conditions that are quite unlike the way people normally see films, (2) often fragment and disrupt the film or the viewing experience, (3) use films or short film stimuli which are not like the films we usually go to see, (4) place little value on self-report data, and (5) rely instead on measurement of behavioral responses.

To explicate the problem of film signification, a more appropriate method would (1) start by studying people doing film-viewing, filmmaking, or film-discussing in everyday situations, (2) avoid manipulating the film-viewing experience, (3) allow viewers to speak for themselves instead of inferring from their behavior what effects a film had on them, (4) take into account the context of the whole film-signification process instead of observing discrete behavioral phenomena in isolation, (5) develop a useful unit for analysis of how and what films communicate, and (6) look for effects across a number of film-viewing experiences as well as effects of a single experience. A phenomenological method is most compatible with these imperatives.

The present study is more concerned with people _talking_ about their experiences of films than with the films per se. While other research methods may be valid for studying other aspects of film signification, phenomenology is particularly suited for studying the intersubjective element of film signification. The basis for using the tenets of Husserlian phenomenology as a set of social scientific methodological assumptions comes from Schutz,[6] whose phenomenology of the social world is concerned with the way in which meaning is made possible in and through social interaction. Schutz argues that the data of sociology are the already constituted meanings of active participants in the social world. He defines meaning as "a certain way of directing one's gaze at an item of one's own experience."[7] Meaning is not something attached to experience, but is caught up in the very act of experiencing. We become consciously aware of meaning only through phenomenological reflection on an already lived experience. If that experience is a perceptual set available to a number of people, their intersubjective reflection on and consensual constitution of meaning from the shared experience is directly available for phenomenological analysis. Thus, in studying how film signification works, it is

[1] Sol Worth and John Adair, _Through Navajo Eyes: An Exploration In Film Communication and Anthropology_ (Bloomington: Indiana Univ. Press, 1972); Richard Chalfen and Jay Haley, "Reactions to Socio-Documentary Film Research in a Mental Health Clinic," _American Journal of Orthopsychiatry_, 41 (Jan. 1971), 91-100.

[2] Herman D. Goldberg, "The Role of 'Cutting' in the Perception of the Motion Picture," _Journal o Applied Psychology_, 35 (1951), 70-71; Roger Penn, "An Experimental Study of the Meaning of Cutting-Rate Variables in Motion Pictures," _Dissertation Abstracts_, 28 (1967), 788A (Iowa); Sol Worth, "Cognitive Aspects of Sequence in Visual Communication," _AV Communication Review_, 16 (1968), 121-45; Dennis F. Lynch, "Clozentropy: A New Technique for Analyzing Audience Response to Film," _Speech Monographs_, 41 (1974), 245-52; John Preston Isenhour, "The Effects of Context and Order in Film Editing," _AV Communication Review_, 23 (Spring 1975), 69-80.

[3] Robert C. Williams, "Film Shots and Expressed Interest Levels," _Speech Monographs_, 35 (1968), 166-69.

[4] J. M. Carroll and T. G. Bever, "Segmentation in Cinema Perception," _Science_, 191 (12 March 1976), 1053-55.

[5] Harold E. Nelson, "The Relative Contribution to Learning of Video and Audio Elements in Films," _Speech Monographs_, 19 (1951), 70-73.

[6] Alfred Schutz, _The Phenomenology of the Social World_, (1932), trans. George Walsh and Frederick Lehnert (Evanston, ILL.: Northwestern Univ. Press, 1967).

[7] Schutz, p. 42.

appropriate to look at the construction of meaning through conversation as a way of getting at the internal process of signification that is going on when an individual watches and thinks about a film. Along with film analysis itself, then, conversation analysis might lead us to a better understanding of how films mean.

## METHOD

Among social scientists, phenomenology is variously regarded as either a valid method for doing empirical research or as a poor substitute for rigorous empirical research. It has been associated with "humanistic" or "naturalistic" perspectives, both to its advantage and to its discredit. The term is too often used loosely to label any kind of vague, intuitive, non-experimental work. While some of what passes for phenomenological research may indeed have little scientific value, there are certain radical assumptions that set phenomenology apart from other methods and that can be applied both rigorously and productively. The questions that can be addressed by phenomenology may not be open to meaningful investigation by other methods. Even though a phenomenological method is far from being universally accepted, it is important that we try to clarify the method by doing research that intentionally follows the epistemological assumptions of a phenomenological philosophy of science, which entails a research method that must be developed in a manner appropriate to the empirical phenomena as they are experienced in the natural attitude.

Giorgi[8] offers a useful contrast between what may be roughly called logical positivistic and phenomenological assumptions: (1) Positive science assumes that measuring a phenomenon is a meaningful way to study it. Phenomenology assumes that measuring a phenomenon is not the same thing as determining its meaning. (2) Positive science typically assumes a passive subject who responds to stimuli, while phenomenology recognizes that a person's behavior reflects intentionality. (3) Where positive science seeks universal repeatability of a phenomenon under identical conditions, phenomenology tries to elucidate essential themes of a particular phenomenon (Husserl's "essences"), which may be known through their varied manifestations. With intentional subjects, phenomenologists would argue, an identical environment in no way implies identical replication of the phenomenon. (4) Finally, positive science assumes that the observed object is independent of the observer, while phenomenology holds that the observer cannot help but influence the phenomenon being observed. An appropriate role for the phenomenologist to play, then, is that of participant observer.

Participant observation is a way of coming to understand and explain a social phenomenon through a discursive process in which the researcher is constitutively involved with the phenomenon. Where positivistic researchers adopt a standpoint outside the lived experience of the subjects, a participant observer assumes the standpoint of the subjects and tries to account for their meanings by participating in the intersubjective construction of those meanings. The researcher's relationship with the subjects is a non-manipulative one, though it is not an invisible one. Part of the participant observer's responsibility is to account for his/her own influence on the phenomenon being studied. Perhaps the best that participant observation can offer is a close approximation of what the meaning of an experience is for people when that experience is not being observed and shaped by a recognizable observer. But the

[8]Amedeo Giorgi, "Phenomenology and Experimental Psychology: II," Review of Existential Psychology and Psychiatry, 6 (1966); rpt. in Duquesne Studies in Phenomenological Psychology: Vol. 1 ed. Amedeo Giorgi, William F. Fischer, and Rolf Von Eckartsberg (Pittsburgh: Duquesne Univ. Press, 1971), pp. 17-29.

advantage of this method is that theoretical categories are derived from the phenomenon as experienced in the natural attitude, instead of being applied to the phenomenon from the outside.

In studying the process of film signification, I am interested in the meanings which emerge in people's experience of a film, and, more specifically, with the _ways_ in which meanings emerge. The underlying question is, "What is the experience of film?" The setting I chose to explore this problem was a film discussion group, of which I was a member. Analysis of the group's discussions and of additional self-report data is in effect a second-level reduction operation, which looks for essential structures of the film signification process as it occurred in our reflection on common film experiences.

The group consisted of seven volunteers from a larger evening school class who were studying images of women in film with me as facilitator. There were six women and one man in the group, ranging in age from 21 to 51. The group met four times outside of class to see and discuss new films which were being shown at local theaters. The members expressed an intense interest in film and a desire to broaden their film-viewing abilities. In this respect, the discussions that were taped and transcribed are rather idealized versions of everyday film talk in that our group had a specific short-term task and avoided extraneous topics. We were particularly concerned with finding meanings in the films. But the talk itself is otherwise as valid to study as any other kind of talk about films, and this group is a fairly accurate approximation of any group of friends who would see a film and then go somewhere to talk about it.

Each person in the group and in the class, including myself, kept a personal film journal with reactions to some fifteen films we saw for the course. Group members also wrote detailed responses to the four films we discussed. A final essay exam and paper were required for the course. The tape transcripts, journals, exams, and papers constituted the material data to be analyzed. The discussion group was the primary source of significative data, but the self-report material collected from all class members was also analyzed to give the findings more thoroughness.

The procedure for analyzing this material was developed from my experience of making sense out of what people were saying about films. It was necessary to organize the data in such a way that the fundamental structures, or essences, of the film signification process might be revealed. Two of the major problems a researcher must resolve in order to analyze group interactions are unitization and categorization of the data. Choice of a unit of analysis will determine how one breaks up or punctuates the material to be categorized. Traditionally, studies of group communication have used either arbitrary time-units, or "natural" units like the act, the interact, the statement, the utterance, or the group phase.[9] While these units are useful for indicating group processes, they have limited value for the analysis of the process of intersubjective signification. What is needed is a unit flexible enough to represent signification ranging from a single sentence to an entire discussion.

The unit of phenomenological analysis developed for this study is called the _signification act_. It is defined as a discrete unit of discourse which is used to make sense out of a particular phenomenon. In an intersubjective set-

[9]Leonard C. Hawes, "The Effects of Interviewer Style on Patterns of Dyadic Communication," _Speech Monographs_, 39 (1972), 114-23; Robert F. Bales, _Interaction Process Analysis_ (Cambridge: Addison-Wesley, 1950); Leonard Hawes, "Elements of a Model for Communication Processes," _Quarterly Journal of Speech_, 59 (1973), 11-21; Dennis S. Gouran, "Variables Related to Consensus in Group Discussions of Questions of Policy," _Speech Monographs_, 36 (1969), 387-91; Ernest L. Stech, "An Analysis of Interaction Structure in the Discussion of a Ranking Task," _Speech Monographs_, 37 (1970) 249-56; B. Aubrey Fisher, "Decision Emergence: Phases in Group Decision-Making," _Speech Monographs_, 37 (1970), 53-66.

ting, a signification act consists of the expression and testing of validity claims about a phenomenon in an effort to arrive at some consensus about its meaning. The phenomenon may be anything from the meaning of a camera angle used in a particular shot to the meaning of an entire film or a set of films. Claims about such phenomena may be tested through discursive validation. Whenever we make sense out of such claims, together or as individuals, we are engaged in a process of signification. The signification act thus becomes an element of the larger set called speech acts, which includes all pragmatic uses of verbal signifying systems. By extension, an interaction that is characterized by related signification acts may best be described as a signification episode, analogous to the speech episode. All speech episodes may contain significative processes to some extent, but the present study is concerned only with those episodes which are defined specifically by the participants as signification episodes.

The purpose of my analysis was to try to punctuate the transcripts and self-reports into fairly discrete signification units in a way that the participants would find consistent with their experience of the process. It would be of little value to try to categorize everything that was said about the films, because not everything was identifiable as a relevant part of a signification act. Only those acts which seemed to contribute significantly to an understanding of the film were selected for analysis.

The major problem of the analysis was to find a set of categories that would be appropriate to the data by virtue of having been derived from the data. Phenomenology does not provide a standard set of categories as such, only the method for choosing categories. For the study of signification, however, semiotics offers an appropriate categorization system in terms of the signifier/signified distinction.[10] Signifiers are the sign-systems which carry the meaning. The signified is that meaning which is carried by the signifier. A signification act requires both a signifier and a signified. For example, in a suspense film, a sequence of shots of a man looking around a deserted street at night, accompanied by slow, suspenseful music, may produce in me a tense premonition of danger. The sequence of shots, the action contained in them, and the music are all signifiers of meaning which, in this case, signified danger. If, in a discussion after the film, I compared this sequence with three other sequences, all of which, I now realize, directly preceded important character transformations, I would be making sense out of these sequences through a signification act which associated three signifiers with a common signified.

While a set of filmic signifiers, signifieds, and signification acts could have been postulated a priori, they would not necessarily have been those most appropriate for analyzing the particular data at hand. This is where the phenomenological imperative becomes essential. Categories which actually emerged in our processes of making sense out of films are the ones to be used in the analysis. These categories were made explicit through the following phenomenological procedure, which is described here in some detail as an example of how one might go about doing phenomenological research. A similar procedure is outlined most succinctly by Colaizzi.[11]

(1) I read through the discussion transcripts a number of times while listening to the tapes to become familiar with the meanings that were constructed.

---

[10]Ferdinand De Saussure, *Course in General Linguistics* (1916), ed. Charles Vally and Albert Sechehaye, trans. Wade Baskin (New York: Philosophical Library, 1959); sections rpt. in *The Structuralists: From Marx to Levi-Strauss*, ed. Richard T. De George and Fernande M. De George (Garden City, N.Y.: Anchor-Doubleday, 1972), pp. 59-79.

[11]Paul F. Colaizzi, "Psychological Research as the Phenomenologist Views It," in *Existential-Phenomenological Alternatives for Psychology*, ed. Ronald S. Valle and Mark King (New York: Oxford Univ. Press, 1978), pp. 48-71.

Statements and interactions which were significant in contributing to the understanding of a film were labelled in the margins according to the type of statement being made or the type of content being discussed. For instance, statements
often took the form of reconstruction of scenes, interpretation of scenes, and
expressions of like or dislike. Among the contents discussed were character
development, moods, and symbols. Analysis of the discussions also revealed such
group processes as steering, asking for and providing information, expressing
confusion or agreement, and providing humor, but these were not labelled for
use in this study because they were not signification acts in themselves. Using
the signification act as a unit of analysis makes the elements of the interaction
process itself irrelevant. This is a different level of analysis from that
which records who says what to whom. It does not matter whether a particular
signification act occurs in one person's statement or among several people.
The act itself can be an intersubjective phenomenon.

(2) I grouped these types of statements and contents into clusters, and
listed every occurrence of each cluster type in the transcripts, with references
to page numbers. This punctuation of the discussions into acts with recognizable beginnings and ends is admittedly somewhat arbitrary, since one act may
overlap or be embedded in another act. To say that an act begins and ends in
certain places is merely a way of lifting it out of the ongoing process of the
discussion to make some sense of how the discussion worked.

(3) Leaving these clusters in rough form, I read the written self-report
data and marked every signification act which exemplified or described a way
of understanding a film. Each act was typed on a separate card along with its
source.

(4) Re-reading the acts recorded on cards, I sorted them into clusters
according to types of statements or types of contents discussed.

(5) I compared the clusters from the tape transcripts with the clusters
from the self-report data, reducing redundancy and eliminating minor clusters,
in order to obtain one set of clusters which represented the typical ways in
which these people made sense out of these films.

(6) Relationships between types of statements and types of contents of
statements were reduced to one-sentence propositions which were written on the
cards or in the margins of the transcripts. These propositions described the
meaning that was given with the signification act but was not stated as such in
it, so that the propositions go beyond the data while remaining true to them.
For example, a common type of content of critical statements was the lack of
realism of a particular character. The resultant proposition would be, "The
realism of a character is criticized," which describes the signification act
being performed by a statement or a series of statements.

(7) Each type of proposition (statement type plus content type) was categorized under that which was being signified (realism, motives, etc.). A card
for each category of signified meaning was filled out with a list of every propositional relationship between that particular signified and any number of signifiers of that meaning, along with the type of act by which signified and
signifier were related (mode of signification).

(8) I re-read each act in the clusters taken from the data to check its
appropriateness for the category of that which was being signified in the proposition used to describe that act. Redundant categories of signifieds and redundant propositions within categories were reduced until the categories became
distinct.

The result of this phenomenological procedure was a propositional model of the film signification process (Figure 1), a description of some of the kinds of signification acts which people may use in making sense out of films. Even though the model is a very general, abstract conceptualization of the signifying process, it remains true to the essential operation of that process and may be a useful first step toward a theory of film signification. As the model is read from left to right, a proposition is constructed which describes a particular signification act. Any number of variations are possible by simply changing one term of the proposition, though not all variations would be meaningful.

Signifiers have been divided into two classes, roughly along the lines of Metz's[12] distinction between film-specific codes and cultural or non-film-specific codes. Film-specific signifiers convey meaning in uniquely filmic ways, while non-film-specific signifiers are common to many media as cultural signifying systems. "Mode of signification" is the type of act which relates signified and signifier for some purpose. Since some acts are actually reports of acts that occurred while watching the film or even before the film in anticipation of what it might be about, it seems useful to include a column called "locus of signification" to identify when the act occurred. This analysis is mainly concerned with those acts which occurred intersubjectively after the film, but these are sometimes extensions of acts that were initiated individually during the film. When two or more films are referred to in a signification act, the locus of signification is said to be "interfilmic."

It is possible to describe the result of some signification acts in terms of a positive or negative attitude toward the film, a deeper appreciation of the film, a recognition of more than one level of meaning, and so on. These results are included in the model as part of the signification act, because the end result of one act may in fact be the beginning of another act. Thus, the arrow shows the possibility of one proposition leading directly to another. Each signification act is situated in some larger context of signification; therefore, a process model rather than a linear model is useful for indicating some of the complexity involved.

## ANALYSIS

The model of the film signification process is not an end result in itself but is a means of analyzing the data. The analysis is a way of testing and refining the model by turning it back to the data from which it was derived. It is appropriate in a phenomenological study to let the participants speak for themselves. The researcher should provide an organizational framework to clarify the structure of what was said. The following examples, then, are included to show that the propositional model can account, in a simple yet useful way, for a basic structure underlying talk about film, a structure by which we are able to arrive at meanings in the experience of films. The model certainly does not account for everything that goes on in people's film experiences, but it does show how we might begin to identify the essences of those experiences. These examples are only a sample of the propositions generated by this data, but they represent some of the more interesting signification acts. All names are fictional except my own.

1. (A) The structure of a section is anticipated during the film, leading to confusion. (B) The purpose of a film is clarified after the film, leading to consensus. (C) The realism of a scene is identified with during the film, leading to appreciation. (Here, the result of one signification act leads di-

[12]Christian Metz, *Film Language: A Semiotics of the Cinema*, trans. Michael Taylor (New York: Oxford Univ. Press, 1974).

rectly into another act. A third act, distinctly separate from the preceding ones, follows immediately.) Discussion, Lumière:

Shirley: (A) This first scene, though, took place in the south of France, at Sarah's country estate, did it not?
Bryan: Yeah.
Shirley: And then they referred to it later in the film, throughout it, but somehow, like Joan, it was very hard for me to go back and remember what they said in the first scene to remember how everything turned out.
Bryan: Yeah, I was expecting her to return to the country estate at the end and tie everything up and put it in a framework.
Joan: Mm hm.
Shirley: And yet it didn't do that at all.
Joan: As a viewer, I would have liked that.
Laura: (B) She really didn't need to, I don't think. I think, you know, it's a movie made for you to think about it later and sort of put it back together, in a way.
Joan: Mm hm. Well, she forces you to do that, there's no doubt. (C) From my own personal experience, what I know about, she portrayed extremely well. There was the one woman who's the mother of four children and pregnant, Laura. She talks about what she's going to do while Sarah and Thomas have supper together. She says, "I'm going to a cafe and have a cup of coffee and that's freedom?" That is such freedom to go to some place where you can watch life go by and not be bothered and sit by yourself--that was such a real and very touching scene to me, that one line, that was absolutely true to life.

2. The realism of a character type is evaluated after the film, leading to consensus. Discussion, Three Women:

Bryan: In the first part, for the longest time, you really laugh at just about everything Millie says. She really makes a fool of herself with everything, all the recipes.
Joan: Mm hm.
Bryan: But on the other hand, maybe he's making a comment that this is how he sees a lot of modern women, having a file of 20-minute recipes, 15-minute recipes . . .
Laura: That's what you're supposed to do, according to Good Housekeeping or whatever.
Anita: Let me tell you, at the office that I work in, that's a major part of the conversation, recipes.
Laura: Or telling each other how to . . .
Anita: Yeah.
Laura: All the girls in my office tell each other how to do this or how to dress or how to do everything. Nobody's supposed to be able to think for themself.

3. The repetition of an action is perceived interfilmically, leading to an impression. (The signification act here is one which occurred across films; it might have had a different meaning if only one of the films had been seen.) Paper, Face to Face, The Marquise of O:

In Face to Face young Jennie pounds on a closed door in a dream sequence begging her parents to come back. The same kind of passionate appeal is made by Julietta through a locked door in The Marquise of O. These two scenes of daughters imploring their parents for understanding and continuing communication are the most vivid of the nine weeks viewing and are indelibly imprinted in my mind.

4. The motive of an action is clarified after the film, leading to understanding. (One person's tentative interpretation of an act in the film is
strengthened here by being tested against others' perceptions.) Discussion,
Lumière:

Shirley: But I wondered if he didn't kill himself because of her. I'm
not--because when she told him that she had found this man that
she wanted to begin a whole new relationship with, and he says,
"Which man," and somehow I had the feeling that he kind of hoped
it was he, I'm not sure.

Anita: I felt the same thing.

Shirley: Did you? And then when it became obvious that it was someone
else, I think he was just--and he had no family and you know this
doctor had told him that there would be times he would want
someone to talk to. And I think he felt that if she was going
to begin a new life, that maybe she was the only one he could talk
to and there wouldn't be anyone for him.

Bryan: That's a good point. It crossed my mind that maybe he was hoping
she would pick him, but I didn't quite understand why he would
kill himself at that point except for the fact that he had a ter-
minal illness. But yeah, that makes sense because the doctor told
him he should be with people. She talked about going to the country estate and wanted him to come.

Shirley: Right, and I think she was the only one he could because all his
other friends seemed to have families and I think he would have
felt like an outsider with anyone else but her.

## DISCUSSION

The propositional model of the film signification process is one way of
conceptualizing how we make sense out of films. It posits the existence of
the signification act as the basic unit of this process. The categories of
each part of the signification act may be viewed as phenomenological essences
of these particular signification experiences, and the propositions may be considered representations of the underlying structure of the signification process. When we attempt to make sense out of a film, what we do is try to
construct coherent signification acts, which take the form of any combination
of propositional elements. The categories listed in this model are very general,
but a more detailed system of categories could be developed by close analysis
of a wider range of data.

The analysis of the data collected for this study, represented by a few
examples above, suggests that the signification process might work in the following way: I view a film, primarily in the natural attitude, as a perceptual
flux of visual and sound images. Perceptions are not yet significations, but
are better described as pre-significations. They are intuitively (that is,
consciously but not reflexively) registered and organized in the forefront of
my consciousness all during the film. At various points during the film, I may
step back from the ongoing perceptual flux to reflect on a set of perceptions
and assign them a tentative meaning, to be tested on subsequent perceptions of
related signs. However, much if not most of the film remains on a perceptual
level.

After the film, I may call certain salient or problematic perceptions into
conscious      reflection in trying to construct what the film means to me. In
doing so, I am engaging in signification acts, either in my own thinking or
writing, or in the discursive testing of my perceptions with those of other
people. When we share our experiences of a film--when different people bring

ut different sets of salient perceptions--a complex signification act is con-
tituted intersubjectively which may transcend the sum of our individual per-
:eptions. It may result in insight and understanding where before there was
one. The perceptions that you talk about may have been temporarily stored in
:he forefront of my consciousness, my intuitive perceptual field, until you
:aused me to bring them into direct consciousness and reflect on them. In the
;ame manner, I may talk about perceptions which you can recall but which had
ot become salient to you until I mentioned them. Together, we can construct
a meaning of the film by testing and clarifying validity claims about our per-
:eptions. We can reach some consensus on what was objectively given to percep-
:ion, and we may even come to recognize the valid co-existence of multiple
evels of signification in a given perceptual event or field.

Signification acts that had been initiated individually during the film
nay be completed after the film by confirmation in others' experiences. My
intuitive experience of the filmic perceptual flux becomes increasingly reduced
:o a finite number of signification acts the more we talk about a film, until I
feel that (1) I have understood the film to my satisfaction, (2) I have not
nderstood it at all and simply give up on it, or (3) I have understood or helped
:o clarify your experience of the film.

What this analysis indicates about the experience of film, as compared with
the experience of unmediated reality, is that the tightly organized perceptual
event that constitutes a film, and that is shared simultaneously by a number of
people, can be a powerful stimulus for growth in people's ability to constitute
meanings from pre-reflective perceptions. Part of the experience of the people
involved in this study was the recognition that they were becoming better film
viewers, particularly as a result of having a chance to discuss the films in
detail. In a sense, they were developing what may be called significative
competence, a skill comparable to communicative competence. In terms of the
model, they were becoming more effective in constructing coherent signification
acts. A discussion facilitator who is trained in the use of the propositional
model may be able to recognize truncated acts and help people form more coherent
acts when they talk about their experiences of films. The acquisition of significative competence, it would seem, is closely connected to the development
of communicative competence. The more we can talk meaningfully about our experience of a film, the richer our experience may be. Experiencing insight
into a film can at the same time be a source of insight into oneself and others.

The generalizability and validity of phenomenological findings are problems
that are far from being resolved. This study certainly has its limitations.
Its purpose is not to predict that all discussions of films operate in this way.
In fact, the range of films used in this study is fairly narrow--they were generally high quality, artistic films with complex women's roles, since that was
the focus of the class. While the participants included some regular working
members of the community, they were all people who elected to take an evening
school course. Most importantly, these findings depended on the availability
of rather lengthy statements and interactions about the films.

At the same time, such limitations are not necessarily weaknesses. Phenomenological research is more concerned with particular meanings in particular
situations than with universals. However, as Schwartz and Merten[13] emphasize,
even though the procedure for phenomenological analysis is grounded in the experience of a particular group, it transcends the experience of that group while
remaining faithful to them. The process by which the model of film signification
emerged in this study may be applied to other groups as well. What is generalizable about this study is the method of analyzing the data, the process of
discovery that I went through, not necessarily the findings.

[13]Gary Schwartz and Don Merten, "Participant Observation and the Discovery of Meaning," Philosophy of the Social Sciences, 1 (1971), 279-98.

The validity of these findings might be tested by the following modifications of questions raised by Psathas[14]: (1) Would the people involved in the study accept my findings as consistent with their own experience, once they reflected on it in a similar fashion? (2) Would this description of the film signification phenomenon allow others who had not been involved in this particular situation to recognize the phenomenon in their own experience? (3) Can the propositional model be used by others as a set of "rules" for performing the same activities? While these questions are as yet unanswered, they do indicate that validation of phenomenological findings is not an impossible or irrelevant task. An extension of this study might involve training coders in this category system to test the reliability of the propositions I constructed in analyzing the data. A further extension would be to apply this procedure for generating categories to other film-discussion situations or even to signification processes other than those related to film--such as discussions of plays, television news, football games, and family problems. The discovery of film signification processes even vastly different from those described here would not necessarily invalidate these findings, as long as these findings met the criteria stated above. As Schwartz and Merten[15] argue, the participant observer "imposes theoretical constructs on a reality which always can sustain more than one viable interpretation of the significance of social action." Continued phenomenological research in many areas of communication, perhaps augmented by specific experimental studies, can lead us to a better theoretical explanation of meaning in human experience.

| Signified | Signifier | Mode of Signification | Locus of Signification | | Result |
|---|---|---|---|---|---|
| The theme of effect purpose values structure technique realism symbolism repetition events roles motive transformation alternatives ambiguity | Film-specific is films a film a section a sequence a shot a technique  Non-film-specific music sound effects dialogue an action an event a motif a dichotomy a symbol a character/type/ role a relationship a myth | anticipated inferred perceived described summarized reconstructed clarified analyzed interpreted reinterpreted evaluated criticized identified with compared questioned reworked rejected | before the film during the film after the film inter- filmically | leading to | insight consensus understanding appreciation an impression a positive attitude a negative attitude confusion interpretation clarification expectations recognition of multiple inter- pretations |

FIGURE 1

A PROPOSITIONAL MODEL OF THE
FILM SIGNIFICATION PROCESS

[14]George Psathas, ed., _Phenomenological Sociology: Issues and Applications_ (New York: Wiley, 1973).

[15]Schwartz and Merten, p. 295.

# 2 / LANGUAGE ACQUISITION AND THE PHENOMENOLOGICAL APPROACH: A VIABLE COMBINATION

ROBIN JOHNSTON
UNIVERSITY OF ILLINOIS

Rarely does one observe the integration and application of the phenomenological method to developmental issues (e.g., language acquistion). The following essay is therefore of a speculative nature with possible implications for future empirical work. One philosopher who both dealt with the topic of language acquisition and advocated the phenomenological approach was Merleau-Ponty. The focus of this paper will be twofold: first, Merleau-Ponty's theory will be explicated and briefly contrasted with that of Roman Jakobson; second, suggestions will be made concerning the applicability of Merleau-Ponty's ideas and methodology for looking at the development of a child's speech. It must be noted at the outset that the orientation of this paper is neither empirical nor an attempt at philosophical exegesis. Rather, it is an initial attempt to integrate two areas that are infrequently combined. It is possible to explain the fruitfulness of such a combination by noting an implicit bias in the early language acquisition research. Specifically, many theorists assume a direct continuity between a child's early speech and later use of conventional language forms. The tendency is "to assume conventionality rather than viewing it as a problem to be accounted for."[1] Merleau-Ponty's method and theory offer an alternative framework from which to both describe and account for the problematicity surrounding a child's movement into conventional speech. As a backdrop to the focus of this paper a few preliminary comments about Merleau-Ponty's theory of intersubjectivity are necessary.

Merleau-Ponty's conception of the development of intersubjectivity assumes "that psychogenesis begins in a state where the child is unaware of himself and the other as different beings."[2] The development of self is postulated as a two phase process: first, in what is labeled a "pre-communication" phase, the child perceives himself as part of "an anonymous collectivity, an undifferentiated group life"[3]; second, on the basis of this original community "both by the objectification of one's own body and the construction of the other in his difference there occurs a segregation, a distinction of individuals."[4] Merleau-Ponty suggests that an undifferentiated system establishes itself within the child. The elements in this system are the child's visual body (the other's body as seen by the child), his introceptive body (the image of one's own body by means of touch), and the other. This initially diffuse, unordered set of relations allows for the "global identification of the child with others."[5] It is only as the child develops an awareness of his body as separate from others

Phenomenology in Rhetoric and Communication, ed. Stanley Deetz. Copyright, 1981, The Center for Advanced Research in Phenomenology and the University Press of America.

[1] Jess G. Delia, "The Development of Communicative Behavior." In Handbook of Rhetorical and Communication Theory, eds. Carroll C. Arnold and John Waite Bowers (Boston: Allyn and Bacon, forthcoming), p. 57.

[2] Maurice Merleau-Ponty, "The Child's Relations with Others." In The Primacy of Perception and Other Essays, ed. James M. Edie (Evanston: Northwestern University Press, 1964), p. 119.

[3] Merleau-Ponty, p. 119.

[4] Merleau-Ponty, p. 119.          [5] Merleau-Ponty, p. 135.

and theirs from his that he is able to discern the possibility of multiple perspectives and personalities (as opposed to assuming self as other). This inability to perceive difference that characterizes a child's early relations with others also typifies his initial relationship with language (the fusion of sign and referent and a lack of symbolic consciousness). Turning now to Merleau-Ponty's theory of language acquisition it is possible to view the following discussion within the frame of his theory of intersubjectivity.

Merleau-Ponty's major interest in language, as noted by James Edie in the introduction to Conciousness and the Acquisition of Language, lies "in the role speech acts play in the bodily and perceptual constitution of our lived-world, of how the structures of speaking are related to, and embedded in and affect perception."[6] For Merleau-Ponty, "speaking is but the refinement, specification and extension of preverbal behaviors which already bestow a human sense on the world."[7] To clarify, during the pre-communication phase a child doesn't separate the communicatee from the communicator. Subsequent perception and understanding of differences between people and things occurs through one's body. At first, the "human body is the vehicle of human communication by reason of its mere physical existence."[8] The significance of the child's early relationship with his environment is that "the primordial human gesture contains in seed all the characteristics of more sophisticated acts of expression."[9] The word "primordial" references "the level of the presence at the world in which there is lived meaning, where the signified is the signification."[10] Fundamentally gesture is meaning. The act of speaking therefore is a building upon preverbal behaviors (the gesture) that are themselves meaningful. The consequences of this for language is that "the conceptual meaning or words must be formed by a kind of subtraction from a gestural meaning which is immanent in speech."[11] What is unique about this philosopher's position is that while admitting to the possibility of different languages saying the same thing in diverse ways, he simultaneously is positing "beneath the level of what these patterned sounds enable one to think conceptually, an untranslatable, primitive level of meaning, distinctive of that language and expressive of its primordial melody, intonation and poetic 'chant'."[12] Investigating the level of meaning beneath these "patterned sounds", (e.g., words having conceptual and referential meaning), leads Merleau-Ponty to focus upon the primitive phonemic processes.

In explicating the significance of phonemes for the language learner, Merleau-Ponty draws upon the work of Roman Jakobson. A phoneme (following Jakobson) is "the element of language which distinguishes one word from all other words identical to it. They are diacritical elements of language. As a consequence, phonemes are essential constituents of words, even though in themselves they are completely deprived of meaning."[13] Phonemes, therefore, have no meaning in and of themselves. It is only their combination, according to the phonological rules of a particular language, that enables a speaker to create words that have some referential or conceptual meaning. However, from Merleau-Ponty's theoretical position "words never completely lose that primitive, strictly phonemic level of "affective" meaning which is already witness

---

[6]James Edie, "Introduction," Consciousness and the Acquisition of Language by Merleau-Ponty, trans. Hugh Silverman (Evanston: Northwestern University Press, 1973), p. xiii.

[7]Edie, p. xiii.

[8]Richard L. Lanigan, Speaking and Semiology: Maurice Merleau-Ponty's Phenomenological Theory of Existential Communication (The Netherlands: Mouton, 1972), p. 46.

[9]Thomas Langan, Merleau-Ponty's Critique of Reason (New Haven: Yale University Press, 1966), p. 126.

[10]Lanigan, p. 46.

[11]Edie, p. xvi.

[12]Merleau-Ponty, Consciousness and the Acquisition of Language, p. 12.

[13]Merleau-Ponty, pp. 25-26.

to another order."[14] The "other" order is the phonemic substructure, the "patterned sounds" which vary depending upon the historical development/use of a particular language. The argument is made for the existence of a level of "affective tonality", a level of meaning which is beneath conceptual thought/words. Language, while not being reducible to this level of meaning, is necessarily dependent upon it in the formation and production of words. The developmental question now becomes apparent. As posed by Merleau-Ponty, "The problem is to know how language has passed from a quasi-biological activity to one which is non-biological but which nevertheless presupposes a whole movement or activity that has integrated it into dialogue."[15] Put another way, how is it possible for the child to move from experiencing signs as gestures (signified is signification) to a mode of being in the world where a dialectic exists between signs and signification? Explaining this movement and the interdependence of these phases in a child's development are important to the communication theorist interested in explaining how symbols become symbolic.

Merleau-Ponty's theory of language is captured in the following presuppositions:

1. Babbling is the ancestor to language.

2. Speech emerges from the "total language" (e.g., the combination of gestures, imitation, etc.) but is structured upon the organs of phonation.

3. A child's involvement in his environment's mode of speech (e.g., pitch, tone, rhythm, etc.) is integrally related to his attraction to language.

4. Prior to speaking the child appropriates the rhythm/stress of his respective language.

   a. Consequently, a child's first words are not spontaneous but rather grounded in an already held repertoire of attitudinal responses.

   b. Additionally, "We cannot say that the appearance of the first word implies a sudden consciousness of the sign-signified relationship."[16] That is, comprehension and production are not linearly related. A child uses his behavior in designative ways prior to the onset of talking.

The child, as Delacroix has remarked, "bathes in language" and being surrounded by the sounds moves himself toward it. The explanation of this movement begins on the phonemic level. Merleau-Ponty states that, "The phonemic system appears as an irreducible reality and language acquisition appears as an integration of an individual into the structure of his language."[17] It is argued that a child's capacity to produce speech is ultimately based not on their articulation abilities but on "the acquisition of phonemic contrasts and their significative value."[18] At first children don't recognize all those sounds having "significative value" within the phonemic system of the adult language. A period of "deflation" of vocal manifestations occurs in most children immediately following the babbling stage. Whereupon, the child loses sounds that may or may not prove useful to his learning his native language. This production difficulty is explained in terms of the child's inability to recognize the significance of particular phonemic patterns. The movement into speech is more problematic for some children than others. The production issue therefore will be raised again when presenting an alternative way to explain this phenomenon. However,

[14]Merleau-Ponty, p. 12.
[15]Merleau-Ponty, p. 12.
[16]Merleau-Ponty, pp. 17-18.
[17]Merleau-Ponty, p. 23.
[18]Merleau-Ponty, p. 23.

to continue with the present line of thought, granting that language acquisition is predicated upon the phonemic processes, (e.g., the ability to differentiate amongst sounds), the question of _how_ a child acquires the phonemic system must now be taken up. Important to the explication of this process is Merleau-Ponty's conception of imitation.

Overall, Merleau-Ponty does not view imitation as some sort of intellectual activity. Cobb's remarks on this point are especially relevant:

> Psychologists have often spoken of learning in the child as though relations with self, world and others originated in contemplative knowledge. Yet ordinary experience shows that in imitating others, in learning to walk, in becoming familiar with an environment, what occurs cannot be explained by the notion that there is first an intellectual act of "knowing" rules, maps or words and then a move to use them.[19]

In other words, in acquiring the phonemic system, the child does not envision the muscular motions that would produce a sound and the reproduce these gestures. Rather, imitation for Merleau-Ponty entails "representing for ourselves not the movement toward an object but the desired object itself."[20] This is true whether talking about a child's relations with others or his learning to speak. The developing organism in an initially undifferentiated relationship with his surroundings imitates not persons but conducts."[21] Language is a particular type of imitation. To clarify, "[Vocal] imitation signifies carrying oneself by one's own means toward a goal (heard speech). The child imitates as he goes along . . . by carrying himself toward the global result."[22] This process of vocal imitation is aided by hearing one's speech and simultaneously determined and limited "by a particular usage which is itself determined by the surrounding phonetic possibilities."[23] Implicit within this discussion of imitation is the idea that phonemes are acquired within a predetermined frame and yet, not necessarily in any predetermined manner.

For Jakobson, the acquisition of phonemes _is_ actually determined by a set of objective laws. In contrast, for Goldstein (with whom Merleau-Ponty aligns himself) "the phonematic development occurs according to a certain phonematic "style" which is not in itself and at the outset prescribed by any necessity."[24] Clarification for what is meant here by a languages "style" comes from Humboldt's concept of _innere Sprachform_. The _innere Sprachform_ "is the reflection in language of the world view appropriate to a given culture."[25] It is within the _innere Sprachform_ or "mental landscape" common to the members of a linguistic community that "pure" thought and language are seen to merge. Most importantly, it is this "nonexplicity thought" that comprises the "style" of a language and concomitantly is what attracts the child to their langauge initially.

In brief summary, Merleau-Ponty places the infant in a world filled with sounds that are "pregnant" with meaning for him. He compares language acquisition to the deciphering of a text. Deciphering in the sense that the child is not born with a key to the code which he is enveloped by. Enticed by a language style, a child moves from what Merleau-Ponty calls "fluent nonthematic signification" to more precise signification. It is however "the value of use that defines language. Instrumental usage precedes signification per se ."[26] There is a point during this movement toward more precise significa-

[19] William Cobb, cf., "The Child's Relations with Others." Merleau-Ponty, p. 96.

[20] Merleau-Ponty, Consciousness and the Acquisition of Language, p. 32.

[21] Merleau-Ponty, "The Child's Relations with Others," p. 117.

[22] Merleau-Ponty, Consciousness and the Acquisition of Language, p. 32.

[23] Merleau-Ponty, p. 32.

[24] Merleau-Ponty, p. 76.

[25] Merleau-Ponty, p. 75.

[26] Merleau-Ponty, p. 52.

tion whereby the child "goes beyond the given elements [phonemic patterns] in order to grasp the significance of the world."[27] Numerous hypotheses have been offered to account for the period of discontinuity observed in children between the period of not "understanding" and that moment of "insight" whereby the code becomes something more than a myriad of sounds (e.g., the process of signifaction suddenly becomes less problematic). Following a brief summary of Roman Jakobson's position, I will return to this issue of discontinuity and offer yet another hypothesis to aid in explaining this phenomenon.

The preceding paragraph outlined two viewpoints concerning the general mechanism by which the phonemic system is acquired; either through a set of objective phonolotical laws intrinsic to a language or by way of Humboldt's concept of innere Sprachform ("world view") which is not governed by any "particular necessity." The former perspective is that of Roman Jakobson. While the significance to this particular paper, (indeed it seems possible to ground these phonological laws in the "menal landscape" of the linguistic community), it is perhaps appropriate to briefly outline Jakobson's position in light of his relationsip to Merleau-Ponty.

As articulated by Holenstein, "There remains a certain indetermination in the development of language--however development is limited by the laws of foundedness, to which the sound system owes its hierarchically structures unity"[28] These laws, perceived to be universal and intrinsic to all sound systems, "act both to maintain the static balance of languages and as determinants in their build-up (in the child's acquisition of language)."[29] Jakobson has isolated the oppositional pair marked/unmarked as being the main ordering principle behind a language's "hierarchical structural unity." The development of the phonemic system "obeys the principle of maximal contrast and proceeds from the simple and undifferentiated to stratified and differentiated, with the simple unmarked terms of a pair of phonemes developing more easily than the differentiated marked terms."[30] Jakobson's assumption and search for eidetic universals, the idea of laws of "foundedness" and his positing of "stages" of phonemic development are in sharp contrast to Merleau-Ponty's attitude that all languages have a unique "style", and his denial of either universal apriori grammars or "successive stages" (e.g., "all possibilities of expression are inscribed in the expressive manifestations of the child."[31]) Recognizing the points of divergence in the thinking of these two men, it nevertheless remains true that both acknowledge the importance of the phoneme and a child's ability to simultaneously distinguish amongst sounds and be able to appropriate those phonemic patterns that have "significative value" in his movement towards speech. The remainder of this paper will focus upon the potential contributions of Merleau-Ponty, both methodological and theoretical to the communication scholar interested in children's speech.

One period of development that needs exploration and explanation is what Merleau-Ponty identifies as "deflation." To reiterate, it is during this time that a child's vocalizations diminish with sporatic "one-word" utterances, only to be immediatly followed by a noticeable increase in verbalizations. As was noted earlier, several hypotheses have been proposed to explain this period of discontinuity between a childs "bathing in language: and the "insight" that the sounds themselves have "significative value." Jakobson offers the following

---

[27]Merleau-Ponty, p. 51.

[28]Elmar Holenstein, Roman Jakobson's Approach to Language: Phenomenological Structuralism, trans Catherine and Tarcisius Schelbert (Bloomington: Indiana University Press, 1974), p. 35.

[29]Holenstein, p. 36.

[30]Holenstein, p. 112.

[31]Merleau-Ponty, Consciousness and the Acquisition of Language, p. 23.

functional account for this observation. "The stability, the selection of sounds and the hierarchical stratification of the sound system after the transition from babbling to speaking can only be explained by the new function of sounds."[32] Jakobson goes on to state that babbling meets the motor and emotional needs of the child. While speech sounds are characterized by elements of social meaning and intentionality. For Jakobson, the child "selects those phonic elements. . .which contribute to the distinction of meaning within a system."[33] Other theorists have suggested the existence of a "babies language" which the child uses for awhile and later switches to the adult language system. Jesse Delia for example, while acknowledging the significance of seeing the child's move to use conventional forms as a problem to be accounted for, simultaneously assumes that the child's possession of a "protolanguage" is an element within the problem. There are difficulties with both of these hypotheses. Do childrens' needs change as dramatically as Jakobson suggests enabling us to propose categories of separate and distinct speech functions? A more viable approach would be to somehow integrate these various periods of needs and dependencies with the particular speech patterns observed in children. Regarding the "baby language" hypotheses, Delia himself asks "When, how and why does a being who has created the beginnings of a new language, give up his newly created linguistic forms for the structure of an already existing language."[34] The question of how and why are important points. One wonders why a child would choose to switch languages if his own had successfully been meeting his needs. It is significant that this switch is posited before the child has interacted with people other than the primary caretaker. In addition, the pragmatic question remains of how the child accomplishes this task in such a remarkably short period of time. Again, there is a need for an integrative approach that takes a child's preverbal involvement with his environment more seriously. One problem these theorists have difficulty accounting for is the prolonged period of "deflation" observed in some children (which is frequently accompanied by a shortened one-word stage).

It is important for those doing developmental research both to account for the "deflation" period and to explain why some children do not follow the "normal" pattern. Our inability to speak to this question is confounded in two ways. First, we implicitly hold the assumption that there is a linear relationship between comprehension and production. Second, the methodology employed in most developmental research impedes our ability to assess the problem objectively. This latter point will be developed shortly. The assumption that comprehension and production are mutually dependent processes is exemplified in our approach to and analysis of the talk of children. We infer comprehension when production is observed (e.g.,we presuppose that the child is cognizant of what he is saying--not only that he is saying). In addition, we do not pay close attention to what the inability to produce speech indicates about comprehension. Holenstein offers a conception of the encoding/decoding process that might allow us to better understand the notion of "deflation." He suggests that "the code is differently structured for speaker and listener."[35] In particular, "The encoding process goes from meaning to sound and from the lexicogrammatical to the phonological level: whereas the decoding process displays the opposite direction-from sound to meaning and from features to symbols."[36] If, as Merleau-Ponty argues, "to learn to speak is to learn to play a series of roles, to assume a series of conducts or linguistic gestures,"[37] than perhaps we need to separate out the actions of listening and speaking for the beginning language learner.

[32]Holenstein, p. 77.

[33]Holenstein, p. 77.

[34]Delia, p. 57.

[35]Holenstein, p. 161.

[36]Holenstein, p. 161.

[37]Merleau-Ponty, "The Child's Relations with Others," p. 109.

It was mentioned earlier that for Merleau-Ponty, imitation is perceived as a movement toward a <u>global</u> result. Coupled now with his suggestion that a child's ability to produce speech is contingent upon an ability to distinguish those sounds having "significative value", it is possible that for delayed language learners, (e.g., those observed to go through prolonged periods of "deflation"), this inability to differentiate sounds having "significative value", (the decoding process of moving from sound to meaning), hinders their capacity to imitate the global goal (heard speech). Consequently, this child does not produce speech when the "normative" scale indicates that he should. While this is a speculative hypothesis, it is important to at least recognize that comprehension and production are not linearly related and that the decoding and encoding processes may be mutually independent systems which only later become mutually interdependent. To reiterate, for those involved in an ongoing dialogue, the speaking and listening roles sometimes occur simultaneously and frequently there is a great deal of overlap. It is conceivable that prior to the onset of speech these roles (linguistic gestures to use Merleau-Ponty's terminology) may be independent processes. Our capacity to adequately explain this deflation period is integrally related and biased by the methodological approach typically employed in developmental research. The remainder of this paper will deal with this issue of methodology and how we might appropriate Merleau-Ponty's thinking.

In order to understand the process of language acquisition, Merleau-Ponty advocates using the phenomenological approach. While he didn't produce a substantial body of "empirical" evidence to justify his claim, the importance in utilizing this method when looking to developmental issues is obvious. Regardless of one's research interest there is necessity for self-reflection about the relationship between what is being looked at and who is doing the looking. Our world is one comprised of relationships and as Merleau-Ponty argues "for us the only way to become aware of that fact is to suspend the resultant activity, to refuse it our complicity . . . to put it 'out of play'."[38] In coming to perceive and interpret these relations the phenomenologist must bracket out (momentarily suspend) his common sense understanding of the phenomenon in question. Both the child and the adult live in a world full of relationships. However, it is a mistake to assume that these are the same type of experiences for the developing infant and the adult. Unfortunately, an infrequently stated but often implicitly held assumption for many developmentalists is to view the child as simply a miniature adult. The work of Dore is a concrete example. He admits to selecting out specific adult forms and to looking for their emergence in children.[39] This conceptual view of the child colors both the way we look at development and our subsequent analysis of these observations.

For the communication theorist, this biased approach is exemplified when we attempt to understand the child's speech development within the framework of what it means to be a "competent adult speaker". The notion of "competent adult speaker" is itself filled with serious complications. However, more to the point is that, in grounding developmenal research on adult structures you are offering a linear explanation. The development of a child's cognitive/communicative abilities are seen in terms of a predefined end. The presupposition here is that a child's view of that world parallels that of an adult. In using adult patterns of behavior (e.g., viewing language acquisition in terms of how talk functions for the adult) one cannot expect to adequately recognize and account for the unique experiential development of the child. Appropriating the phenomenological approach in understanding language acquisition speaks to both the theoretical and methodological problems briefly outlined in this paper. That is, by bracketing out our experiences as competent adult speakers

[38]Maurice Merleau-Ponty, <u>Phenomenology of Perception</u>, trans. Colin Smith, ed. Ted Honerich (London: Routledge and Kegan Paul Ltd., 1962), p. xiii.

[39]John Dore, <u>The Development of Speech Acts</u> (New York: 1973).

and working towards an objective description of a child's patterns of interaction with his environment we are simultaneously allowing for 1) a possible discontintinuity between a child's and an the adult's view of the world and 2) a less subjectively grounded, (e.g., data not based on an adult's intersubjective experience), corpus of data upon which to understand what is "essential" for the child in his making the move into using conventional forms of speech. Finally, to reiterate a point made earlier, this essay has been of a highly speculative nature. It is apparent however that one interested in communication from a developmental perspective can profit from the thinking of Merleau-Ponty. Specifically, it is important for the communication theorist to be sensitive to the relationship between a child's preverbal behaviors and the subsequent acquisition of speech. To merely focus our attention on the latter both ignores the importance of these behaviors and does nothing to further our understanding of how speech suddenly becomes nonproblematic for the language learner. Furthermore serious consideration needs to be given to the methodological approach we take when looking at developmental issues. Employing the phenomenological method makes it possible to circumvent the tendency in existing developmental paradigms to view the infant from an adult frame.

# 3 / ON THE METHOD OF CRITICAL THEORY AND ITS IMPLICATIONS FOR A CRITICAL THEORY OF COMMUNICATION

ROBERT PRYOR
UNIVERSITY OF ILLINOIS

Scholars in speech communication having an interest in developing non-positivistic theories and methods of research must be heartened by the recent appearance in speech communication convention programs and journals of theoretical papers questioning traditional positivist conceptions of social reality and research.[1] Even more heartening to those theorists who are exploring the possible contributions of Marxism to speech communication theorizing must be the increasing attention accorded to Frankfurt Marxism, or German Critical Theory, particularly the work of Jurgen Habermas. Indeed, a recent issue of the Quarterly Journal of Speech[2] contains an essay by Farrell and Aune in which they review the literature of the Frankfurt School and outline certain paths that literature influencing the "critical study of communication" might take: (1) philosophical extensions of the work of the Schools, (2) revising, probing, and extending critical theory's assumptions about communication, and (3) applying aspects of critical theory to alternative conditions and problems. This paper is directed toward the latter two concerns. Specifically, I will attempt to extend critical theory's method and theoretical assumptions to the phenomenon of human communication with the hope of eventually constructing a critical theory of communication. Obviously, this project cannot be accomplished in a single paper. I will be content, therefore, to identify the method of critical theory and its implications for analysis and to discuss some of the central issues a critical theory of communications should address.

Numerous scholars have attempted to define and interpret the nature of the Marxian dialectic in accordance with their own varying perspectives.[3] The result has been confusion: we can speak of an orthodox Marxist dialectic, a structuralist dialectic, a Hegelian-Marxist dialectic, and adding to the confusion are pseudo-dialectics: the phenomenological dialectic and the dialectic seen as simple interaction and reciprocity. Let me be clear that the dialectic of critical theory is a Hegelian-Marxist dialectic. As I see it, the

Phenomenology in Rhetoric and Communication, ed. Stanley Deetz. Copyright, 1981. The Center for Advanced Research in Phenomenology and the University Press of America.

[1] See, for example, J. G. Delia and L. Grossberg, "Interpretation and Evidence," Western Journal of Speech Communication, 41 (1977), 32-42; T. S. Frentz and T. B. Farrell, "Language Action: A Paradigm for Communication," Quarterly Journal of Speech, 62 (1976), 333-49; Dean Hewes, "The Constructivist Approach to Communication Theory: An Alternate View of Human Communication," paper presented to the Speech Communication Association Convention, Minneapolis, Minn., 1978; and L. C. Hawes, "Toward A Hermeneutic Phenomenology of Communication," Communication Quarterly, 25 (Summer, 1977), 30-41.

[2] Actually, the authors list four distinct paths, the fourth being literature that is still being produced by the Frankfurt theorists. Thomas Farrell and James Aune, "Critical Theory and Communication: A Selective Literature Review," Quarterly Journal of Speech, 65 (Feb. 1979), 93-120.

[3] See, for example, Dick Howard, The Marxian Legacy (New York: Urizen Books, 1977), pp. 3-18; Henri Lefevre, The Sociology of Marx (London: Penguin, 1972); Herbert Marcuse, Reason and Revolution, 2nd ed. (Boston: Beacon Press, 1960), esp. the Preface, "A Note on the Dialectic," pp. vii-xiv; Louis Althusser, For Marx, trans. Ben Brewster (New York: Vintage, 1970); and Howard Sherman, "Dialectics as Method," Insurgent Sociologist, iv (1976), 57-64.

dialectic in critical theory is constituted by the concepts of negation, free-dom, and movement, and it involves certain methodological directives: (a) to focus on contradictions in the social world, (b) to search for and focus on emergent structures rather than stable structures which seem to persist through time--emergent structures which relate changing people to changing circumstances (historical-developmental analysis), and (c) to search for the possibilities inherent in social "facts," not being content to identify things as they are, but also to identify things as they might be (analysis directed to the future).

Critical theory is "critical" by the very fact of its being dialectical. What is "critical" is the power of negative thinking "is the driving power of dialectic . . . .," moreover; negative thinking "is the driving power of dialec-tical thought, used as a tool for analyzing the world of facts in terms of its internal inadequacy."[4] Dialectical analysis begins with the assumption that objective reality, the world of things, is not what it appears to be--is other than itself. Objective reality, or the social world, on the surface appears to be orderly, coherent, and stable. Dialectical analysis, however, reveals that underneath this reality there is a struggle, a struggle of opposing for-ces, continually negating each other, producing what we take to be reality. Seeing that the social world is dialectical means that the events and objects which make up the social world in man's perception and understanding of them can be apprehended in terms of contradictory, mutually dependent structures and formations that negate each other and give rise to observable objectifi-cations of reality. Within any observable social phenomena, there can be dis-cerned a myriad of contradictory forces (diversity) which interact with and negate each other. The totality of these negations constitutes the surface appearance of the phenomenon (unity). The world of appearance is, in actual-ity, a world of contradiction. That which is, is constituted by that which it is not--its negation or contradiction. The power of negative thinking is the ability to disclo se the contradictions of societal and everyday life. On society, Adorno writes:

> Society is not consensual, not simple, also not neutrally left to the discretion of categorical forms but on the contrary awaits already the system of categories of the discursive logic of its objects. Society is full of contradictions and thereby determinate; at once rational and irrational, system and fragile, mediated through blind nature and through consciousness.[5]

And in the context of our everyday lives--in the processes of production, social interaction and communication--social relationships appear in forms of objectivity, appear as "things." Their status is taken for granted, as fac-tual and objective, the necessity for their current status or even their very existence is not questioned. As a result, the deep structure of relations between people remains concealed and understanding or awareness of the true historical nature of social conditions and phenomena goes unrecognized.

Critical theory recognizes that the facts and conditions of the social world do not correspond to the categories and concepts that common sense and scientific reason creates for them. In other words, critical theory refuses to accept the given universe of facts as the final context of validation. Facts can always be other than what they really are. Thus, critical theory argues for a transcending[6] analysis of social conditions in light of their

---

[4]Marcuse, "A Note on the Dialectic," pp. vii, viii.

[5]T. W. Adorno, "On the Logic of the Social Sciences," in *The Positivist Dispute in German Sociology*, ed. T. W. Adorno, et al. (London: Heinemann, 1976), p. 26.

[6]Herbert Marcuse, *One-Dimensional Man* (Boston: Beacon Press, 1964), p. xi. Marcuse uses the words "transcend" and "transcendence" in the "empirical," critical sense: they designate tendencies in theory and practice which, in a give society, 'overshoot' the established universe of discourse and action toward its historical alternatives (real possibilities)."

arrested possibilities. In this sense, critical theory is oppositional. At one and the same time, critique affirms the existence of social forms and seeks to change them. Marcuse writes: "Thought 'corresponds' to reality only as it transforms reality by comprehending its contradictory structure. . . . For to comprehend reality means to comprehend what things really are, and this in turn means rejecting their mere factuality. Rejection is the process of thought as well as of action."[7] Marx puts it more forcefully:

> In its rational form it [the dialectic] is a scandal and abomination to bourgeoisdom and its doctrinaire professors because it includes in its comprehension and affirmative recognition of the existing state of things, at the same time also, the recognition of the negation of the state, of its inevitable breaking up; because it regards every histori- cally developed social form as in fluid movement, and therefore, takes into account its transient nature not less than its momentary existence; because it lets nothing impose upon it, and it is, in essence, <u>critical and revolutionary</u>."[8]

The dialectic, argues Marx, recognizes the existence of social facts, but it does not cease with their identification. Social facts must be viewed in light of their historical position and must be analyzed within the context of a particular conception of man, i.e., in terms of what these facts reveal about denied potentialities of men and women under the existing system of dom- ination. The facts at any given moment are to be interpreted as transitory manifestations of an established system and their very facticity denied final validity by a transcendent analysis. Thus, the dialectic exposes the negative elements of society, and it points to those mediating forces which give rise to the positive elements of society, those elements that lead to "progress in the consciousness of freedom."[9]

The foremost purpose of the dialectic, its <u>raison d'etre</u>, is to bring about freedom of thought and action which is the very being of pure human existence. Dialectical thought argues that the experience of the world is unfree; that men, women, and nature exist in conditions of aleination and reification. For Hegel, history is the dialectical progression toward human emancipation through the struggle between alienated objectification and self-understanding.[10] Free- dom is the negation of alienation through self-reflection and self-awareness, i.e., through Reason or dialectical thinking.

The interest or goal of dialectical analysis is to identify those human structures and formations which impinge on the freedom of Reason to develop its potentialities. As such, dialectical analysis focuses on those elements which block free and open communication and on the material conditions which give rise to distorted communication. The goal of a critical theory of com- munication, then, ought to be illuminating the material and intellectual condi- tions for freedom, for achieving a state of affairs in which non-alienating work and free interaction would predominate.[11]

The function of dialectical analysis, then, is to break down the existing state of affairs, to show that it is composed of contradictions, distortions,

---

[7]Marcuse, "A Note on the Dialectice," p. ix.

[8]Karl Marx, <u>Capital</u>, Vol. 1, trans. S. Moore and E. Aveling (New York: International Publishers. 1967), p. 20. Emphasis added.

[9]Hegel, quoted by Marcuse, in "A Note on the Dialectic," p. viii.

[10]Attributed to Marcuse by Phil Slater, <u>The Origin and Significance of the Frankfurt School</u> (London: Routledge & Kegan Paul, 1977), p. 32.

[11]Obviously, this is an ideal state similar in nature to the ideal speech situation as developed by Habermas. See, J. Habermas, "Toward a Theory of Communicative Competence," <u>Inquiry</u>, 13 (1970), 360-75; and <u>Toward a Rational Society</u>, trans. J. Shapiro (Boston: Beacon Press, 1970), pp. 81-122.

and repressions.  To do so, dialectical analysis must destroy the dominate universe of facts which controls the symbolic universe and conceals the true nature of social reality.  Thus Marcus argues that the goal of dialects is to show that negation is so much at the heart of social life that the development of inner contradictions associated with freedom and unfreedom can only lead to qualitative change in society, change to a greater state of freedom.12  As such, dialectical analysis is both synchronic and diachronic.  Interpretation of social reality (that which is) in terms of that which it is not requires historical and developmental analysis:

> Dialectical analysis ultimately tends to become historical analysis, in which nature itself appears as part and stage in its own history and in the history of man.  The progress of cognition from common sense to knowledge arrives at a world which is negative in its very structure because that which is real opposes and denies the potentialities inherent in itself--potentialities which themselves strive for realization.  Reason is the negation of the negative.13

Any critical analysis of communication would have to be historical and developmental in nature; it would have to consider particular forms of communication within a framework of movement.  Thus, any act of communication would have to be analyzed in conjunction with simultaneous progressions of events along several interdependent dimensions.  A critical analysis of communication would have to relate the actors and the act of communication to the particular social context in which the act occurs.  Critique is neither limited to the critique of the individual (subjectivity) nor to the critique of the social (objectivity).  Critique is always critique of the subject and object in dialectical tension.  Critical analysis would see communication as the practice of interacting persons who are socially and biologically determined.  Thus, a critical analysis of communication would be both a critique of the individual creation of communication and the social context in which that creation occurs.

As a form of historical analysis, the critique of communication would account for the development of structures which give rise to the particular communicative encounter and the actors' interpretations or definitions of that encounter.  A critical theory of communcation would be concerned with the historicity of appearance.  To that end, critique would seek to penetrate the surface appearance of social formations to reveal their true, underlying relationships.  Analysis, then, would focus on the emergence of phenomena and the determination of objects over time, as they are formed and decay.

Here we see another facet of the dialectic:  movement.  Dialectic is a process, dialectical formations are fluid, always in movement.  These formations are moments of a particular relationship between elements which are continually being transformed in and through time.  That relationsip can only be understood by understanding the composite of relationships out of which it has arisen, the relations in which it currently exists and those relationshios into which it will develope.  Thus, to render the dialectic static by bracketing it, by freezing it into a single, fixed definition, is to render the concept meaningless.  To understand the dialectic, one must be willing to suspend mechanistic conceptualizations of reality and become receptive to a fluid, unstable, and contradictory reality.

The power of negation, the affirmation of freedom, and the ability of historical, developmental analysis to reveal the irrationality of everyday life,

---

12Marcuse, "A Note on the Dialectic," p. ix.
13Marcuse, "A Note on the Dialectic," p. x.

demands a theory oriented toward a better future. Theory that merely describes social forms as they appear is insufficient. A critical theory would attempt to penetrate the harmonious appearance of social forms to discover hidden dialectical relations. In so doing, critical theory would point out the possibilities inherent in such relationships. Thus, a critical theory of communication would always consider a specific communication event in relation to its possibilities, i.e., what form that particular event could take if circumstances were altered. The critical theorist recognizes that social "facts" are mediated by society; that they need not be accepted as objectively valid or as the final word. Facts are to be seen in light of their arrested possibilities. Thus, the critical theorist continually asks, "Is the observed phenomenon necessary? Could it exist in any other form?" In this respect, a critical theory of communication is emancipatory.

For the critical individual, the recognition of the irrational nature of the "categories of social life" simultaneously becomes their condemnation.[14] Recognizing the irrational nature of society and believing in the possibility of a future, rational society coalesce in the goal of critical theory: the emancipation of man and the establishment of a society based on Reason. According to critical theory, the dialectical forces associated with human interaction precipitate societal transformation eventuating in a classless society where "Reason" prevails and true human freedom is a reality. Such a society, maintains Horkheimer, will be a rational society, "an association of free men in which each has the same possibility of self-development."[15]

How long does man have to await such a society? The answer provided by both Marx and Horkheimer is tied to the dialectic between man and history. History shapes men, but men make history. Thus, a rational society is possible through the actions of men, and when enough men have attained the critical state of mind, when enough men recognize the "sordid state of the world," then the irrationality of capitalist society will be overthrown.[16] The role that critical theory plays in this process is crucial, for it brings to consciousness the tension and struggle of men and women against capitalist society.

## ACTIVITY OR PRAXIS

In addition to being sensitive to dialectical formations in the social world, a critical theory of communication would utilize an understanding of man as an active organism capable of effecting change in his world. For critical theory, the notion of activity or praxis constitutes a fundamental feature of human life. Praxis is crucial for critical theory because it underscores the contention that man has the power to alter his circumstances--to create a better world. Praxis, therefore, renders emancipation possible.

A critical theory of communication would see man as not merely existing in the world, but rather, would see man existing as part of the world. The "world," or objective reality, consists of both the physical or natural world and the social world. The reality of both the physical and the social world pre-dates the individual; this reality is given, and as such, acts so as to negate the individual's freedom of action and constrains possibilities of development. Thus, on one hand, the individual is created by his or her world; on the other, through praxis and interpretation the individual acts upon the world, changes it and himself, and in changing, negates that which once was. Men and women, then, actively intervene in the workings of reality and through

---

[14]Horkheimer, "Traditional and Critical Theory."

[15]Horkheimer, p. 219.

[16]Horkheimer, "The Latest Attack on Metaphysics," in *Critical Theory: Selected Essays*, p. 163.

their praxis re-create reality and re-create themselves. Given this perspective, one realizes that what others call the fundamental paradox of man's exist-
ence--that he is at one and the same time both created by and the creator of
his world--is actually a dialectic between the givenness of the external world
and the practical activity man brings to bear on the world. Communication,
as practical activity, should be seen as an attempt to overcome the tension
between prior social constructions and creativity. Thus, communication
from a critical perspective would be seen as the dialectical moment between
permanence and creativity.

## INTERPRETATION

Habermas' attempt to reformulate the basic Marxist dialectic between forces and modes of production into one between labor, or instrumental action,
and symbolic interaction is uncertaken in order to account for the centrality
of meaning in the social world.[17] In so doing, Habermas' effort marks a contribution to the argument that the process of symbolic interaction or interpretation is a form of praxis; it is a unique form, one that makes other forms
of activity possible, and as such, constitutes a central issue for a communication theory of society.

A critical theory of communication begins with the twin pillars of material
action and interpretation. To understand the phenomenon of communication, one
must account for those entities which make communication possible: acting
subjects interpreting their world in order to make it sensible. A critical
theory of communication must take the process of interpretation as one of its
bases for analysis and focus on the external and internal processes, mechanisms, and structures which give rise to particular definitions of reality
and, by extension, to different models of communication.

What distinguishes critique from other interpretive theories on the issue
of interpretation is critique from other interpretive theories on the issue of
interpretation is critique's demand for a dialectical understanding of the
interpretive process. Within the interpretive process two major dialectical
relationships appear to be operating: the dialectic between praxis and interpretation and the dialectic between socially shared meanings and individual
creativity. With regard to the dialectic between praxis and interpretation,
critical theory argues that individual behavior is a continuous stream of
action and that interpretations emerge from action. That is, one's previous
praxis in the world (and societal praxis) prvides the parameters which give
rise to interpretations. By determining, in part, the substance of interpretations from materializing. Thus, on the one hand, praxis determines interpretation, but on the other, interpretation determines future action in the social
and physical world. Interpretation directs praxis because action is based on
one's definition of the situation. A situation is defined and action results
on the basis of definitions. But the ability to define a situation is
depended on previously defined action schemes. Previous praxis makes interpretation possible, while interpretation makes future praxis possible.

Recognizing the dialectic between praxis and interpretation entails the
stipulation that theory account for the development of social formations im-
pinging on and structuring communicative encounters. Thus, critique, in part,
would focus on the norms, rules and regulations which govern communicative
encounters and the actors' interpretation of them with an eye toward critiquing
their legitimacy in regulating social interaction.[18]

---

[17]See, for example, J. Habermas, "Science and Technology as 'Ideology'," in Toward a Rational
Society, pp. 81-122.

[18]See, for example, J. Habermas, Thoughts on the Foundation of Sociology in the Philosophy of
Language, Fifth Lecture, "Truth and Society: The Discursive Satisfaction of Factual Claims to
Validity," (unpublished manuscript: New School for Social Research, 1977).

A second dialectical relationship operating in the interpretive process is that between socially shared meanings and individual creativity. The act of interpretation is a creative act, but creation does not occur in a vacuum. The creation of new meanings simultaneously implies the destruction of previous meanings. Thus, a tension exists between individual creativity (change) and previously shared interpretations (permanence). Interpretation, a creative act, is always constrained (partially negated) by prior shared social resources: previous interpretations, shared knowledge, language, and so on. Interpretation is dialectical; a tension exists between permanence as manifested in shared social understandings, institutions, and structures and change, as implicit in individual creativity.

From this tension between permanence and change, between historically inherited resources and individual creativity, arises communication. Communication from this perspective is seen as a dialectical resolution between permanence and change. That is, through communicative praxis, individuals attempt to create new understandings and meanings which, in turn, negate previous meanings. But immediately upon their creation, new meanings may become part of the social stock of knowledge and serve to limit, to channel the individual's potential creation of future meanings. Thus, communication, like interpretation, is subject to the same dialectic between permanence and change and to the dialectic between socially shared meanings and individual creativity. Communication seen from this perspective is paradoxical: one cannot communicate without the existence of previous communication. This basis for interpretation and understanding is social, consisting of a socially shared stock of knowledge and language. Communication, an individual creation, is forever constrained by social forms. As such, the attempt to overcome the tension between permanence and creativity is never wholly resolved.

The dialectical nature of interpretation, praxis, and communication leads the critical theorist to investigate the social constraints on individual creativity. For Habermas, this means an investigation of language and speech act theory.[19] However, critique could also be a critique of objective forms of social reality (norms, societal institutions, social roles, communication patterns, etc.) and of subjective understandings of that reality.[20] In the main, critique should be concerned with the dialectic existing between individual creativity and the constraints of externally imposed social reality.

## LANGUAGE

Habermas' contention that the problem of language has replaced the traditional problem of consciousness in social philosophy and that the transcendental critique of language supersedes that of consciousness gives added weight to the argument that a critical theory of communication should account for the role and impact of language in social interaction.[21] Moreover, since critical theory is concerned with the practical impediments to the realization of free and open communication, one of the major issues a critical theory of communciation would have to confront is that of language.

The negative power of the dialectic reveals the contradictions inherent in social reality, that the true nature of existence is one of alienation and unfreedom--of domination. This domination is not merely economic and political

---

[19]See, J. Habermas, "Toward a Theory of Communicative Competence," *Inquiry*, 13 (1970), 360-75; and "On Systematically Distorted Communication," *Inquiry*, 13 (1970), 205-18.

[20]Marcuse argues that "all objects thus 'contain' subjectivity in their very structure." "A Note on the Dialectic," p. viii.

[21]Habermas, quoted in T. A. McCarthy, "A Theory of Communicative Competence," in *Critical Sociology*, ed. Paul Connerton (London: Penguin Press, 1976), p. 471.

but is an integral feature of social reality. The social world is negative because that which is observable, which is real, denies its own potentialities which strive for realization.[22] Thus, domination, like freedom, is at the root of human existence. Domination is a product of the interaction between people; its expression is most clearly found in language. Domination occurs linguistically when one party or class of people is able to impose meanings on another.[23] Such domination is strengthened and solidified (legitimized) when the dominated sector fails to reflect on the lanaguage or on its own material and social conditions.

Marcuse argues that in contemporary civilization the will to reflect on one's material and social conditions has been blunted by the forces of science and technology. The rapid advancement of science and technology has necessitated the creation of a new language whose objectives are functionalty, simplicity, manipulation, and control. This new language eliminates the desire for reflection; thus, Marcuse calls it a "one-dimensional" language.[24] In addition to eliminating reflection, science and technology now provide an ideological justification for existing social conditions. According to Marcuse, "science, by virtue of its own method and concepts, has projected and promoted a universe in which the domination of nature has remained linked to the domination of man."[25] This new domination is spread by a "one-dimensional universe of discourse," a form of linguistic behavior which blocks conceptual development, represses conscious existence, "repels recognition of their facts, and of their historical content."[26]

Not only does one-dimensional language spread the domination of science and technology, it also becomes, in itself, an instrument of control. One-dimensional language is anti-historical, anti-critical, and anti-dialectical--a closed language which does not demonstrate or explain but communicates decision, dictum, and command.[27] Marcuse maintains that this one-dimensional language controls by reducing the linguistic forms and symbols of reflection, abstraction, development and contradiction and by substituting images for concepts. It denies or absorbs this transcendent vocabulary, it does not search for but establishes and imposes truth and falsehood.[28]

One of the principle tasks for a critical theory of communication is to break through this closed universe of discourse, to develop and speak a language which is not the language of those in control. The critical theorist must speak the language of contradiction, must break up and "demythologize" through reflection the dominant meanings of one-dimensional language. This requires a particular style of discourse, a discourse built on negation which seeks to affirm the positive. Such discourse is reflective, two-dimensional, and metaphorical.[29] In a sense, dialectics and poetics meet on the same ground. Their purpose is to transcend the immediacy of everyday existence, to break through barriers of natural thought, and to show us alternative forms of existence.[30]

[22]Marcuse, "A Note on the Dialectic," p. x.

[23]P. Bourdieu and J. Passeron, Reproduction in Education, Society, and Culture, trans. Richard Nice (London: SAGE Publications, 1977), p. 4.

[24]Marcuse, One-Dimensional Man, pp. 84-120.

[25]Marcuse, One-Dimensional Man, p. 166.

[26]One-Dimensional Man, p. 97.

[27]One-Dimensional Man, p. 101.

[28]One-Dimensional Man, p. 103.

[29]See, F. Jameson, Marxism and Form (Princeton: Princeton University Press, 1971), pp. 6-8.

[30]Marcuse, "A Note on the Dialectic," pp. x-xi.

A critical theory of communication, then, must account for the role of language in influencing, directing, and controlling our everyday lives. Critical theory sees language dialectically as the medium through which contemporary praxis and historical formations meet. Language is seen as a creative, generative system which makes for the possibility of understanding. At the same time, language must be seen as a system of constraints on the vehicle of meaning. That is, although language allows us to create more than was there previously--allowing the generation of knowledge--it allows such only within a specific structural framework. Language is a public medium; as such, constraints exist on how meanings are used. A critical theory of communication would concern itself with those constraints, their development and transcendence.[31]

## SUBJECT-OBJECT

The question of the subject-object relationship is of major importance for critical theory in that it encompasses the relationship of the theorist to the object of study, the question of value-free research, and the relationship of social theory to social practice. Mainstream social science typically assumes that the observer is able to remove him/herself from what he or she observes, that he/she can and does function independently of the reality he or she studies. This implies that some standard of objectivity has been reached. Thus, objectivity entails the separation of fact from value in an effort to create a value-free social science.

Based on a dialectical conception of social reality, critical theory rejects the subject-object dualism. Epistemologically, in the process of constructing reality a contradiction exists between the subjective and objective moments of impression formation.[32] Even in the temporary unity of the experienced object, the antithetical aspects of the moment are retained, although they are synthesized into a working perceptual alliance. But the different components of this new working reality encounter other objective forms, which, through negation changes the internal composition of the subject making it non-identical with its own previous identity, and so on. The unity of the experienced object, then, is a unity of opposites wherein subjectivity is the form of the objective (the how of reality), and the objective defines the subjective.[33] Adorno writes that, "In Hegel, the productive activity of the mind also and simultaneously appropriates its own product, just as the product appropriates [shapes] the subject."[34] In other words, the various categories through which the world is interpreted are products of the very same object world they are formed to order and explain. As such, subjectivity cannot exist without objectivity and vice versa. The two are inseparable, they are "moments" of one and the same process.

Positivist social theory strives to limit the inevitable subjectivity in research. Such efforts are futile. Rather than trying to abrogate subjectivity, argues Adorno, we should "bring this subjectivity back to its objectivity," through self-reflection.[35] Methodologically, this means reflection on the knowledge-interest relationship, on the pre-suppositions and goals of theory,

---

[31] In addition to praxis, interpretation, and language, a critical theory of communication should account for the influence of ideology on the process of communication. However, space does not permit consideration of the question of ideology and communication. See, for example, Claus Mueller, The Politics of Communication (London: Oxford Press, 1973); and Alvin Goulder, The Dialectic and Ideology and Technology (New York: Seabury, 1976).

[32] T. W. Adorno, "Subject and Object," in The Essential Frankfurt School Reader, ed. A. Arato & E. Gebhart (New York: Urizen Books, 1978), 487-511.

[33] Adorno, "Subject and Object."

[34] Adorno, quoted by Arato and Gebhardt, p. 402.

[35] Adorno, "Subject and Object."

and reflection on the social impact of theory. It means that "we should be inside and outside the object simultaneously."[36] Politically and socially, "self-reflection leads to insight due to the fact that what has previously been unconscious in a manner rich in practical consequences."[37]

Adorno's dialectical depiction of the nature of impression formation constitutes a critique of the traditional value-free position in social science. The very process of the scientist's impression formation alters social reality: the researcher cannot help but influence the object of study. To separate the subject from that which is studied--objectivity reality--would be misleading. As such, the positivist belief in apparently neutral techniques of verification for testing statements about social reality is nonsense. In actuality, the process of social inquiry and investigation is itself a product of a "framework of controversial, ideologically committed visions of the world."[38]

Recognizing the social nature of social research implies for a critical theory of communication continual re-evaluation of the theory-practice relationship. Theory does indeed direct praxis. At the same time, however, praxis itself (i.e., the actual development of economic, social and political relationships influences theory. Practice continually poses new problems and repeatedly calls original theoretical propositions into question. A critical theory of communication, therefore, must continually renew itself in light of changes in communicative practice. A critical theory of communication must be reflexive.

A critical theory of communication rejects the value-free position in social theory and research. The value-free position is a myth; as such, the question is not whether social scientists should strive to be value free, but rather which values are to be pursued and which alternatives exist. Thus, the choice for the social scientist becomes a choice of whose interests will be served by his or her work. For the social scientist, the alternatives available are to continue to serve groups in power, or to alter his or her skills to serve the interests of society as a whole. The social scientist who ascribes to critical theory serves the interests of the latter. Horkheimer put it a little differently: either the theorist should give expression to the contradictions of everyday social life and interaction or offer legitimizations for the continued existence of the domination of the present order.[39] Critique, in this case, provides a theory and method for doing the former.

In summary, a critical theory of communication could not be content with describing some isolated aspect of communication. Rather, critique would have to come to terms with the nature of communication as a dialectical event and would have to recognize the inevitability of praxis as concomitant with theory's role in the social world. To achieve this end, a critical analysis of the nature of society and communication's role in it is necessary to reveal the inadequacy of the natural attitude of everyday understanding. The goal of a critical theory of communication would be a re-awakening of consciousness so that people may realize their actual condition as active organisms employing taken for granted cultural meanings as tools for the construction and re-construction of social reality and subsequent praxis. A critical theory of communication, rather than being satisfied with attempts to describe the categories of meaning and their mutual relations, would seek to reveal the role of inter-

---

[36]Adorno, quoted by Arato and Gebhardt, p. 403.

[37]J. Habermas, *Theory and Practice* (London: Heinemann, 1974), p. 23.

[38]J. J. Wiatr, "Sociology-Marxism-Reality," in *Marxism and Sociology*, ed. Peter Berger (New York: Appleton-Century-Crofts, 1969), p. 29.

[39]Max Horkheimer, "Traditional and Critical Theory."

retation and action in reaffirming and modifying categories so that human beings
might realize the historical relativity of the alienating and estranged world
in which they exist.  In other words, communication theory would become a form
of social criticism oriented toward the increasing emancipation of individuals
from social structures which distort their development.  Obviously, a critical
theory of communication cannot solve all the problems encountered in theorizing
about communication; it does, however, offer a better way of understanding the
nature of social reality and the problems involved in social praxis because it
begins by questioning the "given."  Critical theory refuses to accept the "given
facts" as the context of validation and, as such, provides the theorist with a
chance to reflect on what it means to do social research, to reconsider what
communication theory could be, and to re-evaluate what interests or purposes
such a theory might serve.

Timothy Stephen
Bowling Green State University

Speech communication scholars are currently stressing a need for
theoretic advancement.[1] Fisher, for example, has surveyed dominant theoretic
perspectives within the discipline. It is noteworthy that of those which he
identifies, not one originated within our own field of inquiry. According
to Fisher, speech communication has imported most of its major theories and
methodologies from other disciplines, primarily psychology and sociology. Yet
the discipline of speech communication predicates its domain upon the belief
that there is something truly unique as well as scientifically useful and
socially productive in the study of human communicative phenomena. Scholars
emphasize that our scientific interests are different from those of psychologists, sociologists, and other social scientists in our prevailing interest
in symbolic phenomena. Many feel that this interest defines or should define
the parameters of the domain of scientific inquiry which is speech communication.[2]

The methodologies and theories which our field has imported, with the
exception of those advanced by symbolic interactionists, were not developed
with human symbol usage in mind. Rather, they were developed to meet the
needs of other specialized domains of inquiry which do not particularly identify themselves with a science of symbolic processes. Current methodological
approaches within our field deemphasize or deny communication as process.[3]
Similarly, they deny communication as symbolic. Questions pertinent to a
symbolic view of communication await the development of methodologies which
are true to a symbolic, processual reality.

This essay will sketch elements of theories of symbolicity which help
to explain weaknesses and strengths of current methodological orientations.
The emergent, systemic nature of symbolic processes is considered in view
of concepts and tenets of traditional methodologies. Guidelines are presented for constructing symbolic methodologies. Finally, the concept of
prediction is considered from the perspective of a symbolic science.

The arguments developed assume an interaction between the elements of
a set of available methodologies and the theoretic advances which are possible
within a discipline of inquiry. For example, prior to the development of
advanced inferential statistics, the science of agriculture depended upon

Phenomenology in Rhetoric and Communication, ed. Stanley Deetz. Copyright, 1981, The Center
for Advanced Research in Phenomenology and the University Press of America.

[1]See, for example, V. Cronen and L. Davis, "Alternative Approaches for the Communication
Theorist: Problems in the Laws-Rules-Systems Trichotomy," Human Communication Research, 4 (1978),
120-128; B. Fisher, Perspectives on Human Communication (New York: Macmillan, 1978); and G. Miller,
"The Current Status of Theory and Research in Interpersonal Communication," Human Communication
Research, 4 (1978), 164-178.

[2]Compare with K. Campbell, "The Ontological Foundations of Rhetorical Inquiry," Philosophy and
Rhetoric, 3 (1970), 97-108.

[3]D. Smith, "Communication and the Idea of Process," Speech Monographs, 39 (1972), 174-182.

the farmer's and the researcher's hunch. The relationship between dependent variables, such as crop yield, and independent variables, such as soil composition and climatic conditions could not be clearly examined and specified.

The field of speech communication's research endeavors characteristically utilize one of two methodologies: either an historical-critical or an experimental-statistical methodology.[4] Neither of these methodologies were invented with the study of symbol usage in communication in mind. The historical-critical methods were imported from disciplines interested in the past and the experimental-statistical methods were imported from disciplines studying natural phenomena such as agriculture, physics, and medicine. The historical-critical methods fall short of advancing a science of symbolic processes in their relatively exclusive emphasis on content analysis of public forms of communication. The experimental-statistical methods fall short through their inherent postulation of invariant, sign or signal relationships among a species that is characteristically symbol using. Phenomenological psychologists have stressed that a science interested in characteristically human phenomena must have a methodology which attends to the description of meanings.[5] A science of symbolicity shares this emphasis but is also in need of methods which attend to symbolic processes involved in the construction, transformation, and sedimentation of meaning.

To focus on communication as a symbolic process is to stress that humans operate within a subjective, semantic universe and that this universe is forever transformed by present experiencing. The relationship between experienced phenomena and the phenomena themselves is arbitrary, which is to say that it is dependent upon the unique symbolic processes of the experiencing being. Humans create meaning from the experience of a stimulus rather than extract meaning from properties inherent to the stimulus itself. If a stimulus was to convey the same meaning for every being that encountered it, then the nature of the relationship between the stimulus and the experiencing being would not be symbolic, but a sign or signal relationship. In a symbolic relationship, meanings are arbitrary, varying from one person to another, while in sign or signal relationship meanings are fixed and invariant. Since humans reside in a universe which is an almost wholly symbolic one, we understand human experience by empathically understanding the unique symbolic transformations a given being enacts when encountering an aspect of experience.

The nature of symbolic processes may be more specifically stated. The relationship between the human experience of a stimulus object and the object itself is metaphoric, emergent, or systemic. Elements of a stimulus object are understood through a combining of present experiencing with aspects of the total symbolic store in such a way that present experience is transformed by encountering the symbolic store and, reciprocally, the symbolic store is transformed as it encounters present experiencing. Thus, meanings arise through a systemic interaction among symbolic elements; they are metaphors which subsume aspects of total being as well as aspects of present experiencing. The nature of this process accounts for and predicts emergent and novel human transactions and emphasizes semantic transformations which mediate between stimuli and experience. The process of experience and, more specifically, the process of communication is therefore a process of metaphoring.[6]

---

[4]C. Arnold, "Rhetorical and Communication Studies: Two Worlds or One?" *Western Speech*, 36 (1972), 75-81.

[5]A. Giorgi, "Toward Phenomenologically Based Research in Psychology," *Journal of Phenomenological Psychology*, 1 (1970), 75-98.

[6]Compare with R. Romanyshyn, "Metaphors and Human Behavior," *Journal of Phenomenological Psychology*, 5 (1975), 441-460.

In signal communication, by contrast, the process does not involve a remaking or recreation of reality. Rather, the process is a linear one in which reality, in the form of a stimulus, directly presents itself. When signal communication is present, the process is mechanical and direct rather than metaphoric and transformational. This distinction between signal and symbolic relationships has helped in understanding communicative phenomena and has been employed by scholars such as Burke[7] and Langer[8] to distinguish among uniquely human communicative phenomena and communicative phenomena in general. An emphasis on symbolic processes directs attention from a search for sign-like invariances in human communication, centering instead upon meaning and upon the formal aspects of symbolic experience.

Insofar as human experience is symbolic and metaphorically structured, the relationship between experience and behavior is no more direct for a symbol using being than the relationship between stimulus and experience. If human communication were sign-like, a scientific method which treated it as such would be appropriate. Since human communication is symbolic, however, current methodologies which ignore or deny symbolic processes are inappropriate. When communication is viewed symbolically, the study of overt behavior with its accompanying assumption of sign-like relations between experience and reality is not a study of communication.

The literature addressing experimental methods isolates various sources of error which may jeopardize a researcher's understanding of phenomena. Campbell and Stanley[9] have written a useful tract devoted to an analysis of this problem. To the authors' list of twelve factors which may confound the interpretation of research results, a thirteenth may be added. This effect, which is a consequence of the symbolic nature of human communication may be titled "The Emergent or Metaphoric Effects of Symbol Usage." This effect is present as a source of error to the extent that the researcher fails to treat the concatenation of metaphoric transformations which occur along the way to a final version of a research report. All too frequently researchers would seem to assume that (1) the presence of some experimental stimulus elicits a sign-like response in a subject; (2) that the subject's behavioral response is a sign-like representation of an experience of the stimulus; (3) that a sign-like relationship operates between the behavioral response and a statistic which is computed to represent that response; (4) that there is a sign-like relationship between a researcher's experience of a statistical representation and the nature of conclusions reported in a research monograph and an auditor's experience of the research monograph. In fact, each step in this chain is symbolic and metaphorically transformational. The nature of this process calls into question the utility of current experimental-statistical research procedures for investigating symbolic aspects of communication. If these methods are to be at all useful to a science of symbolicity, they must at least be recast.

## CONTRASTING METHODOLOGICAL ORIENTATIONS

The experimental-statistical methods are presently modeled in accordance with the study of phenomena of the physical sciences and behavioral psychology. In this respect they are designed to investigate sign-like relationships among phenomena. However, methodologies which would advance

[7] K. Burke, <u>Language as Symbolic Action: Essays on Life, Literature, and Method</u> (Berkeley, California: University of California Press, 1966).

[8] S. Langer, <u>Philosophy in a New Key: A Study in the Symbolism of Reason, Rite and Art</u>, 3rd ed. (Cambridge, Massachusetts: Harvard University Press, 1960).

[9] D. Campbell and J. Stanley, <u>Experimental and Quasi-Experimental Designs for Research</u> (Chicago: Rand McNally, 1963).

a science of the symbolic aspects of communication must assess processes involved in the creation of meaning and in the transformations of experience which occur through communication. The difference in the type of method required by a science of symbolic communication and extant experimental-statistical techniques is highlighted by an examination of four god terms of experimental-statistical methodology: objectivity, control, validity, and reliability.

## Objectivity

Traditional methodologies wish to approach what is purported to be an "objective" view of communication phenomena. Research projects are considered objective to the extent that researchers are personally removed and disen-franchised with phenomena under consideration. As has been argued, however, it is impossible to gain objectivity by increasing the length of the infer-ential chain which begins with a subject's experience and ends with publica-tion of a research report. As the length of the transformational chain increases, the likelihood that aspects of the lived experience of the subject will be accurately represented in the research report drastically decreases. Due to the nature of communication, the subject experiences through metaphor-ing. Each time an experience is communicated it is passed through another process of metaphoring. In traditional methodologies, the researcher must interpret metaphors of metaphors in an amount proportionate to the number of steps in the transformational chain. Thus, in order to understand a subject's symbolic process, it is desirable to decrease the length of the chain, putting the researcher in closer proximity to the subject.

In another sense, traditional methodologies consider research to be ob-jective to the extent that the researcher is removed from the interpretation of research results. The idea is that in objective research, the data will speak for themselves. What is meant by "data" is numerical transformations of a subject's overt behavior. It is, however, impossible to remove the researcher's interpretive process from the research situation. The researcher selects variables of interest by interpreting a situation in a certain fashion. The researcher selects, through interpretation of a situation, a method of transcribing behavior into numerical representations which are further inter-preted into a statement about the outcomes of the research. Rather than treating these inevitabilities as contaminating or confounding, a symbolic science views them as important instances of symbolic processes which them-selves hold interest for study.

The communication researcher traditionally strives for objectivity through movement away from phenomena of interest. However, since symbolic phenomena manifest themselves in symbolic ways, objectivity in research may never be fully achieved. The research process is and will remain a symbolic process of communication. The question which a communication researcher might usefully consider, then, is what sort of representation of the phe-nomena will yield results subject to the least amount of interpretation with the highest possible degree of correspondence with the lived experience of the subject? Another way to pose this question is to ask how many steps are involved in the transformational chain? On the one hand, the researcher may utilize a design in which a survey is administered by a research assistant and is subsequently coded into numerical representations which are then sub-jected to computer analysis and finally to the researcher's own interpretation. On the other, the researcher may opt for a procedural format which transcribes a subject's verbal transformation of an experience more or less directly into the research report. Rather than striving for "objective" methods for sym-bolic research, it is suggested that the scholar might more usefully strive for methods which are "responsive" to the subject's experience and modes of communicating with regard to that experience. An allegiance to a principle of responsivity would move the researcher toward a greater degree of participation with the symbolic experiencing of subjects.

## Control

Traditional experimental approaches to communication inquiry emphasize the concept of "control." Kerlinger[10] asserts that techniques of experimental design have "one grand purpose: to control variance" and McGuigan[11] maintains that "the word 'control' implies that the experimenter has a certain power over the conditions of his experiment." Within this traditional view, control is maintained through the use of research designs through which an experimenter arranges stimuli in such a way that subjects are presumed to encounter some known conditions. The responses of subjects are generally interpreted through a process of abstracting from their symbolic experience to a numerical language which is subject to the logic of social statistics.

If it is assumed that meanings arise through a process of metaphoring, then experimental conditions will be experienced and known metaphorically by subjects, and this, in turn, brings into quesiton traditional methods of variable control. With a view of reality as socially constructed, symbolic, and metaphoric, the researcher does not presuppose a constancy of experience among subjects exposed to a similar or identical stimulus-set. The meanings which are assigned to stimuli will vary from one subject to the next. This variance may be considered a source of error by those interested in communication as sign, but it is precisely the object of study in symbolic investigations. The idea is to understand the range of meanings which may emerge in a situation and to achieve a precise idea of the transformational calculus which governs the dynamics of semantic emergence. Within this perspective, it is necessary to shift the emphasis in the design of research from a concentration on controlling conditions to an emphasis upon developing techniques for understanding emergent experience.

The amount of experimental and statistical control inherent in the research project is related to the responsivity of the research and to the degree of correspondence between the subject's symbolic experience and the research report. The greater the experimental control, the less the responsivity of the design and the lower the degree of correspondence. As Miller and Nicholson[12] have noted, the use of statistics and other types of control, "reflects a compromise between generalizability and precision." As traditional experimental controls are deemphasized the researcher may indeed be less able to measure precisely communication as sign. This does not mean, however, that the researcher is similarly handicapped when the object of study is symbol. In symbolic research precision is reflected by the degree of correspondence between the experience of a subject and the research report. This will increase with decontrol and heightened responsivity in research design.

Traditional methods of control were devised to serve a science interested in the construction of a set of abstract generalizations or "laws" positing invariant sign relationships among communicators. A symbolic science must grapple with the problem of describing phenomenological aspects of symbolic processes. This requires research procedures that are responsive to symbolic relationships and whose emphasis leads to giving first priority to understanding differences in the ways subjects interpret communication situations rather than in attempting to control them.

[10] F. Kerlinger, Foundations of Behavioral Research, 2nd ed. (New York: Holt, Rinehart and Winston, 1973), p. 300.

[11] F. McGuigan, Experimental Psychology: A Methodological Approach, 2nd ed. (Englewood Cliffs, New Jersey: Prentice-Hall, 1968), p. 120.

[12] G. Miller and H. Nicholson, Communication Inquiry: A Perspective on a Process (Reading, Massachusetts: Addison-Wesley, 1976), p. 167.

Validity
   A third term which has acquired a sort of divine status in the annals of
experimental-statistical research is "validity."  In the traditional approach,
validity exists in the extent to which experimental conditions correspond to
lived experience.  Validity in instrumentation rests upon the correspondence
between aspects of experience recorded by a measuring tool and nuances of
experience the instrument is purported to measure.  The greater the validity
of an instrument, the more readily its results may be generalized to individuals in the population.  Experimental designs attempt to achieve validity by
creating artificial stimulus conditions which correspond to stimulus conditions
which occur naturally.

   Traditional interpretations of the concept of validity deemphasize the
symbolic nature of experience and instead emphasize direct, invariant signal
relationships.  Emergent symbolic processes which predict a dissimilarity
of interpretation of experimental conditions or measuring devices are treated
as contaminating factors which jeopardize validity.  An emphasis on the
symbolic aspects of communication directs researchers toward understanding
exactly those processes that create differential meaning within a communicative
context.  The traditional interpretation of the notion of validity, on the
other hand, treats these processes as "error variance."

   It is highly questionable that validity in the traditional sense can
ever be achieved.  Whether a research procedure is seen as a valid representation of an aspect of lived experience is dependent upon whose perspective is
used in  making the determination.  The world of researchers and social
scientists generally differentiates itself from the world of subjects in terms
of episteme.  Kerlinger argues that the non-scientist interprets the world
through an epistemology of common sense.  Scientists, however, know the world
through a process of controlled observation and through the use of research
procedures which posit explicit decision rules for establishing truths and
verifying ideas.  The experimental-statistical paradigm is held in esteem
insofar as its epistemology is reasoned to yield more credible conclusions.
This juxtaposition of epistemologies to fortify the traditional approach as
the more desirable is nonproductive from a symbolic perspective.  The question
should not be one of "which is the better method" but rather of identifying
the varieties of epistemic contexts.

   Burke approaches the problem in his discussion of terministic screens
where he argues that symbolic truths are relative to the particular sub-uni-
verse of symbols and meanings in which one operates.  Similarly, Thayer[13]
conceives of social groups as epistemic communities in which one's meanings
and ways of determining meanings are confirmed.  Thus, validity coefficients
determined on the criteria of traditional approaches to research may be expected to have little correspondence to a subject's interpretation of the
amount of validity inherent in a research situation.  Again, it is precisely
this variance which is of interest to the student of symbolic communication.

   The investigator of symbolic aspects of communication processes is guided
by two premises.  The first posits communication as metaphoric; the second
views meaning as emergent.  Hence, traditional orientations to the idea of
validity in research must be recast.  Symbol usage differentiates among people
and separates them from direct knowledge of a natural, positive universe.  The
study of symbolic communication thus looks not at what is valid across subjects
but instead at how various subjects find validity in their everyday experiences.

   [13]L. Thayer, "Knowledge, Order, and Communication," in Brent Rubin and John Kim, eds., General
Systems Theory and Human Communication (Rochelle Park, New Jersey: Hayden Book Co., 1975), pp. 237-
245.

## Reliability

An experimental truth is held to be "reliable" to the extent that it may be demonstrated repeatedly through empirical tests. Similarly, a reliable measuring instrument must demonstrate an ability to discriminate among communicators through time and under a variety of specified conditions. These interpretations of the concept of reliability have served a science interested in treating communication as sign-like. However, a science interested in understanding symbolic operations is concerned with communication processes which transform people and which are used by people to transform the experiences of others. The symbolic emphasis highlights emergence, a reality which is generated through communication with others, and the time-bound nature of truths. Thus, the traditional notion of reliability is radically deemphasized in symbolic research. Symbolic inquiry is interested in developing an understanding of the transformational characteristics of conditions rather than in viewing them as impediments to the advancement of knowledge. Finally, it is interested in the uniqueness of experience rather than in its repeatability. The notion of reliability, as with those of objectivity, control, and validity, is realigned to assist in the accumulation of knowledge of the symbolic. The four terms, all central within the traditional approaches to communication research, reflect an interest in different sorts of communication phenomena than those which interest the student of symbolicity. Traditionalists use extant research procedures to extract sign-like relationships among communicative events. A symbol oriented science, by contrast, is interested in describing the nature of varying processes of symbolic action. A methodological issue which confronts the student of symbolicity is, of course, how to tap into symbolic processes and semantic structures in a way that will yield useful analytic material.

## GUIDELINES FOR SYMBOLIC INQUIRY

One method for attaining useful symbolic data employs an empathic dialog between subject and researcher. This dialog has two aims. First, to establish as accurately as possible the meaning the subject creates for understanding and coping with the research situation itself. The researcher is concerned with the effects of the research project's intrusion into the experience of the subject. The researcher seeks to assess the manner in which his or her presence influences the subject's symbolic process. The second aim of the empathic dialog is in approximating the meanings a subject creates with respect to research variables. The nature of the dialog is such that researcher and subject "team up" to formulate useful conclusions about the nature of symbolic processes.

The researcher is not limited to verbal dialog in obtaining useful data. The emphasis of study lies in the description and analysis of processes involved in the construction and evolution of meaning. It may be advanced by attending to characteristics of contexts in which the subject participates or by observing the subject interacting with others or with objects. It is important to note, however, that as the researcher moves from direct verbal contact with subjects, the extent to which the researcher must rely on inference increases. All research involves inference but open and direct contact with subjects helps to ascertain levels of inference in data and allows a check on the accuracy of results.

Methods of symbolic research may take many forms. Among these are participant observation, content analysis of written or verbal material, and interviewing subjects and their significant others. Since there is no well developed line of symbolic research to use as a methodological guide, the range of methods cannot be specified. A method is appropriate for the study of symbolic processes to the extent that it is able to account for the relationship between the symbolic epistemologies of researchers and those of subjects. The appropriateness or adequacy of a proposed method is dependent upon the nature of the research question under investigation. A chosen method may need to be discarded or modified once the researcher has gained exposure to the symbolic realm of the subject and has become sensitive to a method's adequacy in treating the research question. Rather than define any one set of methods as appropriate for symbolic research, it is more productive to indicate the issues that are pertinent to a research project which would treat symbolicity. Such projects are productive to the extent that the research report is true to the lived experience of subjects. Also, they are productive to the extent that the researcher has considered the effects of semantic intrusions brought about by the subject's experience of the research project. Finally, such projects are productive to the extent that they further our understanding of the emergent, metaphoric processes of communication. Current methodologies have not progressed very far in treating any of these issues. Consequently, the symbolic researcher carries a considerable burden of creativity.

There is a noticable movement within several social science disciplines toward the combining of available objective and subjective methodologies to construct a composite approach to the study of social phenomena. Denzin[14] and Olson and Cromwell[15] are outstanding among advocates of this position. Denzin calls for the combination of participant observation with other methods such as survey research and the analysis of documents to form a "triangulated" approach to research. Similarly, Olson and Cromwell argue for a "multi-method multi-trait" approach which combines methods varying with regard to the reporter's frame of reference (insider versus outsider) and the type of data (subjective versus objective). It is believed that the combination of methods will overcome the increasingly well documented fact that scientific understandings of phenomena are highly contingent upon whose perspective is used as a data source and the type of instrumentation employed.[16]

Giorgi[17] has, however, cautioned that the use of composite methodologies "merely brings together . . . abstract views without making a concrete synthesis." Insofar as it remains for traditional approaches to demonstrate their value for symbolic analyses, there seems no compelling reason to assume that when used in combination with one another, traditional methods will show any greater contribution to knowledge of the symbolic than they do individually. The combination of methods seems likely to lead to exactly the problem the symbolic researcher wishes to confront, i.e., how to understand and describe operations of varying epistemologies and the differing symbolic processes which accompany them. The symbolic researcher is not interested in the construction of a single method which will yield up a picture of an objective, hard and true reality. Rather, the researcher is interested in utilizing meta-level methods to understand and describe methods of knowing (epistemologies) in the first place. Such a desire moves the researcher to pursue genuine innovations as opposed to combining traditional methods.

[14]N. Denzin, The Research Act: A Theoretical Introduction to Sociological Methods (Chicago: Aldine Publishing, 1970).

[15]D. Olson and R. Cromwell, "Methodological Issues in Family Power," in R. Cromwell and D. Olson eds., Power in Families (New York: Sage, 1975), pp. 131-150.

[16]The literature addressing marital and family interaction offers clear examples of this sort of methodological relativity where researchers are keenly aware of the problem. See, for example, D. Olson, "Insiders' and Outsiders' Views of Relationship: Research Studies," in G. Levinger and H. Rausch, eds., Close Relationships: Perspectives on the Meaning of Intimacy (Amherst, Massachusetts: University of Massachusetts Press, 1977), pp. 177-135.

[17]A. Giorgi, "Convergences and Differences Between Phenomenological Psychology and Behaviorism: A Beginning Dialog," Behaviorism, 3 (1975), pp. 200-212.

## PREDICTION IN SYMBOLIC RESEARCH

Social psychologists,[18] sociologists,[19] and communication researchers[20] alike have placed a premium on the role of prediction in science. This traditional view of science is founded upon an emphasis of sign-like aspects of communication and social behavior. An interest in symbolicity, however, dictates an interest in emergent meaning and in the epistemological functions of communication. This emphasis militates against assigning a central role to prediction for two reasons. First, prediction and systemic emergence are somewhat contradictory terms. We may predict on an abstract level that meanings will combine in systemic ways and that the process of communication will be essentially metaphoric. However, we cannot predict the emergent outcomes which follow the combination of specific semantic elements. The second reason for reconsidering the utility of prediction for a symbolic science is, simply, that so little is currently known about the nuances of symbolicity. The science of the symbolic aspects of communication is in its infancy. Therefore, here, as in any other fledgling science, first concerns appropriately lie in the description and cataloging of phenomena of interest. Prediction is always secondary to useful description. Nevertheless, the role of prediction in a science of the symbolic may need to be conceptualized differently than in traditional, sign oriented research. This is so not only because of the systemic nature of symbolic material but also because of the particular communicative relationship between social scientist and subject.

The traditional view of communication research fails to consider the symbolic relationship between subjects and researchers both in the research situation itself and also in the larger cultural milieu. Gergen[21] has analyzed interface of science and society. He argues that scientific theories of social behavior are quickly consumed by the larger society through ever widening channels of the mass media. Once popularized versions of scientific thought become well known, the assumptions about the society upon which a theory was based are no longer tenable. The social body is transformed as it learns what scientists think about it. Society and science thus form a feedback loop as social theories influence the society they address, transform it, and consequently present scientists with a new type of society to study.

Science legislates meaning. This occurs not only through educational channels but also as scientists serve as consultants to government, industry, and other agencies of social policy. Lasch[22] has examined the history of scientific influence upon social policy and family life during the twentieth century. He notes changes in public attitude and action which are attributable to the dicta of social scientific thought. Similarly, Warwick and Linninger[23] acknowledge this feedback phenomenon, labeling it "the self-

---

[18]M. Shaw and P. Constanzo, Theories of Social Psychology (New York: McGraw-Hill, 1970), for example.

[19]See, for example, H. Blalock, Theory Construction: From Verbal to Mathematical Formulations (Englewood Cliffs, New Jersey: Prentice-Hall, 1969) and P. Reynolds, A Primer in Theory Construction (Indianapolis: Bobbs-Merrill, 1971).

[20]See, for example, A. Bochner, "On Taking Ourselves Seriously: An Analysis of Some Persistent Problems and Promising Directions in Interpersonal Research," Human Communication Research, 4 (1978) 179-191; Miller, and Miller and Nicholson.

[21]K. Gergen, "Social Psychology as History," Journal of Personality and Social Psychology, 26 (1973), 304-320.

[22]C. Lasch, Haven in a Heartless World (New York: Basic Books, 1975).

[23]D. Warwick and C. Lininger, The Sample Survey: Theory and Practice (New York: McGraw-Hill, 1973), p. 55.

defeating prophecy" which occurs as research "results lead to a change in public or official awareness, which, in turn, reduces the likelihood of the predicted behavior."

The traditional view of communication research assumes that through the use of random sampling, random assignment, and double blind experimental designs, research purposes could be masked from an unassuming subject population. However, the research on research studies[24] has served to highlight basic flaws in such assumptions. Subjects are as involved in creating meanings pertinent to understanding researchers and researcher situations as researchers themselves are interested in creating meanings pertinent to the understanding of their subjects. The empirical-statistical approach has regarded the communicative relationship between subjects and researchers as something of a contaminating influence and has developed progressively refined techniques for separating the two. As this occurs, however, the researcher becomes less directly involved with subjects and consequently less able to adequately assess symbolic processes. The more removed the researcher becomes from the subject, the longer the chain of inference between the lived experience of subjects and the research report and the more abstraction and the less applicability the results possess for any particular person.

## SUMMARY AND CONCLUSION

This essay has argued that an incongruity exists between the nature of communication phenomena and the means used to assess communication phenomena. The field of speech communication posits symbolic processes as its differentia among the social sciences. At the same time, however, the predominant methodological approaches used in speech communication research are only applicable to a study of communication treated as signal or sign, not as a symbol. Historical-critical and empirical-statistical methods dominate studies conducted in the field. Neither of these were devised with the study of emergent symbolic processes in mind.

The empirical-statistical approach distances the researcher from the subject and decreases the probability that results will be reflective of symbolic process. Researchers interested in studying the symbolic aspects of communication processes must exercise inventiveness and creativity in devising research methods which are appropriate to such an interest. Methods are productive to the extent that they include the subject's phenomenal reality as a legitimate and necessary source of data. The researcher is encouraged to view the subject as a cooperative partner to the research project rather than as a naive, sign-using member of a population of unassuming individuals. The role of prediction for the researcher investigating symbolicity is viewed as secondary to that of description.

---

[24]See, for example, R. Rosenthal and R. Rosnow, eds., <u>Artifact in Behavioral Research</u> (New York: Academic Press, 1969).

# DISCUSSION / SUBDUED THOUGHT AS DISCOURSE*

RICHARD LANIGAN
SOUTHERN ILLINOIS UNIVERSITY

Human worlds are constructions, deconstructions, and reconstructions of conscious experience. This a priori condition of human communication informs our daily sensitivity for marking out Culture from Nature. The lived experience that we call 'time' is Nature's version of the experience of consciousness. And, the living consciousness that is Culture becomes the 'space' of experience. These temporal and spatial marking of Culture as the Symbol and Nature as the Symbolic are desperately familiar to us in the vicarious text and context of the discourse which mediates consciousness and experience. The very essence of discursive engagement is the marking of human wants (as themes of cultural desire) and needs (as themes of natural desire). Yet, the concrete presence of discourse is but the voice of subdued thought--the embodied dialectic of desire. Indeed, "the problem is to what extent thought that can and will be both anecdotal and geometrical may yet be called dialectical."[1]

These four papers share a common problematic in the theme of subdued thought in discourse. That theme is the dialectic tension between the narrative of personal incident and the epic of social structure. The papers subsequently display a common logic for discursive phenomena in various styles of human communication which include:

1. How consciousness emerges in experience: the construction of the Symbol in the Symbolic in Tim Stephens, "Toward a Phenomenological Methodology for the Study of Symbolic Communication."

2. When consciousness emerges in experience: the construction of the Symbolic in the Symbol in Robin Johnston, "Language Acquisition and the Phenomenological Approach: A Viable Combination."

3. Why experience emerges in consciousness: the reconstruction of the Symbol in the Symbolic in Robert Prior, "On the Logic and Method of Critical Theory and Its Implications for a Critical Theory of Communication."

4. What experience emerges in consciousness: the deconstruction of the Symbolic in the Symbol in Bryan Crow, "Toward a Phenomenology of Film Signification."

In short, the papers represent a progressive movement in conscious experience from Symbology, to Eidetic Symbology, to Critical Symbology, and to Productive Symbology.

---

Phenomenology in Rhetoric and Communication, ed. Stanley Deetz. Copyright, 1981, The Center for Advanced Research in Phenomenology and the University Press of America.

*This title belongs, of course, to Claude Levi-Strauss whose classic study La Pensee sauvage (1962) bears this same denomination. I have used my own translation ("subdued thought") rather than propogate the insensitivity of the "savage mind" usage.

[1] The Savage Mind (sic), anon. trans. (Chicago: University of Chicago Press, 1966), p. 245.

## SYMBOLOGY

Tim Stephen's paper is an explication of the emancipatory cognitive interest that the discipline of Speech Communication has in shifting research methodologies from the Symbol to the Symbolic. His analysis is insightful by suggesting that the contemporary specification of communication behavior as a process rather than a state is not matched respectively by appropriate research methods.

This is to say, the discipline recognizes that state descriptions of interpersonal communication are mechanical, linear, and direct in being inappropriately geometric. The state description is by definition communication as signal at the level of natural desire. The appropriate technology of the Symbol for such 'invariance under transformation' is a research design in the "experimental-statistical" tradition. The heuristic guideposts are, of course, objectivity, control, validity, and reliability. Stephens correctly suggests that in the paradigm shift from state to process conceptions of communication, i.e. from rhetoric to dialectic, a parallel shift in methodology has not (or is only beginning to) taken place. His diagnosis is clear and concise. Process communication is metaphoric, transformational, and reversible in being appropriately anecdotal for fulfilling cultural desires. Process is Symbolic. In short, the technology of research can remain intact. But the criteria in methodology need to be reformulated as new constructions. Objectivity should constitute responsiveness to experience. Control should be the use of differential interpretation. Validity should be the structural coherence in metaphoric shift. And, reliability should be the uniqueness of experience as the constant in every present possibility. The final test of how consciousness emerges in experience is the ability to account for the relationship between symbolic epistemologies of research and those of the subjects.

## EIDECTIC SYMBOLOGY

Robin Johnston's paper is an explication of the knowledge-constitutive interest that the discipline of Speech Communication has in shifting research data from the Symbolic to the Symbol in the study of language acquisition. Following the work of Saussure and Jakobson, it is clear that linguistic analysis cannot be accurately modeled exclusively on an adult language behavior context taken to be representative of mature, rational thought. This mistaken Symbolic view of language elements hypostatizes the categories for competence and performance which result in the generation of predictable data, but not in the location and description of data per se. The logical type is mistaken for the token in use. In short, the phonemic marking of Nature (the Symbolic) is an inappropriate research guide in the dialectic of language acquisition and use. Rather, the gesturally eidectic markings of Culture (the Symbol) as proposed by Merleau-Ponty should be utilized. Language belongs to the constitutive world of play, not to the regulative world of work.

A child's first words are not spontaneous, unique insertions of personality in the world of Nature. Sound is not a creation de novo. Articulate sound is speech in the repertoire of cognitions, affections, and conations of the human world of Culture. The child appropriates the rhythm and style of that repertoire (the Symbolic) and nominates a lived reality (the Symbol). The phenomenon of "deflation" in the child's acquisition behavior suggests a concrete, experiential proof for the validity of Merleau-Ponty's thesis, as Johnston so clearly argues in her paper. Thus she suggests the care and perspective that researchers must engage when recording and explicating the dialectic between language acquisition in the child and language behavior in the adult speaker.

## CRITICAL SYMBOLOGY

Robert Prior's paper is an explication of the purposive-rational interest that the discipline of Speech Communication has in reconstituting the dialectic relation between the Symbol and the Symbolic. That is, a basic question of critique is raised with respect to the analysis of communicative behavior. Why does cultural desire as social purpose require a rationality grounded in natural desire? An answer following the view set forth by the German Critical Theorists of the Frankfurt Institute tradition and championed by Jurgen Habermas is the reconstruction of rational interests structured on the essence of the observer's relation to observed social phenomena. Here, the research program of Critical Theory is fairly explicit. One begins to reconstruct Nature in Culture, i.e. locate the Symbol (natural desire) in the Symbolic (cultural desire), by explicating the very process of dialectic in discourse as action.

The subdued thought in discourse as communicative actions must be analyzed and demystified by (1) focusing on the conditions in the social world, (2) searching for and focusing on the emergent rather than the stable structures which relate changing people to changing circumstances, and (3) searching for possibilities inherent in social facts. In short, we must ask what is and what can be discursively grounded as a "rational society."

Thus, the dialectical foundations of the social world are best exposed by a critique of experience as it emerges in consciousness. This is especially the case for Critical Theory since consciousness is a reconstituted ideal of social needs and wants mediated by the dialectic of ideology. Experience becomes social consciousness within the rational structures of Culture that are uncovered by a critique of the natural condition: human desires.

## PRODUCTIVE SYMBOLOGY

Bryan Crow's paper is an explication of the knowledge-legitimizing interest the discipline of Speech Communication has in deconstructing the dialectic relation between the Symbolic and the Symbol. With the technology of film the shifting movement between the natural and cultural states of consciousness is deconstructed into the infrastructure and preconscious condition of dynamic experience. As such the problematic for a phenomenology of the cinematic experience becomes how people play in order to understand and appreciate films. That is, the researcher has to determine what experience emerges in the consciousness created by the interaction between (1) film and viewers and (2) viewers and viewers with respect to the film.

Crow's analysis is provocative in determining that film is a Symbolic experience (constrained by a natural attitude) that becomes a Symbol in consciousness (liberating a personal commitment). In brief, social knowledge is legitimated by talk. In this case, what experience a film provides is displayed in consciousness as the new meaning in communication about oneself, others, and a shared situation of perception. From a research point of view, Crow's theoretical procedure in locating the self-other-world connection is informed by the work of Schutz (and Merleau-Ponty).

Thus, the phenomenological researcher progressively works through (1) the act of experiencing (description), (2) the reflection on lived experience (reduction), and (3) the construction of meaning through conversation (interpretation). This three step methodology allows Crow to locate and express the dialectic of desire that is contained in the film experience. Using a sophisticated phenomenological procedure that incorporates the semiology of Metz in the reductive step of the analysis, Crow constructs a propositional model for describing phenomenological data (more correctly, "capta"). The laudatory result is the deconstruction of film experience as a "signification act" which consists of the experience and testing of validity claims to achieve consensus. In particular, signifier and signified code distinctions are used to specify speech acts within larger logical sets of "signification episodes." Crow's study is an exemplary demonstration of excellence in applied empirical research in the phenomenological tradition that can serve as a model for further investigations into the subdued thought in discourse.

# 5 / TOWARD A PHENOMENOLOGICAL PERSPECTIVE FOR RHETORICAL CRITICISM

CAROLE BLAIR
UNIVERSITY OF IOWA

In his essay, "The Experience of Criticism," Rosenfield suggests that the province of the rhetorical critic lies in "experiencing" phenomena. The response that ensues from this phenomenologically-based experience is an "appreciation by one released to reality [which] involves a monadic sense of thankful-ness, a gratitude that which might-have been-otherwise is as it is."[1] It is, according to Rosenfield, a pleasurable experience. Included among the advantages of such a concept of criticism is the position that questions of objectivity and subjectivity are rendered irrelevant.[2]

Richard Gregg argues that the phenomenological "orientation" requires an attempt to determine the cognitive structure which is determinant of the rhetorical act:

> Operating on the assumption that a person's perception and cognitive reality determine his attitudes and behavior, the critic focuses his energy upon discovering, defining, and describing those images which are active within the confines of the rhetorical act. He understands that the recipients of any rhetorical effort bring to the situation individual images of themselves and their reality which may in some form coalesce into shared group or public images. Such images form a screen, actively sifting and sorting, interpreting and coloring, evaluating and judging, and finally accepting or rejecting all messages which pass through it.[3]

Thus, according to Gregg, the critic attempts to determine the rhetor's view of the world.

These explanations of the critic's response are not necessarily inaccurate, but they are incomplete from both phenomenological and critical standpoints. The intent of this discussion is two-fold; it will attempt to indicate: 1) that the critic's experience should go beyond "appreciation" as Rosenfield describes it and the determination of the rhetor's value structure as Gregg suggests, and 2) that the subjectivity/objectivity consideration is important in understanding the critical potential of phenomenology. Although Rosenfield's view seems to be predicated upon the existentialist interpretation of phenomenology, these statements appear to be valid in applications of either Husserlian reductive phenomenology or existentialist phenomenology; both of these stances will be considered here.

_Phenomenology in Rhetoric and Communication_, ed. Stanley Deetz. Copyright, 1981, The Center for Advanced Research in Phenomenology and the University Press of America.

[1] Lawrence W. Rosenfield, "The Experience of Criticism," _Quarterly Journal of Speech_ 60 (December, 1974), 494.

[2] Rosenfield, pp. 489-96.

[3] Richard B. Gregg, "A Phenomenologically Oriented Approach to Rhetorical Criticism," _Central States Speech Journal_ 17 (May, 1966), 85.

## HUSSERLIAN PHENOMENOLOGY

The initial reduction required by Husserlian phenomenology is a shift from the "natural standpoint," which is described in this way:

> I am aware of a world, spread out in space endlessly, and in time becoming and become, without end. I am aware of it, that means, first of all, I discover it immediately, intuitively, I experience it. Through sight, touch, hearing, etc., in the different ways of sensory perception, corporeal things somehow spatially distributed are for me simply there, in verbal or figurative sense "present," whether or not I pay them special attention by busying myself with them, considering, thinking, feeling, willing.[4]

In order to move beyond this standpoint which contains "nothing of conceptual thinking," the subject must shift the focus of attention, concentrating upon his/her different acts of experience.[5] Thus, the subject is able to conceive of the objective world in a different manner and from a new perspective, in seeking the eidos or "immutable" and "necessary" characteristics of the object under consideration.[6] Simply stated, this initial reduction allows the mind a freedom of "movement" to engage an object from a variety of stances, much like bodily movement in the spatial/temporal world of the natural standpoint would allow various visual percepts of the same object.[7]

The second, or phenomenological, reduction, attempts to "reach reality as it is immediately given in primordial experience;" its goal is to know the Lebenswelt or the lived-world.[8] Raval describes the result of the phenomenological reduction as the "pure being of one's self focussing its light on the pure being of an object, and both stand revealed to each other. . . ."[9] Essences are here fully comprehended in terms of consciousness as it intends the object.

Rosenfield's description of the critical experience and response clearly is inconsistent with Husserlian phenomenology conceived in terms of the two reductive processes. Rosenfield would have the rhetorical critic remain at the natural standpoint level. He explains the stance of the critic in this way:

> we can as well understand aletheia as a receptiveness to the unhiddenness of reality, to the self-evident features of Being that dis-close (manifest) themselves to the witness. The opposite of dis-closed reality that radiates the truth of Being will be the unreal. . . .[10]

---

[4]Edmund Husserl, *Ideas: General Introduction to Pure Phenomenology* (1913), trans. by W. R. Boyce Gibson, reprinted in *The Age of Analysis*, ed. by Morton White (N.Y.: Mentor Books, 1956), p. 105.

[5]Husserl, p. 105.

[6]Joseph H. Kockelmans, "What is Phenomenology?" *Phenomenology: The Philosophy of Edmund Husserl and Its Interpretation*, ed. by Kockelmans (Garden City, N.Y.: Anchor Books, 1967), p. 31.

[7]See R. K. Raval, "An Essay on Phenomenology," *Philosophy and Phenomenological Research* 33 (December, 1972), 219-21.

[8]Kockelmans, p. 34.

[9]Raval, p. 222.

[10]Rosenfield, "Experience of Criticism," p. 493. Although Rosenfield does not assume the natural standpoint explicitly, his description of the stance is remarkably similar to the description of that found in Kockelmans, pp. 27-9, and in Husserl's *Encyclopedia Brittanica* article on phenomenology.

No reduction is sought in Rosenfield's scheme; yet the enunciated goal of the critic is to know the world.[11] Naturally, the strict adherent to Husserl's phenomenology would deny that the goal could be attained without reduction. He/she also would argue that, according to Rosenfield's analysis, the rhetorical critic's goal is founded upon the same premise as that of the natural scientist, strictly objective knowledge.[12] This conclusion clearly is not in accord with the sort of "appreciative" response that Rosenfield expects from the critic. If pure Husserlian phenomenology is implied, the distinction between objectivity and subjectivity is important to criticism. The movement away from the natural standpoint, initially to eidetic reduction, and finally to the phenomenological reduction, necessitates a consideration of the objective/ subjective dichotomy. The inconsistency of the stance and the desired response in Rosenfield's scheme, considered in terms of reduction, is indicative of the need for this sort of analysis.

The reductive model also explicates the pluralistic nature of rhetorical critism, a characteristic which Rosenfield attempts to discredit. He argues that: "A critic who comes upon a critical object in a state of mind such that he has a 'set of value' handy (or, indeed, any other system of categories) does not engage in a critical encounter so much as he processes perceptual data."[13] According to this reasoning, the critic's possession of a predetermined or preconceived framework within which he/she seeks the essence of the communicative act-object invalidates the process.[14] However, in the eidetic reduction, critical frameworks, if not explicitly encouraged, certainly evolve as a result. This initial reduction requires that the critic assume various stances or perspectives from which he/she perceives the object of the enquiry.

From this perspective, the value of the numerous extant critical stances is easily defensible. In studying the communicative act-object from as many stances as possible, our knowledge of it is increased. The critic's choice of stance is, of course, characterized by subjectivity, and the derived conclusions are subjective as well. If "incomplete" knowledge of the essent constitutes subjectivity, the conclusions reached by the eidetic reducation clearly are subjective. The act-object can be engaged from an infinite number of perspectives, and the critic's knowledge, to that extent, is always incomplete.[15] However, subjectivity should not be considered objectionable in the critical enterprise.[16]

The transcendental reduction also can be described as inherently subjective but for a slightly different reason. Presuppositions are suspended or bracketed at this stage, however, the phenomenological relationship between the critic and the act-object entails a subjectivity in itself, as Stewart argues:

> The fact that the noema does not change with each different noetic act demonstrates that noesis and noema are distinct. The perceiving of a

[11] See Ibid., 494.

[12] See Kockelmans, p. 28. Also see Edmund Husserl, The Idea of Phenomenology, trans. by William P. Alston and George Nakhnikian (The Hague: Martinos Nijhoff, 1973), p. 37.

[13] Rosenfield, "Experience of Criticism," p. 491. Emphasis added.

[14] That pluralism in criticism is explained in another of Rosenfield's essays, "The Anatomy of Critical Discourse," Speech Monographs 15 (March, 1968), 50-69.

[15] On the concept of infinity of stance in the eidetic reduction, see Ludwig Landgrebe, "The Phenomenological Concept of Experience," Philosophy and Phenomenological Research 34 (September, 1973), 9-11; J. Quentin Lauer, The Triumph of Subjectivity: An Introduction to Transcendental Phenomenology (N.Y.: Fordham University Press, 1958), p. 15.

[16] This assertion will be expanded further on in the paper. At this point, it may be defended simply by arguing that, to the extent that Husserlian phenomenology provides an acceptable foundation for the critic, subjectivity is not to the detriment of criticism because the system actually necessitates it.

tree, then is a meeting or encounter between these two distinct elements, consciousness and its objective correlate. . . . As Edie summarizes, "phenomenology is clearly not a realism or an empiricism. . . ." It is not a description of the 'real world,' but it is a description of the experience of the perceived world as the primary reality. . . . The world has no meaning in itself because meaning always involves consciousness . . . one cannot be "purely objective," because noema is also inextricably bound up with noesis.[17]

The meaningful interpretation of the act-object then is dependent in part upon the critic-as-subject. The critic actively experiences while the object of the critical act is experienced.

Subjectivity in the method should not be a cause for alarm, but it also should not be ignored. Merger of the objective and subjective obscures the possibilities of the critic from the standpoint of the reductive process. The reductive critical response clearly will be different from the response of the critic operating within the natural standpoint, as indicated by the juxtaposition of Rosenfield's concept of critical experience with the basic processes of reduction.

## EXISTENTIALIST PHENOMENOLOGY

The existentialist position is, of course, somewhat different, but if anything, the subjective consideration looms even larger in this realm. The existentialist's primary concern is the "impact of intentional consiousness on the subject or person's concrete world."[18] Spielburg describes this difference in emphasis:

Its subject-matter is human existence or "human reality," not consciousness, as in phenomenology. It studies existence in its involvement in a situation within a world. Consciousness, however, reflective as well as pre-reflective, is part of the encompassing structure of existence. . . . The ultimate objective of existentialism is not theoretical justification, but the awakening to a special way of life, usually called "authentic existence."[19]

The focal point in Heidegger's phenomenology, for example, is Dasein which is described as the "exposure of the horizon for interpretation of the meaning of Being in general."[20] Heidegger's hermeneutic method was directed toward discovering the essence of being, but his description of Dasein also indicates that it is the perceiving measure of other objects.

Sartre explains the coming-to-be of the self as "mediated" by everything that is not the self. In other words, the Other negates the self, and it is through this contact with the Other that the being of the self is clarified:

[17]John Stewart, "Foundations of Dialogic Communication," Quarterly Journal of Speech 64 (April, 1978), 189; also see Raval, p. 218. Rather than considering this argument as a statement of a reality-appearance dichotomy, and an ontological position, it is more helpful to understand it as an epistemological statement which claims that the critic's experience of the rhetorical act gives the act meaning. Without the subject's experience, the object has being, but has no essential characterization. Meaning is given to the object in the experience of it. See Stanley Deetz, "Words Without Things: Toward a Social Phenomenology of Language," Quarterly Journal of Speech 59 (Feb., 1973), 44.

[18]Stewart, p. 19.

[19]Herbert Spielburg, "Husserl's Phenomenology and Sartre's Existentialism," in Kockelmans, p. 225.

[20]Martin Heidegger, "Being and Time," in Basic Writings, ed. by David Farrell Krell (N.Y.: Harper and Row, 1977), p. 58.

Thus self-consciuosness is first a syncretic relation without truth between a subject and an object, an object which is not yet objectified and which is this subject himself. Since the impulse of this consciousness is to realize its concept by becoming conscious of itself in all respects, it tends to make itself valid externally by giving itself objectivity and manifest existence. It is concerned with making the "I am I" explicit and production itself as an object in order to attain the ultimate stage of development. This state in another sense is naturally the prime mover for the becoming of consciousness; it is self-consciousness in general, which is recognized in other self-consciousness and which is identical with them and with itself. The mediator is the Other. The Other appears along with myself since self-consciousness is identical with itself by means of the exclusion of every Other.[21]

Jaspers explains essentially the same idea more clearly when he describes existential philosophy as that which "does not merely focus on objects, but illuminates and brings to bear the thinker's own being."[22]

The critical objective, according to Sartre's analysis, must be a concept of the rhetor's "self-awareness" or pour soi.[23] This is not unlike Gregg's description of the goal of the critic, "discovering, defining, and describing those images which are active within the confines of the rhetorical act."[24] The objective is a consideration of the pour soi, made explicit to the critic by a determination of the "underlying value judgements present in a discourse, for such judgements are a direct result of the rhetor's concept of reality."[25]

The existentialists generally reject the reductive concept of Husserlian phenomenology, but their stance is also subjective. The existentialist philosopher clearly seeks a subjective stance by virtue of the fact that his/her concentration is upon the subject and its self-awareness.

Rosenfield's concept of critical experience obviously is more in tune with the existential position, but it remains incomplete. Gregg's analysis is entirely different but also lacking an essential element. When the two stances are considered in combination, the synthesis comes much closer to describing the perspective of the critic, but one crucial component remains untouched.[26] This can be illuminated by an examination of Husserl's three modes of intentionality.

## MODES OF INTENTIONALITY

Brentano's categorization of mental phenomena are reinterpreted by Husserl as the modes of intentionality, as Morrison explains: "for Brentano there are three basic classes of mental phenomena: presentations, judgments, and feelings.

[21]Jean-Paul Sartre, Being and Nothingness, trans. by Hazel E. Barnes (N.Y.: Simon and Schuster, 1978), p. 319.

[22]Karl Jaspers, cited in Ernst Breisach, Introduction to Modern Existentialism (N.Y.: Grove, 1962), p. 111.

[23]See Stewart, p. 193.

[24]Gregg, p. 85. See also Richard L. Lanigan, "Merleau-Ponty's Phenomenology of Communication," Philosophy Today 14 (Summer, 1970), 81.

[25]Gregg, p. 89.

[26]There seems to be a tension between the notions of phenomenological perspective and phenomenological method in criticism. The Rosenfield perspective or attitude does not lead subsequently to any specific workable method or objective, does not explicate a method. Both provide a firm orientation for the predispositions of the critic, but they do not attempt an explanation of the ways in which the phenomenologically-predisposed critic would engage in the critical act itself.

Husserl interprets these as ways of intending an object. Thus, one way of intending an object is to present (e.g., perceive) it, another is to make a judgment about it, etc."[27] Thus, the basic orientation of the critic should be founded in these three areas in combination.[28]

Presentation is the prerequisite of feeling and judgment. It consists of that which is the <u>object of</u> feeling and judgment. For the Husserlian, it is the <u>potentially</u> essential phenomenon, the result of the natural stance, the act-object to be reduced eidetically and phenomenologically. It is the content of the phenomenon. Existential presentation is the subject's ideation of the Other-as-self with emphasis on the subject's self as "negated." Gregg's proposed perspective for the critic emphasizes presentational intentionality because it seeks the essential content in the Husserlian sense, or the Other's being-in-the-world, in accord with the existentialist stance, depending upon the interpretation placed upon it.

Feeling is one of the responses issuing from the original experiential stance. Rosenfield explains it very well in his description of the critic's appreciation. Feeling occurs as an aesthetic response to the presentational intentionality. In other words, it is the affective intentionality of the presentational phenomenon. The subject may intend happiness, dismay, pleasure, anger, etc., in terms of the original presentational intentionality.

Both Gregg and Rosenfield overlook the third mode of intentionality, judgment, in their formulations of criticism's goals. Although description and appreciation are both important elements in the process, critical analysis is usually considered imcomplete without some sort of final judgement or evaluation.[29] While both Rosenfield and Gregg mention the critical judgement function very briefly in the aforementioned discussions or in previous ones, it is neither emphasized for its own merit or considered as a response to the original presentation.[30] The subject must evaluate the phenomenological essence or the concepts residing in the <u>Lebenswelt</u> of the rhetor in order to complete the critical act. Such is the conclusion of rhetorical critics as well as phenomenologists.

## THE PHENOMENOLOGICAL CONTRIBUTION

The potential contributions of phenomenology to rhetorical criticism are numerous, whether one considers the original conception presented by Husserl or the modified theory of the existentialists. A phenomenological perspective reveals the importance of the subjectivity-objectivity dichotomy in terms of its method, the kinds of information and responses that can be derived, and the relationship of the subjective to the objective. The methods emphasize and provide justification for a subjective stance, and they explain the ways in which the critic-as-subject response to the information derived from the method.

[27]James C. Morrison, "Husserl and Brentano On Intentionality," <u>Philosophy and Phenomenological Research</u> 31 (Sept., 1970), 38.

[28]Although some of the existentialists disagree with Husserl's concept of intentionality, it is unlikely that they would object to these modes as perceptive ones because they aid the subject in defining his/her own <u>pour soi</u> in light of that of the Other (rhetor).

[29]Most rhetorical critics agree that some sort of judgments or evaluative measures should be made. See Marie Hochmuth Nichols, <u>Rhetoric and Criticism</u> (Baton Rouge: Louisiana State University Press, 1963), p. 78; Donald C. Bryant, <u>Rhetorical Dimensions in Criticism</u> (Baton Rouge: Louisiana State Univ. Press, 1973), pp. 34-40; Karlyn Kohrs Campbell, <u>Critiques of Contemporary Rhetoric</u> (Belmont, California: Wadsworth, 1972), pp. 13-24; Edwin Black, <u>Rhetorical Criticism: A Study In Method</u> (N.Y.: Macmillan, 1965), pp. 1-9; Bruce E. Gronbeck, "Rhetorical History and Rhetorical Criticism: A Distinction," <u>Speech Teacher</u> 24 (November, 1975), 318-19; Carroll C. Arnold, <u>Criticism of Oral Rhetoric</u> (Columbus, Ohio: Charles E. Merrill, 1974), p. 16.

[30]Gregg, p. 85; Rosenfield, "Anatomy of Critical Discourse," pp. 50-69.

The differences in perspective when a critic "moves" from the natural standpoint through the eidetic and transcendental reductions provides one reason for the emphasis upon the subjective/objective split.  The natural standpoint, as Husserl conceived it, considers the experiencing and perceiving of "real objects [as] there, definite, more or less familiar, agreeing with what is actually perceived."[31]  The implication is the objective, "pre-scientific" nature of the field of experience.[32]  The subject, through the two reductions, ultimately seeks a "transcendental subjectivity," a definitive shift from the natural standpoint.[33]

The subjective is stressed heavily in existential phenomenology as well, but the emphasis varies from that of Husserl and his adherents.  According to Copleston's account, the existentialist subject is of primary importance, viewed as "actor" rather than "spectator," and the focus of the inquiry is that which "arises out of [one's] own personal existence as an individual human being."[34]  Instead of the Husserlian attempt to understand objects in the world through the self, the existentialist seeks a comprehension of the self in terms of the world.

Whichever perspective is assumed, the subjectivity/objectivity division is important.  Lauer describes the dichotomy and its importance for the Husserlain: "Husserl was saying that an act of consciousness and its object are . . . the subjective and objective aspects of the same thing.  Thus, to know an act of consciousness adequately, which is to say essentially, is to know its object."[35]  The statement would have to be modified to suit the existentialist so that the goal would be to know the subject essentially.  However, Lauer's argument summarizes one of the conclusions of this discussion, that both the objective and subjective facets of phenomena are important considerations in an understanding of critical stance and process.

Phenomenology provides a defense for subjectivity in the critical process.  Because the attainment of critical knowledge is theoretically an infinite process, the statements that critics make concerning communication will always be synecdochical in terms of evidence.  In other words, the derived knowledge, as well as the method, is subjective in nature.  Defense of that subjectivity, however, is implicit in the assumptions of phenomenology.  Merleau-Ponty explains: "If we are to know what anything is--and this the phenomenologist will do--we must examine the consciousness we have of it: if this does not give us an answer, nothing will."[36]  The conclusion, of course, is that the method which the critic uses, although characterized by subjectivity, is the sole means of approaching essential knowledge of rhetorical acts, and of responding to them.

The responses generated within the critical act are understood in terms of presentational, affective and judgmental intentionality.  Presentation is the "content" of the rhetorical phenomenon, the consciousness of which is affectively and judgmentally intended.  It is the means by which the critic grasps the rhetor's Lebenswelt or the underlying values in a message, as in Gregg's position.  Feeling or affective intentionality, the response stressed by Rosenfield, is

[31] Husserl, in Age of Analysis, p. 105.

[32] Husserl, The Idea of Phenomenology, p. 37.

[33] George Nakhnikian, intro. to The Idea of Phenomenology.

[34] Frederick Copleston, Contemporary Philosophy, 2d. ed. (Paramus, N.Y.: Newman, 1972), pp. 127-29.

[35] Lauer, p. 17.

[36] Maurice Merleau-Ponty, "La Structure du Comportement," quoted in Lauer, p. 7.  While Merleau-Ponty emphasized that subjective analysis is the only means by which we gain knowledge, Kierkegaard stresses that it is the best one; the "concluding Unscientific Postscript to the 'Philosophical Fragments'" (1846) A Keikegaard Anthology, ed. by Robert Bretall (Princeton, N.J.: Princeton University Press, 1946), pp. 207-31.

important because it especially exemplifies the fact that the critic-subject, because of his/her character of being-in-the-world, is not an objective yardstick for measuring the worth of the rhetorical act. The critic expresses the phenomenon, the encounter of the self and the object.[37] Judgment is the final mode of intentionality, resulting from, and interacting with, the others. It is the claim issued by the critic concerning his/her analysis of the rhetorical act, and its evidence lies in the presentational and affective intentionalities.[38] While any of the three modes of intending an object may be pre-eminent in a critic's work, they are all important. The variance of emphasis of the intentional modes together with the infinite number of possible stances in the eidetic reduction, explain and justify the disparity and number of extant critical models. In any case, the critic evaluates the rhetorical act through his/her cognitive and affective intending of it.[39]

Phenomenology then provides a method of knowing and responding to discourse, as well as a justification for the nature of the method and responses. The critic, purposefully conscious of the rhetorical act, presentationally, affectively, and judgmentally, can know, feel, and judge the discourse essentially.

---

[37]See William Luijpen, *Phenomenology and Humanism: A Primer in Existential Phenomenology* (Pittsburgh: Duquesne University Press, 1966), p. 87.

[38]Note that the judgmental component lends another premise to the position on subjectivity. It is demonstrably true that two critics may not judge a single discourse in the same way. The judgment is dependent upon the imposition of the individual subject in the critical act.

[39]Importantly, this is not a methodological exegesis; it is intended as an explanation of pre-methodological critical stance, and in that sense, it isolates only the variables of intentionality composing the critical act. There will be no attempt to pattern them into a working model for the rhetorical critic here.

RICHARD DANIELS

UNIVERSITY OF WISCONSIN-MADISON

In the philosophical treatise Being and Time, in the section on the method of the treatise, Martin Heidegger states that the word "phenomenology" primarily signifies a methodological conception.[1] To explain, in part, this signification of the word, Heidegger analyzes the word into its two constituents: "phenomenon" and "logos." The word "phenomenology" derives its meaning from certain senses of the Greek words which correspond to these two constituents. Thus, according to Heidegger, one constituent, "the expression 'phenomenon' signifies that which shows itself in itself, the manifest."[2] Phenomenon is the "object" of phenomenological research, but it is not an object in the ordinary sense of the word "object." To say that phenomenon is "that which shows itself" is to say that in the way that the phenomenon is--or we could say, in the mode of its existence--it shows, or reveals, itself. In phenomenology, the object of research is the mode of something's existence.

From this, we should understand that phenomena are not facts (i.e., not empirical facts); they are not what is characteristic of something. Facts are stated; phenomena cannot be stated. They cannot even be put into words. Yet to say all of this could be misleading, since there are phenomenological facts. But phenomenological facts are not empirical facts. Phenomenological facts are the facts of experience. As such, they are not expressed by descriptions but in them. One will either be able to see them or not. Depending upon which, such descriptions will either be accepted or rejected. Empirical facts are what is characteristic of something other than experience itself. They are expressed by statements. Such statements are either true or false. Thus, it is not that phenomenon exists, but in the way that it exists, that it shows itself.

Although phenomenological facts are expressed in descriptions, phenomena are not what something is about; they are neither the topics nor the themes of something. That they are not about something, but the mode of something's existence, is the reason why they cannot be talked about. We can neither be told of phenomenon nor about it; we can only be shown it. That phenomenon is something which can only be shown, knowledge of it must be obtained in perception. We must learn of it in perception, for it is the manifest.

The sense of logos, which is the other constituent of the word "phenomenology," is logos as discourse. According to Heidegger, logos "as 'discourse' means . . . to make manifest what one is 'talking about' in one's discourse. But this is not true of any discourse; it must be genuine discourse. Heidegger states that "so far as it is genuine, what is said is drawn from

Phenomenology in Rhetoric and Communication, ed. Stanley Deetz. Copyright, 1981, The Center for Advanced Research in Phenomenology and the University Press of America.

[1] Martin Heidegger, Being and Time, trans. John Macquarrie and Edward Robinson (New York: Harper and Tow, Publishers, 1962), p. 50.

[2] Heidegger, p. 51.

what the talk is about, so that discursive communication, in what it says, makes manifest what it is talking about, and thus makes this accessible to the other party." In short, such discourse "lets something be seen."[3]

Thus, on the one hand, phenomenon is "that which shows itself in itself"; and on the other hand, logos as discourse is discourse which "lets something be seen." Putting the two constituents together, Heidegger states that the word "'phenomenology' means . . . to let that which shows itself be seen from itself in the very way in which it shows itself from itself."[4] Simply, phenomenology is discourse which lets the phenomenon be seen.

Although phenomenology is primarily a method, just as the object of phenomenological research, the method is not a method in the ordinary sense of the word "method." By the word "method" we ordinarily mean a definite, well-defined procedure. The method of phenomenology cannot be such a procedure; it can be neither definite nor well defined. Heidegger states:

> The more genuinely a methodological concept is worked out and the more comprehensive it determines the principles on which a science is to be conducted, all the more primordially is it rooted in the way we come to terms with the things themselves, and the further is it removed from what we call "technical devices."[5]

Not that the methodological concepts of phenomenology could not be made into "technical devices." They could be, but then we would not really understand them. For "whenever a phenomenological concept is drawn from primordial sources, there is a possibility that it may degenerate if communicated in the form of an assertion." Heidegger states that in the form of assertions, the concepts of phenomenology "get understood in an empty way."[6]

There are primarily two reasons why the methodological concepts of phenomenology when put in the form of assertions, get understood in an empty way. First, because of the nature of the object of phenomenological research. The object is something that we cannot be told of, or about, but must be shown. Second, the object must be seen in the "very way" in which it shows itself. A method that accomplishes this must be of the same nature as the object (i.e., it too must be something which is shown). And, therefore, just as knowledge of the object, knowledge of the method must be obtained in perception.

Thus, to be really understood, the method of phenomenology must be engaged in, or it must be seen within the context of research. That phenomenology is primarily a method, and that knowledge of the method must be obtained in perception, the form of the knowledge of the method will be skillful knowledge. Critical for understanding phenomenology is understanding the distinction between "knowing that" and "knowing how." To "know that" is simply to possess some information. To "know how" is to know how to do something. It is a matter of having a skill. To really understand phenomenology, we must know how to engage in the method. And if we do not know how, we must simply engage ourselves in research and obtain that knowledge. We can be guided in our research by the idea that to engage in the method is to create discourse which lets the phenomenon be seen.

This then calls for such an engagement. The research which follows is, in part, phenomenological and, in part, rhetorical, in that the implications of

[3]Heidegger, p. 56.
[4]Heidegger, p. 58.
[5]Heidegger, p. 50.
[6]Heidegger, pp. 60-61.

the phenomenon revealed have rhetorical significance. Thus, let us proceed to The Fundamentals and the fundamentalist movement.

The rhetoric of the fundamentalist movement of the early twentieth century in the United States is pervaded by violence. The rhetoric shows itself to be aggressive, emotional, and hostile. The dominant tropes are the metaphors of war. Consider these two passages. J. Frank Norris:

> I believe with all my soul that future generations will write about this Fundamental Movement as historians now write up the Reformation and Wesley Revival and other great awakenings. And as revolutions have rent and torn to pieces all political alignments and governments of the world, so we are now in the greatest religious revival that time has ever witnessed since, perhaps, Pentacost.

> What if the present-day denominations are smashed to smithereens? It ought to be. They are unscriptural.[7]

Courtland Myers:

> I also say to you that we ought to make war, strenuous war, and fight to a finish, against foreign innovation in our religious world. . . . Go back to the fountainhead and you will find the crimson stream has its source in the rank German theology that has been forcing its way into the veins and arteries of all our religious life. We ought to fight to the finish.[8]

We could easily find other fundamentalist rhetoric displaying such metaphors.[9] In The History of Fundamentalism, Stewart G. Cole judges Courtland Myers's statements to be representative of the fundamentalists.[10] In "Modernists and Fundamentalists Debate Restraints on Freedom," Allan H. Sager characterizes fundamentalism as "an aggressive conservative movement."[11] In Voices of American Fundamentalism, C. Allyn Russell concludes that the fundamentalist's "aggressive, acrimonious attitude came to be their hallmark."[12] In The Fundamentalist Controversy, Norman F. Furniss observes that "violence in thought and language was an outstanding feature of the fundamentalist movement."[13]

The rhetoric of the fundamentalist movement confirms the observations and judgments of these historians but with one important exception--twelve pamphlets entitled, The Fundamentals: A Testimony to the Truth.[14] These twelve pamphlets are recognized to be the most comprehensive expression of fundamentalism. It is in The Fundamentals that the "Five Points" are originally set forth: the infallibility of the Bible, Christ's Virgin Birth, his Substitutionary Atonement, Resurrection, and Second Coming. The "Five Points" was the essential

---

[7]J. Frank Norris, Voices of American Fundamentalism, ed. C. Allyn Russell (Philadelphia: Westminister Press, 1976), p. 27.

[8]Quoted in The History of Fundamentalism, Stewart G. Cole (Westport: Greenwood Press Publishers, 1931), p. 74.

[9]See, for example, William B. Riley, Current History, Vol. 26, p. 437, or A. Z. Conrad, Jesus Christ at the Cross Roads (New York: Revell Press, 1924), p. 13.

[10]Cole, p. 74.

[11]Allan H. Sager, "Modernists and Fundamentalists Debate Restraints on Freedom, 1910-1930," America in Controversy: History of American Public Address, ed. Dewitte Holland (Dubuque: Wm. C. Brown Publishers, 1973), p. 281.

[12]C. Allyn Russell, "Conclusion," Voices of American Fundamentalism (Philadelphia: Westminister Press, 1976), p. 213.

[13]Norman F. Furniss, The Fundamentalist Controversy, 1918-1931 (New Haven: Yale University Press), p. 36.

[14]The Fundamentals: A Testimony to the Truth, eds. Amzi Clarence Dixon and Reuben A. Torrey (Chicago: Testimony Publishing Company, 1909-1912).

doctrine of fundamentalism.  Furthermore, the pamphlets are considered instrumental both in the fundamentalist movement and in the controversy between the conservative fundamentalists and the liberal modernists within the Protestant church.  Some attribute the origination of the fundamentalist movement to the pamphlets.[15]  Some do not consider the pamphlets as originating the movement but as bringing it to fruition.[16]  Some contend that the controversy between the fundamentalists and the modernists became full blown with the publication of the pamphlets.[17]  Although there is disagreement as to the kind of influence the pamphlets had, all agree they were instrumentally important.  Yet the character of the rhetoric of the pamphlets is in complete contrast to that of the movement generally.  The rhetoric is not aggressive; it is not emotional; it is not hostile.  In A Religious History of the American People, Sydney E. Ahlstrom judges that the pamphlets exhibit "dignity, breadth of subject matter, rhetorical moderation, obvious conviction, and considerable intellectual power,"[18]  Ahlstrom's judgment is accurate--as we shall see-- which raises the question, How could The Fundamentals be instrumental, given their rhetorical moderation, either in the origination or fruition of a movement marked by rhetorical excess?  The answer to this question lies in the pamphlets themselves.

The Fundamentals were published between 1909 and 1912.  They were published in reaction to the modernists within the Protestant church.  The conservatives were alarmed by the growing strength of the liberal modernists.  The pamphlets were an attempt to stem this growing liberal strength.  This is alluded to in the forward of the pamphlets:  "Two intelligent, consecrated Christian laymen bear the expense because they believe that the time has come when a new statement of the fundamentals of Christianity should be made."[19]  The five points that the pamphlets set forth became for the fundamentalists "the fundamentals of Christianity."  The controversy between the fundamentalists and modernists revolved around the five points, but particularly the first point--which encompasses the other four--the infallibility of the Bible.  Where the fundamentalists believed in the infallibility of the Bible and deferred to it as the religious authority, the modernists questioned both this belief and this authority.

Because the controversy primarily revolved around the question of authority, Allan H. Sager concludes, "The question at root was thus less one of the theology than of epistemology--what is the ground of religious knowledge."[20]  Sager's conclusion is the result of his focus on the topics of the controversy.  We need to penetrate the topics and consider the human phenomenon that lies behind them.  To conclude that the root of the controversy is epistemological gives an intellectual cast to the character of the controversy.  The character of the rhetoric, though, with the exception of the pamphlets, is not intellectual but emotional.  And if the rhetoric is not a cover for a lack of integrity, then it is a release and an accurate reflection of the character of the controversy.

The root of the controversy between the fundamentalists and the modernists goes deeper than epistemology.  The modernist not only questioned biblical authority but showed that the Bible was not valuable to him in the same way that it was to the fundamentalist.  He showed this by his treatment of it.  Shailer Mathews states:  "The Modernist is attempting to utilize the methods of the his-

---

[15]See Furniss, p. 13.

[16]See Cole, pp. 52-53.

[17]See Sager, p. 294.

[18]Sydney E. Ahlstrom, A Religious History of the American People (New Haven: Yale University Press, 1972), p. 816.

[19]The Fundamentals, op. cit., p. ii.

[20]Sager, p. 305.

torical and allied sciences to discover the permanent values in his religious inheritance."[21] The Bible is the modernist's most important religious inheritance, yet within his religion it held no permanent value. The modernist sought to discover--or, perhaps more accurately, recover--the permanent values of the Bible with methods outside of his religion. To apply historic and scientific methods to the Bible is to treat the Bible as any other text. It is not to treat the Bible as it is in The Fundamentals: religiously as Scripture, as a sacred text.

The methods of the modernist became his way of thinking on religious matters; and it is not a religious way of thinking. Again, Shailer Mathews: "Modernism is . . . the historical method of thinking about the Bible and Christian doctrine."[22] To think historically instead of religiously about the Bible, the modernist acknowledges more than a difference in epistemology from that of the fundamentalist. For the fundamentalist the Bible is an absolute authority and the source of religious knowledge; the fundamentalist seeks this knowledge within his religion. For the modernist the Bible is a religious document and a source of religious values; the modernist seeks these values with historic and scientific methods. Thus, not only is the "ground of religious knowledge" different; the relationship the fundamentalist and the modernist have to the Bible is different. This suggests more than a difference in understanding or knowledge; it suggests a difference in experience. The root of the controversy is not simply epistemological; it is metaphysical.

That the root of the controversy is metaphysical is shown in the pamphlets. Moreover, it was by making the root of the controversy manifest that the pamphlets derived their influence. This is not to suggest a causal connection between the pamphlets and their power; rather, it is to juxtapose the character of the movement--thus the disposition of the fundamentalists--and the character of the pamphlets. That the two are in contrast, it must be what the pamphlets make manifest that gave them their power. The character of the movement was aggressive, emotional, and hostile. Although we find nothing of an aggressive, or hostile character in the pamphlets, we find something of an emotional character. What we find of an emotional character is the manifestation of a felt loss: the loss of a reality. A loss that would be secured by the triumph of modernism. The pamphlets show this; the fundamentalists must have sensed it. We should now closely examine the pamphlets to capture a sense of it ourselves.

The modernist's employment of historic and scientific methods in the study of the Bible became known as "higher criticism." The title "higher criticism" designated specifically that field of study which attempted to determine the historical origins, the dates, and the authorship of the books of the Bible. It was essentially the study of the Bible's literary structure. Several whole chapters and sections of others in The Fundamentals are devoted to a critique of higher criticism. In the critique, the pamphlets themselves offer criticism of the Bible. The criticism is of a different form from that of higher criticism though. It is in the form of this criticism that the root of the controversy is shown.

In the pamphlets there are primarily two charges made against the higher critics. First, the higher critics do not understand what it means to say that the Bible is the Word of God. In a chapter of the pamphlets entitled "The His-

[21]Shailer Mathews, "Fundamentalism and Modernism," *American Review 2*, Vol. 1 (January-February, 1924), p. 1.
[22]Mathews, p. 1.

tory of Higher Criticism," Canon Dyson Hague states: "the Bible does not merely contain the word of God; it is the Word of God."[23] Similarly, in the chapter "Inspiration," L.W. Munhall states: "the Bible plainly teaches that its words are inspired, and that it is the Word of God."[24] The significance of the word "is" in these statements is given critical treatment in the pamphlets. Secondly, the higher critics lack religious faith, and such faith is a necessary condition for the perception of Biblical truth. Higher criticism, states Hague, "demands at once the ability of the scholar, and the simplicity of the believing child of God.[25] He contends that "unbelief was the antecedent, not the consequent, of their criticism."[26]

These two charges are transformed into major points of interpretation in the pamphlet's criticism of the Bible. In the chapter "Life in the Word," Philip Mauro articulates four dimensions of significance of the phrase, "the Word of God is a LIVING Word."[27] That is, he explicates the meaning of the word "living" as it is used to refer to the words of the Bible. The first two dimensions are concerned with what it means to say that the Bible is the Word of God. The second two dimensions are concerned with faith as a necessary condition for the perception of Biblical truth. Though Mauro's criticism is uncommon in its resourcefulness, it is representative of these points. It should, therefore, serve well as an example of the pamphlet's criticism.

Mauro's criticism begins with an expression of hope:

If one is able to apprehend, however feebly, the tremendous fact that the Word of God is a LIVING Word, such knowledge will go far towards affording him protection from what is perhaps the greatest danger of these "perilous times."[28]

The danger, of course, is the unbelief of modernism and the heresy of higher criticism. But hope lies in knowledge of the Bible. That Mauro's hope lies in "knowledge" might lead one to conclude that his criticism conforms to the idea that the controversy is epistemological in nature. But the meaning of the word "knowledge" in this passage turns on an understanding of "to apprehend the tremendous fact that the Word of God is a LIVING Word." The "tremendous fact" is a phenomenological fact, not an empirical fact. To gain such an understanding is the purpose of his criticism.

The first dimension is articulated by means of comparison; indeed, the criticism is largely composed of a series of comparisons. The Bible is compared to various kinds of living things. The Bible is shown to share certain attributes with certain kinds of vegetation; it is shown to share certain attributes with animals. Comparisons are made between the Bible and people. For example, just as people have the ability to adapt to new circumstances and cultures, so does the Bible. The Bible is capable of "adapting itself and its message to all people, and of speaking in all languages, tongues and dialects."[29] In another example the Bible is likened to a friend to whom we go in times of need, and who is capable of responding to our particular problem. Just as a friend "will have something new to say, as changed conditions and situations require it," so does the Bible: "from the most familiar passage there comes again and again a new message." The Bible shows a "perpetual freshness."[30]

[23]Canon Dyson Hague, "The History of Higher Criticism," The Fundamentals, p. 105.

[24]L. W. Munhall, "Inspiration," The Fundamentals, p. 59.

[25]Hague, p. 88.

[26]Hague, p. 99.

[27]Philip Mauro, "The Life in the Word," The Fundamentals, p. 9.

[28]Mauro, p. 9.

[29]Mauro, p. 31.                              [30]Mauro, p. 14.

Each comparison is accompanied by a passage from the Bible that either supports the claim of the comparison or illustrates it. The effect is persuasive. Through the display of this series of comparisons one is not simply told <u>that</u> the Bible is a living thing; one is told to <u>view</u> the Bible as a living thing. For the comparisons offer pictures and in their repetition and vividness the pictures persuade the act. Thus, the comparisons do more than articulate a dimension of significance of the word "living"; they also show it. We are both told and shown that the words of the Bible are "living" similar to other living things.

The second dimension of significance is the Bible's transcendence; the Bible transcends the object of comparison once the comparison is made complete. For example, though people generally can adapt to different cultures, learn several languages, and even different dialects within languages, no single person could learn all the languages and dialects of the world. It is not logically impossible, but it is practically impossible. Yet the Bible, in a sense, speaks all the languages and dialects of the world by having been translated into all of them. Thus, the Bible transcends people.

The comparisons show a progression in the Bible's transcendence of living things. The Bible is first compared to vegetation and shown to transcend it, then to animals, and then to people. Finally, the progression of transcendence ends with Jesus Christ as the object of comparison. The Bible "bears the same resemblance to other writings that Jesus . . . bore to other men. It is given in human language just as he came in human flesh. Yet there is between it and all other books the same difference as between Him and all other men, namely, the difference <u>between the living and the dying</u>."[31]

The comparisons build on one another in progression so that in the the end the words of the Bible are not only viewed as living, but the Bible itself is viewed as a living <u>being</u>. The progression of comparisons transcend, as in Cartesian ontology, from the lower forms of being until they reach God. The Bible is not just the word of God. The Bible is itself a being, not a human being, but a divine being. The Bible is God. This is the mode of the Bible's existence. And just as God is everlasting, so is the Bible. It is in this sense that "the Word of God is a LIVING Word." Yet to say it is not to "apprehend the tremendous fact." There is a necessary condition of faith.

The third and fourth dimensions that Mauro articulates are concerned with the condition of faith. There is a condition of faith that one must attain in order to understand fully the meaning of the word "living" as it is used to refer to the words of the Bible. An auditor of the Bible is required to do more than recognize the attributes that the Bible shares with other living things, although he must do at least this; the auditor is required to more than understand that the Bible transcends the various objects of comparison until it reaches Christ, although he must do at least this too. There is a certain relationship that the auditor must develop with the Bible. In reference to the Bible's perpetual freshness, Mauro states: "This characteristic will be recognized only by those who know the Book in that intimate way which comes from living with it, as with a member of one's family."[32] Similarly, to understand that the words of the Bible are "living" words one has to form an intimate relationship with the Bible. It is necessary for the auditor to live with the Bible for the Bible to live for the auditor.

The auditor must live as a son or daughter to the Bible, for the auditor is subservient; he is a child of God:

[31]Mauro, p. 12.
[32]Mauro, p. 14.

> [T]he Bible . . . claims the right to exercise, and assumes to exercise, <u>authority over man</u>. It speaks as one <u>having authority</u>. It issues commands to all. It does not simply advise or commend one course of action rather than another, as one would address an equal, but it directs men imperatively what they shall do, and what they shall not do. . . ."[33]

The auditor is not engaged in a dialogue with the Bible; the Bible speaks and the auditor listens. But there is a dimension in the auditor's relationship with the Bible that serves to justify his subservience:

> We go to it not so much to learn the thoughts of other men, as to learn our own thoughts. We go to other books to find what was in the hearts and minds of their authors; but we go to this Book to find what is in our own hearts and minds. To one who reads it with ever so little spiritual intelligence there comes a perception of the fact that his Book understands and knows all about him. It lays bare the deepest secrets of his heart, and brings to the surface of his consciousness, out of the unfathomable depths and unexplorable recesses of his own being, 'thoughts and intents' whose existence was unsuspected. It reveals man to himself in a way difficult to describe, and absolutely peculiar to itself. It is a faithful mirror which reflects us exactly as we are. It detects our motives, discerns our needs; and having truthfully discovered to us our true selves, it counsels, reproves, exhorts, guides, refreshens, strengthens and illuminates.[34]

For the higher critic the Bible is a religious document and an object of criticism. But for the auditor of the Bible who is a "believing child of God"--what we might call an authentic auditor as opposed to a critical auditor--he is himself the object of criticism and the Bible is his critic. The Bible "lays bare the deepest secrets" of the auditor; it "brings to the surface of his consciousness . . . 'thoughts and intents' whose existence was unsuspected"; it then "counsels, reproves, guides, refreshens, strengthens, and illuminates." The Bible does criticism of the auditor.

But the Bible can only do criticism if the auditor is in the necessary condition of faith. The expression "believe on" is used by Mauro in his criticism. He states: "The Bible plainly declares it, and those who believe on the Christ of God know also by experience the beginning of a new kind of life in their souls."[35] This expression is used repeatedly in the Gospel of John; for example, "He that believeth on the Son hath everlasting life." This expression seems to capture the sense of the necessary condition of faith of the authentic auditor of the Bible. The expressions "believe that"[36] and "believe in"[37] have received analysis by philosophers of religion, but apparently the expression "believe on" has not. Simply, to say that one "believes that . . .," is to make a tentative assertion; to say that one "believes in . . .," is to express an involvement with another. The expression "believe on" seems to encompass both of these other belief expressions. It seems to both make an assertion, but not simply tentatively, and express an involvement. One who "believes on . . .," is in a condition or state of belief. So that to say that one "believes on" Jesus Christ is to express a state of belief that one is in. The authentic auditor of the Bible is in such a state.

---

[33]Mauro, p. 23.

[34]Mauro, p. 29.

[35]Mauro, p. 48.

[36]Bernard Williams, "Tertullian's Paradox," <u>New Essays in Philosophical Theology</u>, eds. Anthony Flew and Alasdair MacIntyre (London: Cambridge University Press, 1965).

[37]Donald D. Evans, <u>The Logic of Self-Involvement</u> (London: SCM Press Ltd., 1963).

The hope of Mauro's criticism is for the auditor of the Bible to apprehend the "fact that the Word of God is a LIVING Word." Hope lies in such knowledge. Given the view of the Bible as God and the belief condition of the authentic auditor, this suggests that the <u>fact</u> that the Word of God is a LIVING Word that the auditor apprehends, is not the intellectual apprehension of a fact, but a <u>fact experienced</u>, a phenomenological fact. That is, this view of the Bible and the belief condition shows the criticism to do more than articulate the meaning of the word "living," the criticism pictures the experience of the meaning of the word. This distinction is similar to that between a description of a performance and the performance itself. The criticism performs when it pictures. Mauro states: "In going to the Bible we never think of ourselves as going <u>back</u> to a book of the distant past, to be a thing of <u>antiquity</u>; but we go to it as to a book of the <u>present</u>--a living book."[38] And to go to the Bible as a living book it is necessary to experience the words of the Bible as living. It is not enough to know that the words are living, except in Mauro's special sense of "knowledge" (i.e., to experience them as living). And to experience the words of the Bible as living words is to experience them as <u>spoken</u> by God. Reading the Bible must approach the writing of it; and the writing is said to have been inspired by God.

In <u>The Bible at a Single View</u>, Richard C. Moulton states: "The Bible is not a treatise on God; its theme is the intercourse between God and man."[39] Moulton's inclusion of the word "theme" in this statement fails to capture what the Bible makes manifest. It fails where Mauro's criticism does not. Moulton's statement should read: The Bible is not a treatise on God; it is intercourse between God and man. This is what the authors of the pamphlet must mean when they say that the Bible does not merely contain the word of God, but <u>is</u> the Word of God. This is what Mauro must mean by capitalizing all the letters of the word "living." This is a dimension of significance of the word "living" that his criticism does not articulate, possibly because it cannot. The criticism makes this dimension manifest. It makes manifest an experience that is on the borders of language and words can only suggest it. But when the Bible is viewed as God and certain belief conditions are met, the Bible speaks and the auditor listens.

The difference then between the authentic auditor of the Bible, in the criticism of <u>The Fundamentals</u>, and the modernist's historical way of thinking about the Bible is more than a difference in understanding or knowledge, at least in the way we have come to mean these words; it is a difference in experience or reality. It is the difference between reading a religious document and having a religious experience. For the authentic auditor, the Bible is a present religious reality; for the modernist, it is a flawed record of a past reality. And a difference in reality is a metaphysical difference.

<u>The Fundamentals</u> derived their authority among fundamentalists by showing what was at the root of the controversy. They pictured for the fundamentalist what he only latently sensed: that the religious reality of the Bible was being rejected within his own church, that the world of the Word was being lost. Knowing this, we should not understand it as a defense of the fundamentalist movement. The rhetoric of the movement, with the exception of <u>The Fundamentals</u>, should not be defended. It is aggressive, emotional, and hostile. And yet we can now better understand why it is of this character. A world was at stake in

---

[38]Mauro, p. 31.

[39]Richard G. Moulton, <u>The Bible at a Single View</u> (New York: The MacMillan Company, 1918), pp. 7-8.

the controversy with the modernists:  the world of the Bible.  Without this world the mode of the Bible's existence could not be seen.  Without this world the Bible could not be heard.  For the fundamentalists such a loss was intolerable.  For us, if we have sensed something of what the fundamentalists must have sensed in <u>The Fundamentals</u>, we will not be able to as comfortably persist in this world of dark silence.

# 7 / A PHENOMENOLOGICAL APPROACH TO THE CRITICISM OF SOCIAL MOVEMENTS

## VALERIE ENDRESS AND KAREN BRUNER
### INDIANA UNIVERSITY

A phenomenological approach to rhetorical criticism is based on a belief that man must first symbolize his environment into cognitive structures and then act on the basis of such cognitive perceptions.[1] Working on the basis of this assumption, the critic must focus upon discovering, defining, and describing those images which are active within the confines of the rhetorical act.[2] In other words, it is necessary for the critic to study the philosophical and phenomenological underpinnings prompting the rhetor to action.

The cognitive structures may indicate philosophical predispositions, reasons for action, and can also aid the critic in understanding the impetus behind rhetorical choices made by individual speakers or groups. Such an approach, based on select concepts of phenomenology, is particularly useful for developing a holistic view of rhetorical acts, rather than concentrating on isolated speeches in the historical situation. Black points out that, "There is little predisposition among neo-Aristotelian critics to comprehend the discourse in a larger context, to see it, for example, as the movement study would, as part of a historical process of argument."[3] It may well be profitable to study social movements from this perspective.

Herbert Simons observed in 1970 that the standard tools of rhetorical criticism were designed for microscopic analysis of particular speeches, and therefore, were largely inappropriate for analyzing the discourse of social movements.[4] Two years later, Robert Cathcart mirrored Simons' view with a request for "new approaches to the rhetorical criticism of movements."[5] Now, at the brink of a fourth decade of social movement research, rhetorical critics are still searching for an acceptable theoretical foundation to develop appropriate methodologies. The lack of progress in theory development was recently noted by Charles Stewart who observed, "We know little about how social movements design and transmit persuasive messages to various audiences or how channels affect design and transmission."[6]

The purpose of this paper is three-fold: (1) to suggest the utility and functions of social movement criticism founded on concepts derived from

Phenomenology in Rhetoric and Communication, ed. Stanley Deetz. Copyright, 1981, The Center for Advanced Research in Phenomenology and the University Press of America.

[1] Richard B. Gregg, "A Phenomenologically Oriented Approach to Rhetorical Criticism," Central States Speech Journal, (May 1966), p. 83.

[2] Gregg, p. 85.

[3] Gregg, pp. 89-90.

[4] Herbert W. Simons, "Requirements, Problems, and Strategies: A Theory of Persuasion for Social Movements," The Quarterly Journal of Speech, 56 (February 1970), p. 2.

[5] Robert Cathcart, "New Approaches to the Study of Movements: Defining Movements Rhetorically," Western Speech Journal, 36 (Spring 1972), p. 82.

[6] Charles Stewart, "One Last Attempt to Define Social Movements," Indiana State Speech Association Convention, Indianapolis, 28 Oct. 1977.

a phenomenological base, (2) to demonstrate where previous literature has not succeeded in building a comprehensive evaluative framework, and (3) to present an organizing perspective of social movement variables, enabling critics to adapt analysis to particular movements from a phenomenological perspective.

As a starting point, social movement criticism, independent of any particular methodological perspective, should consider what conditions in the rhetorical situation give rise to a social movement. The critic must also examine why people join social movements. In asking such questions, it becomes important then for the critic to understand the basis for the perceptions, attitudes, and beliefs of participants in the rhetorical act. For it is these perceptions that become instrumental in shaping the language choices and rhetorical strategies of movement leaders and members and their respective audiences. The critic must also ask, then, what rhetorical strategies are necessary to sustain a voluntary membership. By studying how a social movement forms and develops, examination continues as to what variables influence a movement's success or failure. For example, the critic might consider the impact of changes in the rhetorical situation, the results of the communication of membership needs, the effects of varying audience responses, and the rhetorical choices made by movement leadership and members to explain movement effectiveness. Finally, analysis of movement rhetoric may provide information to help both movements and audiences better understand how a more effective communication process could be adopted for the needs of groups in question. Most importantly, social movement criticism could pose generalizable observations to predict the problems, strategies, and effectiveness of future movements. The range of potential questions a social movement critic may pose include:

(1) What situational conditions, personal motives, and forms of rhetoric attract and sustain social movement members?

(2) What influences a movement leaders' choices of rhetorical strategies in communicating to both members and outside audiences during different phases of a movement's development?

(3) What effect do responses from differing audiences have on a movement?

(4) What effect does a movement's internal communication between leaders and members have on its external messages?

(5) Is there a link between the success of a movement, the rhetorical situation, leadership rhetoric, choice of audience, and access to varied communication channels?

Previous studies have provided extensive discussion on necessary variables to be considered by social movement critics. Such discussion served an important purpose in isolating necessary descriptive concepts. Past literature, however, failed to show how such concepts fit into an overall framework. For example, Crandell's preoccupation with breaking down a movement into "exact" phases guided future critics to examine the parts of a movement, rather than to evaluate the movement as a whole.[7] Griffin advised the movement critic to isolate rhetoric from historical and social variables and to classify rhetoric as "pro" or "anti."[8] Although Griffin's later application of Burkeian

---

[7] S. Judson Crandell, "The Beginnings of a Methodology for Social Movement Studies in Public Address," The Quarterly Journal of Speech, 33 (February 1947), pp. 36-39.

[8] Leland M. Griffin, "The Rhetoric of Historical Movements," The Quarterly Journal of Speech, 38 (April 1952), pp. 184-188. See also Leland M. Griffin, "The Rhetorical Structure of the New Left Movement: Part I," The Quarterly Journal of Speech, 50 (April 1964), pp. 131-135. It is our belief that Griffin essentially failed to extend his use of Burkeian theory by ignoring what Burke terms as ratios designed to demonstrate the relationships and component parts of the pentad.

precepts constitutes a functional method for describing social movements from a rhetorical perspective, his failure to analyze the relationships among the components of the pentad leaves the rhetorical critic with no theoretical starting point. Though Griffin defines a movement's structural characteristics, he ignores analysis of the persuasive efforts of movement leaders and members. However illuminating a description may be, it is insufficient to account for the ways in which a movement unfolds, or more particularly, the role that communication plays in that process.

In applying an organizational model to the study of social movements, Simons took a significant step forward in investing the criticism of social movements with a sound theoretical underpinning. The restriction imposed by the limited sources of motivation in organizational contexts, however, makes the model somewhat inadequate. Hahn and Gonchar maintained that "intertwining traditional categories of analysis facilitates insights into the complexity of social movement rhetoric."[9] They tried to avoid a misunderstanding of terms by relying upon classical categories, but in so doing, failed to distinguish their critical method from the classical descriptive model.

Cathcart's emphasis on dialectical tension as the defining characteristic of social movements limits one's critical focus to a communication response representing only the "tip of the iceberg."[10] Like Cathcart, Andrews argues that a movement assumes form only after the occurrence of dialectical tension and response from the establishment.[11] This assumption, however, ignores the initial developmental stages of a movement and the internal communication between participants and leaders and their subsequent effects on a movement's persuasive strategies.

In sum, critical approaches for the analysis of social movement persuasion have been primarily descriptive and unable to evaluate complex interactions. The diversity of concepts has not been integrated into an overall view. Each new approach, trumpeting new and unexplored areas of social movements, only added to the confusion in that it did not follow from a systematic and coherent theoretical base. The problem is somewhat akin to the picture of a beginning mechanic dismantling a car engine. As the mechanic proceeds, he lays out all the parts with no regard for part relationships and functions. With all the engine parts laid out before him, it is impossible for the mechanic to understand how the materials work together. When it comes time for the mechanic to put the engine back together, he realizes that while he is familiar with each separate part, he has no overall conception of how the entire engine functions. The situation is also faced by the social movement critic when attempting to work with the many variables discussed in the literature. Thus, the primary task of this paper is to suggest a phenomenological perspective to the criticism of social movements.

## AN ORGANIZING PERSPECTIVE

The critic of social movements, drawing upon tenents of phenomenology, must emphasize the interplay of contextual systems, recognizing the cognitive structures of communicators interacting within the framework of a social movement's transmission of messages to societal audiences and vice versa. It is essential for the critic to discover the reasons underlying value judgements

---

[9]Dan F. Hahn and Ruth M. Gonchar, "Studying Social Movements: A Rhetorical Methodology," The Speech Teacher, 20 (January 1971), p. 47.

[10]Robert Cathcart, 87. Observation made by Stewart in convention presentation.

[11]James R. Andrews, "The Passionate Negation: The Chartist Movement in Rhetorical Perspective," The Quarterly Journal of Speech (April 1973), pp. 196-197.

made by senders and receivers in the communication process. In doing so, the critic must then determine the degree to which value judgements of the intended audience and rhetor coincide with the resulting rhetoric.[12] These conceptions of audience and receiver have a decided impact on the rhetoric evolving in a situation.[13] Alterations in attitudes and perceptions may lead to changes in the public and internal dialogue of both social movements and its audiences.

Essentially, the audience image of the rhetor must be evaluated along with the rhetor's image of the audience.[14] Because the vehicle for transmitting this image is primarily through language, the critic must, of necessity, study language choices made by the rhetor for specific rhetorical purposes.[15] To illustrate, social movement proponents may try to create a negative image of the establishment. Success for the social movement rhetor may be determined by whether or not an audience might conceptualize the "evil" establishment in their minds. By creating a negative image of the establishment for movement participants, the rhetor establishes a target for movement attack and action.

The perspective we propose allows for the breakdown of the movement and its audiences into component parts, indicates the lines of communication, and recognizes the potential communication gatekeepers who filter the movement's messages to participants, leaders, and audiences. Such information guides the critic toward determining the inter-relationships between social movement subsystems and toward a recognition of the functions of communication in the movement.

A movement's beginnings may be traced to persons responding to motivational exigencies in the rhetorical situation (Figure 1). Some research suggests that a group of dissatisfied individuals will be sustained only through appeals generated by both motivational and mobilizational rhetoric. Motivational exigencies are the reasons for action, problems, or unmet needs and dissatisfactions that serve as the impetus for persons to act out the desire for change.[16] Mobilizational appeals represent persuasive efforts designed to sustain social movement participants and function to establish and maintain a movement's organization.[17] Examination of both motivational and mobilizational appeals reveals reasons for the movement's beginnings and its philosophical and organizational base.

Messages communicated to the external environment by the social movement assume the form of strategic indicators. Strategic indicators may be defined as messages communicated to external audiences either through direct channels in the form of books, pamphlets, and person-to-person or through indirect filters, such as the media. The media represents an important filter and gatekeeper for the communication of messages between social movement leaders, participants, and audience. The functions of the media may vary depending upon the nature of the movement and the constraints placed upon such systems for satisfying and maintaining a general reader and viewer audience.

Movement messages are conveyed to an audience comprised of opponents, proponents, uncommitted observers, and decision-makers. The opposition con-

---

[12]Gregg, p. 89.

[13]Gregg, p. 88.

[14]Gregg, p. 89.

[15]Gregg, p. 85.

[16]Ralph R. Smith and Russel R. Windes, "The Rhetoric of Mobilization: Implications for the Study of Social Movements," *Southern Speech Journal*, 42 (Fall 1976), p. 2.

[17]Smith and Windes, p. 2.

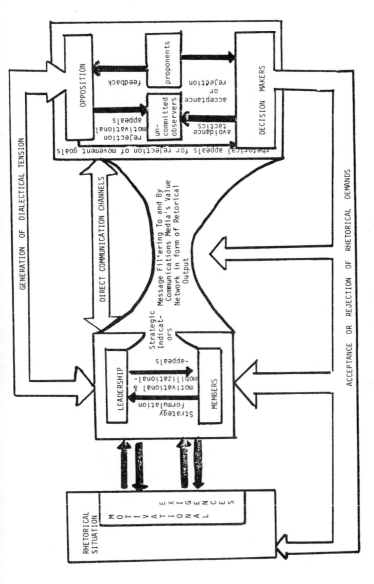

THE RELEVANT ENVIRONMENT

FIGURE 1

sists of those persons attacking the movement's ideologies and organization. Dialectical tension orignates from the opposition's response to the movement. This group communicates motivational appeals directed toward uncommitted observers who are typically targets for appeals to reject movement aims. Uncommitted groups are observers who are neutral to the movement's aims and are largely unaffected by its messages, at least, in the short run. Proponent groups include observers who adhere to the movement's aims, and profess belief in what the movement is attempting to accomplish, but who take little action other than verbally supporting it. Decision-makers represent persons or groups capable of providing solutions or of initiating some form of action or response to the movement's demands. The opposition, proponents, and decision-makers may employ varying rhetorical strategies to persuade uncommitted observers to reject or accept movement goals. An audience's acceptance or rejection of a movement's rhetorical demands transmits a message back to the movement and, in turn, the rhetorical situation is influenced. Acceptance or rejection of the message affects the movement's structure, spokespersons, and members. A social movement, then, is continually transforming due to internal and external influences.

The model attempts to place diverse variables into a logical framework in which a social movement might function. Although our goal is to order systems and relevant components, an obvious liability of the model involves the failure to establish and explain relationships between various parts. Because the evidence that would clearly establish the nature of the relationship among the constituent elements has not been identified, the model nonetheless presupposes certain functional relationships on logical grounds.

Such relationships not shown in Figure 1 may be clarified by Figure 2 which attempts to illustrate how and why a social movement evolves, the direction of movement messages, what rhetorical interactions aid or deter a movement's achievement of goals, and the impact of different messages on varied audiences. The functional model (Figure 2) is based on the assumption that if a group of dissatisfied persons are to achieve long range change, then, organization necessarily evolves and leadership emerges. If an organization does not form, then, temporary action or no action may occur, but eventually interest in the problem quickly dies.

A second assumption of the model is that a leadership relying solely on motivational rhetoric again faces the possibility of extinction. However, the inclusion of mobilizational rhetoric greatly increases a movement's chances for survival. Through the use of such rhetoric, leaders provide direction, purpose, and legitimate avenues for action and expression of discontent.

A third assumption in the model stipulates mobilizational rhetoric as a primary influence in the further development of a movement's structure. Through the structure, lines of communication are defined. If the membership is not able to provide feedback on movement goals, purposes, and actions, members soon may lose interest and react through other channels. The onus of responsibility again falls on the movement leadership. Without engaging sufficient portions of the membership, the movement may fail.

A fourth assumption introduced by this model maintains that a movement potentially communicates different strategic indicators to varied audiences. For example, a movement communicating subversive and affirmative rhetoric,[18] could outwardly appear self-defeating and contradictory. But, if the critic

---

[18]Walter R. Fisher, "A Motive View of Communication," *The Quarterly Journal of Speech* (April 1970), p. 132.

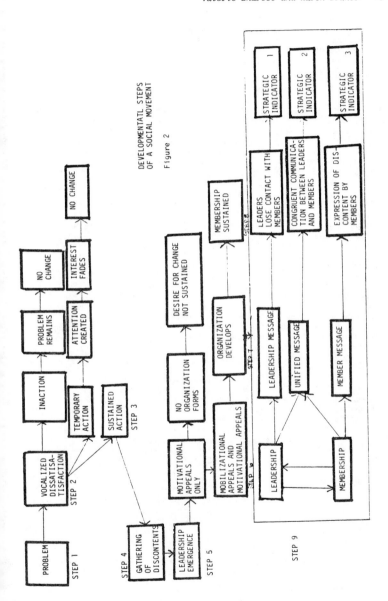

DEVELOPMENTATL STEPS
OF A SOCIAL MOVEMENT

Figure 2

recognizes that a movement addresses four distinct audiences, the differing messages are logical outcomes of attempts to assess the needs of different respondents. Ultimately, a movement's success or failure depends upon acceptance, rejection, and feedback from the various audiences necessary to address.

## CASE STUDIES

The purpose of the case studies is not to provide a full-blown analysis of a movement's rhetoric, nor to illustrate in depth how each of the components discussed inter-relate. Such a study must necessarily follow. Our primary intent is to briefly describe how the movement variables work together in an overall framework. Examples from two contemporary movements, the Peace People Movement of Northern Ireland (Figure 3) and the New Left Movement (Figure 4) serve to illustrate concepts developed in Figure 1 and Figure 2.

### Peace People Movement

The rhetorical situation in Northern Ireland reached such an intensity in 1976 that public response seemed inevitable. Deaths resulting from sectarian violence were the highest number reported since 1972.[19] The need for group action was critical in August when three children were killed by an IRA car pursued by British soldiers.[20] While the public angrily responded to the incident at first, motivation to initiate change promised to quickly die unless a movement was formed and a program for action developed and sustained. It was from this situation that the Peace People Movement emerged.

As a case study, the Peace People Movement has two advantages. First, mobilizational appeals were predominant in the crisis period when the movement precipitated intense responses from the Irish Republican Army, Sinn Fein, loyalist opposition groups and dissidents within the Peace Movement. Second, the movement illustrates how the media was crucial in reporting and interpreting the movement's message in its attempts to gain legitimacy, ward off opposition, and attract financial support and membership.

The failure of the movement leadership to initiate an autonomous organizational structure during the movement's inception period prompted a haphazard early growth. Though attracted to the movement's goals, many members who participated in peace marches between August and December of 1976 were only temporarily committed. Once the marches ended, the Peace People lost a sizable portion of participants due to both the lack of direction and failure of the movement leadership to initiate immediate mobilizational appeals.[21] However, after formal structural guidelines were developed, movement spokespersons employed other channels of persuasion to mobilize remaining participants.

A magazine, Peace by Peace, was developed and distributed internally throughout the organization and to interested proponents in the external environment. A clearly defined functional structure was established for community-level Peace Committees. Spokespersons developed a movement constitution and written strategies for peace.[22] For example, the movement magazine potentially had the effect of clarifying the movement's intent, leadership goals, and peace committee responsibilities. However, the impact of the magazine in fulfilling such purposes was limited due to the long time periods between issues. The same problem arose when the leadership published statements of the movement's

[19] Facts on File: World News Digest with Index, 36 (December 31, 1976), pp. 1007-1008.

[20] The London Times, August 15, 1976, p. 1.

[21] Richard Deutsch, Mairead Corrigan Betty Williams, (Barron's: Woodbury, New York, 1977), p. 148

[22] Deutsch, pp. 134-137.

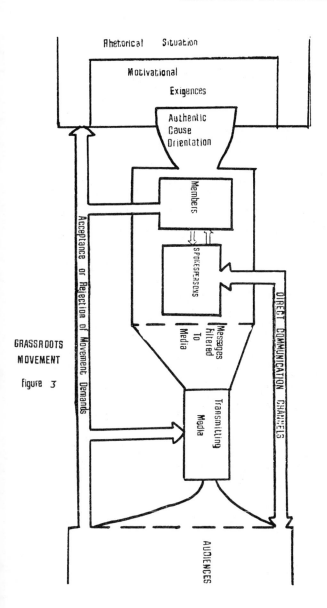

GRASSROOTS
MOVEMENT

figure 3

philosophical base months after the movement's inception. By then, factional groups developed, peace committees were in disarray, and the media were focussing public attention on movement problems.[23]

A formally recognized leadership was instrumental in establishing clearly defined communication networks between peace committees and the executive office. Gradually, however, the role of the movement leadership became one of spokespersons who symbolized or represented the movement to the external environment, rather than who coordinated the day-to-day responsibilities of the movement's central office in Belfast.

This symbolic spokesperson role created potential rhetorical problems for the movement leadership in their communication of messages to the movement participants. The leaders were accused of using Peace Prize money for personal reasons rather than for movement purposes.[24] Their travels to foreign countries to raise money and support provoked sharp criticism for not being accessible to movement followers. The leaders responded by formally stepping down from their positions. The new and present chairman, Peter McLachlan, set the tone for future movement leadership by stating, "My style will be one of withdrawal rather than being at the front of things."[25] By withdrawing from their roles as movement spokespersons, the original leadership shifted media and public attention away from them and back to the movement and its purposes.

The opposition's response created dialectical tension between the movement and opposition groups. In late September of 1976, the provisional IRA threatened that "if any of our volunteers are murdered or imprisoned as a result of the peace movement, these informers must be prepared to accept the consequences, even though they may claim they acted in the interests of a spurious peace."[26] Two months after the movement began, the provisional Sinn Fein, political wing of the IRA, produced a leaflet declaring its aim to cut attendance at peace rallies in Northern Ireland, Britain, and Southern Ireland.[27] In the same period, there was also an increase in violence and bombings by the Provisional IRA which was reported as "an attempt to reestablish credibility after considerable losses due to the success of the peace movement."[28] Ulster's Secretary of State explained the reaction as a "lashing out in anger to counteract the wave of feeling generated by the peace movement."[29] The Peace People countered the opposition by sending members to visit guerillas in prison and by offering "escape routes" to spirit opposition terrorists out of the country.[30] Such strategies reflected an intent to communicate in contexts or through channels that might reduce the dialectical tension between the movement and the opposition groups.

A strong internal organization now requires the Peace People Movement to communicate rarely with the external environment. Rhetorical strategies originated not from a single source, but grew to be eventually determined from a confirmed consensus by the entire movement membership. Thus, the movement's rhetoric adopted a group orientation reflecting the needs and goals of a movement now centered upon implementing programs at the grass roots level in Northern Ireland communities. Primary concern presently is with maintaining a clearly established organizational structure and lines of communication between movement spokespersons and participants.

[23]*The London Times*, October 19, 1976, p. 12 and October 27, 1976, p. 2.

[24]"Ulster's Peace Women," *Newsweek*, March 27, 1978.

[25]"Ireland's Peace Groups: Low Key But Consolidating," *The Christian Science Monitor*, (October 15, 1978).

[26]*The London Times*, September 28, 1976, p. 1.

[27]*The London Times*, October 10, 1976, p. 1.

[28]*The London Times*, October 26, 1976, p. 2.

[29]*The London Times*, October 26, 1976, p. 2.

[30]*The London Times*, June 21, 1977, p. 2.

## The New Left Movement

The social and political discontent of the 1960's was perhaps most visible in the student activists of the New Left (see Figure 4). Defined primarily as a movement of white middle-class youth, the membership was typically associated with a post-war, post-depression generation.[31] As historian Irwin Unger explained, "It was a movement of youth; it was bold and playful as well as erratic and unstable."[32] Overwhelmed by what the membership believed to be the impersonal powers of the industrial-military bureaucracy, students were alienated in a society with which they could no longer identify. Thus, the student rhetoric of the 1960's was characterized by a violent rejection of traditional affluency. At the same time, the membership became a champion of the poverty stricken minority classes of America. With the advent of the publication of Galbraith's The Affluent Society and Michael Harrington's expose on American poverty, The Other America, the rhetorical situation gathered its tools for the formulation of protest.[33]

What were the "major crises," then, that presumably activated the New Left? In contrast to the singular motivational exigence giving rise to the Peace People Movement, students appeared to have joined the movement for a variety of reasons. Some members entered the organization in hopes of personal enrichment--to give meaning and purpose to their discontented lives. Others joined the movement in hopes of changing the social structure of the country. Still others joined for individual causes such as racial advancement, women's rights, student rights, and in protest of American domestic and foreign policy.[34] In essence, the members' reasons for joining appeared to be as many and as diverse as the membership itself. For many members, subjective experience, rather than any specific objective goal, seemed to be the force that drew them together.

In order to counter such a problem of diversity, a consistent cause orientation was created by a group of clever intellectual leaders. Their duty appeared to have rested upon providing the terms of the argument and influencing directions of membership groupings. The problem charismatic leaders faced was in mobilizing support from discontents who had joined the cause for varied reasons. For example, in mid 1962, Robert Haber and Tom Hayden of the SDS combined forces at their annual convention to assemble the Port Huron Statement. The document was designed to recruit membership as well as set apart the New Left Movement and distinguish it from New Left organizations of the past.[35]

The Port Huron Statement found fault with nearly every aspect of America: "racism, cold war, the threat of nuclear holocaust, and poverty in the midst of plenty, all tarnishing the image of American virtue."[36] Such a statement was sufficiently vague to enlist as many members as possible--regardless of the true source of their discontent. Not only were problems outlined, solutions were proposed. All told, the Port Huron Statement provided the students with a solution that was only a short step beyond the New Deal--Fair Deal-- New Frontier tradition of Roosevelt, Truman, and Kennedy.[37]

[31] Irwin Unger, The Movement: A History of the American New Left: 1959-1972, (New York: Harper and Row, 1974), p. 29.

[32] Unger, p. 29.

[33] Unger, p. 58.

[34] Unger, pp. 38-39.

[35] Tom Hayden, The Port Huron Statement (New York: SDS, 1962), p. 42.

[36] Hayden, p. 53.

[37] Hayden, p. 12.

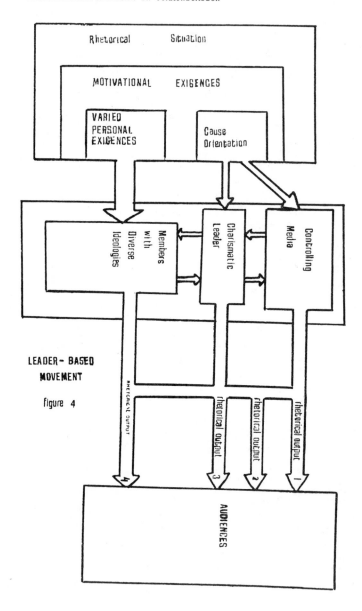

LEADER- BASED
MOVEMENT

figure 4

Although a base was provided for the New Leftist ideology, the members failed to provide feedback to the leadership in the form of a shared and unified consensus. Rather than filter their messages through the leaders or the news media, the membership tended to communicate their personal goals to the target audiences directly.

As with a formal organization, the New Left Movement had to maintain a hierarchy of authority and a division of labor so that members could be persuaded to take orders, perform tasks, and sacrifice time and money for the sake of the movement rather than for personal causes.[38] However, the New Left Movement experienced considerable difficulty in accomplishing such a task. A number of factors led to the New Left's lack of organizational structure. By the nature of its ideology as a participatory democracy, the New Left's structure shunned effective organization. The movement held a great distaste for institutions and bureaucracies and viewed a leadership-hierarchical structure as a form of authoritarianism.

In theory, the New Left organization viewed all members as equal. As a result, many members acted independently of each other, causing at times, confusion and turmoil. At the same time, it was especially important for the leadership to organize and coordinate activities encompassing a wide variety of issues. Thus, one of the major rhetorical problems within the movement was a sharp difference between the philosophical position expressed and the absence of an organizational structure requisite for dealing with its concerns.

Compounding the movement's problems, leaders from each faction of the New Left tended to work separately, further factionalizing the movement as a whole. For example, during the final stages of the movement, the SDS split into smaller organizations such as the Revolutionary Youth Movement, the White Panthers, and the Weathermen. Ideology largely depended on the action of a few individuals. The split of the movement into such diverse groups created further rhetorical problems because each group tended to assume its own rhetoric. Therefore, not only were there conflicting messages being conveyed from the movement to its audiences; messages communicated within the internal structure were also in conflict. Often, members were left in confusion as they watched their organizational leaders quarrel and continually change alliances.

Thus, the New Left Movement had considerable problems in maintaining loyalty to the organization because of factionalized ideals among the members and leadership. A formal hierarchy of authority was never actually established. Therefore, any activities initiated by members were largely an individualized effort.

The movement's audience received conflicting messages not only from the members and leaders, but from the news media as well. As a third source of interpretation of the movement's activities, the media tended to impose a drama-centered view on the strategic indicators. Historian Norman Fruchter noted the persuasive role played by television in the transmission of the New Left Movement's message:

> Television affected and molded the quality of youth protest, when protest became the daily fare on college campuses. It has even been claimed that without television there would have been no New Left. Marches and building occupations were staged for the six o'clock news, and New Left leaders were defined as those who gave interesting interviews to David Susskind or Mike Wallace. This is a great exaggeration, but toward the end of the radical decade, a thoughtful man of the Left would claim that the ability of the young rebels to manipulate television imagery both made and broke the Movement.[39]

[38]Theodore Roszak, The Making of a Counter Culture (New York: Anchor Books, 1968), pp. 42-84.

[39]Unger, p. 54.

While the movement's messages were extremely diverse, their audiences were of a similar nature.  In the case of the New Left, strategic indicators were directed toward three audiences comprised of strong, right-wing conservatives of the establishment (OPPOSITION), moderates and left-wing sympathizers (PROPONENTS), and finally, right and left-wing decision-makers.

The New Left failed to secure adoption of its demands by the establishment.  Reasons point to the regressive tendencies within the movement's organizational structure.  As the author of The Movement explained, "The inner imperatives of SDS . . . made it forget its need to keep in touch with the hopes and needs of some constituency outside itself and was obviously a fundamental cause of its collapse."[40]

Had the movement directed rhetorical appeals to students and discontents, or proponents, instead of appealing to decision-makers, it may have succeeded in moving America to the left--securing at least partial adoption of their policy.  Instead, the movement was forced to engage in defensive and subversive rhetoric in order to counter the opposition's generation of dialectical tension.  Because of their preoccupation with subversive rhetoric, the movement failed to secure adoption of their ideology by the establishment.

## CONCLUSIONS

To date, social movement criticism has demonstrated promise in its capacity to explain the motivations of societal groups to bring about change. Reviewed as a whole, however, individual studies have employed differing methods with little success due to the lack of a coordinated perspective. This paper established a possible organizing perspective by emphasizing the usefulness of a framework based upon phenomenological precepts for social movement criticism.

In building such a framework, it is necessary to first map out frequent structural interactions in order to establish a normative base for evaluating the rhetoric of social movements.[41]  The need for testing and further amplification of the structure mapped out through the models and case studies is obvious.  Social movement critics must also determine how movements may change internally and externally during different phases of development. Through such considerations, social movement criticism can begin  to achieve the organizing perspective necessary for the building of sound rhetorical theory.

Finally, future research should attempt to establish relationships between different forms of rhetorics and movements.  Direction of research may lead the critic to determine whether a link exists between structure and types of rhetorical strategies emerging from a particular structure.[42]  Once this groundwork is completed and a tighter theoretical structure developed, social movement critics may begin the task of evaluation from a much clearer perspective.

---

[40]Roszak, p. 36.

[41]Jackson Harrell and Wil A. Linkugel, "On Rhetorical Genre: An Organizing Perspective," Philosophy and Rhetoric, 12 (Fall 1978), pp. 262-270.  The authors present ideas easily adapted to theory development for social movement criticism.

[42]Direction of research may lead the critic to determine whether a link exists between structure and types of rhetorical strategies emerging from a particular structure.  For example, as a result of a social study using this framework, possible relationships may be drawn between a leader-based movement and subversive rhetoric.  Charismatic leaders in a leader-based movement potentially could be using rhetoric of a subversive nature most frequently to sustain a membership against the establishment.

KRISTIN LANGELLIER
SOUTHERN ILLINOIS UNIVERSITY

The French word l'histoire presents an ambiguity which suggests the relationship between history and story. That is, from both a record of events and their recounting, l'histoire (his-tory) as personal narration emerges to mediate history and philosophy.[1] The narrative in literature names a similar equivocation. For we have the double articulation of a story- intelligible as a world, or a narration; and a -telling attributable to a speaker, or narrator. Narrative therefore questions the relationship which grounds both narration and narrating.

Correspondingly, two theories of literature--a poetics and a rhetoric-- treat narrative in two different ways. Structural poetics, on the one hand, defines the narrative as literary discourse which articulates a world of meanings. Analysis of narrative as a model of intelligibility focuses upon the conventions of writing which a reader must possess in order to recognize the world articulated. Such conventions of narrative fiction explain the effects of literary discourse upon readers as cultural norms. Roland Barthes, for example, in explicating le roman nouveau, extends structural poetics to assert that writing becomes truly writing only when it prevents one from answering the question 'who is speaking?'[2] Rhetoric, on the other hand, relies directly upon the identity of a speaker and listener in order to account for literary discourse. The voice, or point of view of a speaking subject, explains effects on readers as rhetorical choices about narrating as an enunciative act. For example, Wayne C. Booth's rhetorical analyses account for fiction prior to le roman nouveau.[3]

Although structural poetics and rhetoric as theories of literature explain literary discourse in different ways, i.e., as writing or speaking, both assume reading as an infrastructure. Reading in the case of structural poetics involves judgments about cultural norms of writing; reading in the context of rhetoric requires judgments about persons who speak. In either case, reading names the fact of human experience which both a poetics and a rhetoric must describe and explain as narrative.

The explication of a human fact requires a methodology employing experiential data and personalistic ontology, i.e., phenomenology.[4] More specifi-

Phenomenology in Rhetoric and Communication, ed. Stanley Deetz. Copyright, 1981, The Center for Advanced Research in Phenomenology and the University Press of America.

[1] Maurice Merleau-Ponty, In Praise of Philosophy, trans. John Wild and James M. Edie (Evanston: Northwestern University, 1963).

[2] Roland Barthes cited in Jonathan Culler, Structuralist Poetics: Structuralism, Linguistics, and the Study of Literature (Ithaca, N.Y.: Cornell University, 1975), p. 200; for an application to the oral interpretation of literature, see Mary Frances Hopkins, "Structuralism: Its Implications for Performance of Prose Fiction," Communication Monographs 44, No. 2 (June 1977), 93-105.

[3] Wayne C. Booth, The Rhetoric of Fiction (Chicago: University of Chicago, 1961).

[4] Maurice Roche, Phenomenology, Language, and the Social Sciences (London: Routledge and Kegan Paul, 1973); see also Don Idhe, Experimental Phenomenology: An Introduction (New York: Capricorn, 1977).

cally, a phenomenology of human communication takes conscious experience--the meaningful relationship between person and lived world--as its data base.[5] Phenomenology explains experience through the explicit proposition of implicit meanings in a series of reductions. In the question of narrative, the conscious experience of reader constitutes the data base for a phenomenology such that reading is defined as the performance of text.[6] In other words, my concern is with reading in performance, such as narrative as oral interpretation, narrative as silent readings, and narrative as interpersonal communication. Thus, for a phenomenology of narrative I describe reading as performance which constitutes narration, or a lived-world; I reduce narration to the constitution of speaker and listener, or narrating; and finally, narrative names the experience of reading as human communication which situates person (narrating) and lived-world (narration).

## NARRATION

What is it to read narration? Structural poetics suggests that at least the reader expects a meaningful world--a story about something. In a novel,

> words must be composed in such a way that through the activity of reading there will emerge a model of the social world, models of individual personality, of the relationship between individual and society, and perhaps most important, of the kind of significance which these aspects bear.[7]

Narration names a linguistic description of conscious experience where literary discourse functions as the relationship between story and world. Whether traditional or le roman nouveau, narration is mimetic to the extent that it signifies a world as a degree variation within the range of human experience. In reading, one performs a story, according to literary norms, about something related to cultural norms. Conventions of reading refer to individual and institutional models articulated such that cognitive, affective, and conative meanings emerge.

Placing structural poetics within performance has the force of situating narration and reader within reading which articulates meanings as intelligible social models. Put another way, narration in performance is a social system of relationships in the sense of an ecosystem of organism (narration) and environment (reader).[8] Ecosystem specifies a system of communication with coding relations between subsystem and the larger contextualizing environment. The relationship between narration and reader is a question of punctuation, that is, the setting of boundaries which gives information exchanged within the ecosystem meaning. The exchange of information within the ecosystem of narration defines language as discourse in distinction from ecriture.[9] In reading, narration has meaning as a function of significant units which contrast and combine with each other within and between levels.[10] Narration as text without center weaves codes as a world of meanings experienced in performance.

[5]Richard L. Lanigan, "Phenomenology of Human Communication," Philosophy Today 23 (Spring 1979), 3-15.

[6]Eric E. Peterson, "Oral Interpretation as Performing Performance," Speech Communication Association Convention, Minneapolis, 3 Nov. 1978.

[7]Culler, p. 189.

[8]Anthony Wilden, System and Structure: Essays in Communication and Exchange (London: Tavistock, 1972).

[9]Roland Barthes, Writing Degree Zero, trans. Annette Lavers and Colin Smith (Boston: Beacon, 1970).

[10]Umberto Eco, A Theory of Semiotics (Bloomington: Indiana University, 1976), pp. 261-276.

How information is exchanged in the ecosystem of narrative relationships such that the reader recognizes a story defines discourse. Discourse articulates a world according to modes, or manners of experiencing a world. When discourse supplies information referring to cultural objects and events, the narrative relationship to the story is thematized. The reader recognizes codes relatively unmediated and correlative with the time and space structures of concrete reality. A world is experienced as seen; the reader is shown a story in the dramatic mode. Characters in scene, for example, are identifiable as individual and social models. What cannot be naturalized as referential, as showing a world, may be ascribed to a narrator whose codes mediate the story. The narrative relationship to the reader defines the story experienced as told in a lyric mode, such as summary and description which collapse and elaborate time and space. Thus, modes of showing and telling structure narrative relationships in the ecosystem of narration to create a meaningful world.

Essential to story-as-shown and story-as-told is the undifferentiated experience of world, the movement between showing and telling within the epic mode.[11] What relates world and narration is reading as performance of text. According to Barthes, in *S/Z*, "what we hear, therefore, is the displaced voice which the reader lends, by proxy, to the discourse. . . it is significantly the voice of reading."[12] Here Barthes merely throws in relief what reading already implies: the shared experience of a social text in which characters, narrators, and readers name relationships which are functions rather than static entities. The boundaries of narration that mark arbitrary starting points are within a system of differences transformed in performance. Reading recovers information concretely experienced in a social world of relationships which is dynamic. The voice of reading constitutes the object of consciousness for a phenomenology of narrative.

Narration as ecosystem is constituted as text in transformation according to structural shifts in reading. The dramatic mode or the lyric mode stands in relationship to the epic mode, a metonymic shift. And, any reading of the story stands in relationship to other readings, a metaphoric shift. Initial boundary conditions do not limit, therefore, reading as interpretation. Narration as ecosystem displays both equifinality (different modal choices discover a similar story) and multifinality (similar modal choices reveal different stories). Text is its own justification within reading as performance prior to any causality reliant upon a subject or object posited prior to reading.

A phenomenology of narrative constitutes narration as the experience of a story about something, a lived-world. Jonathan Culler insists that "if structural analysis is to make sense as an intellectual enterprise it must specify clearly what are the facts about human experience which it attempts to explicate."[13] Structural poetics must take place within a phenomenology which reveals judgments of literary and cultural norms as experienced. The phenomenological description of narrative as ecosystem reveals that narration is already a performance in reading. Narration as lived-world discovers the significant elements for a structural analysis.

The ecosystem of narrative constitutes text as a story regulating a discourse which constitutes a context. Narration constitutes reader as the voice of reading, but not conversely. Narration offers information about meanings: we know what the story says as the experience of narration. What it means

[11]For an explication of the epic mode in the group performance of prose fiction, see Robert S. Breen, *Chamber Theatre* (Englewood Cliffs, N.J.: Prentice-Hall, 1978).

[12]Roland Barthes, *S/Z*, trans. Richard Miller (New York: Farrar, Straus, and Giroux, 1974), p. 151.

[13]Jonathan Culler, "Phenomenology and Structuralism," *Human Context* 5 (1973), 42.

emerges through choices in narrating. The phenomenological description of narrative explicates the context for choices about meaning within a structural poetics. To discover narrative choices, we turn to a rhetoric phenomenologically grounded.


## NARRATING

The description of narrative as ecosystem discovers a world of meanings interpreted according to individual and social models such that to read narration continues a process of meaning-production in history as performing. The experience of narration presents meanings--thematically and nonthematically--to displace life-world with lived-world. Within a phenomenology of narrative, narration is always already a performance, always already read--a discourse before objectification and explanation. A phenomenological grounding in performance for structural poetics defines narration as a concrete linguistic description of a figure-ground correlation which may be viewed from several perspectives as specific narrating choices. The appropriate question about narrative emerges as the hermeneutic "how?" rather than the "what?" of information to be naturalized.[14] Narration as performance interrogates narrating as performing. Or, how do we read narration?

Telling structures story. The movement to phenomenological reduction takes the mode of experiencing as its object of consciousness--narrating as perspective on the figure-ground correlation of narration. A traditional theory of rhetoric explains narrating as the point of view between a speaker (author or narrator) and listener (reader) which conditions the story as variables of "person" and degree of omniscience. Point of view understood phenomenologically claims its situation within performing. Narrative stance replaces narrator or reader to specify how the epic mode discloses the lived-world of narration. Narrating does not produce a story as a message sent by a speaker to a listener such that there is coincidence of subject and object or coincidence of subject and subject. Rather, in narrating we live through an experience structured in lived-space and lived-time prior to states of speaking and listening. Dialogue names the narrative stance for narrating as communication which constitutes the rhetorical dimensions of speaker and listener.

Gusdorf defines communication as "a search for the you and the I and the you tend to join together in the unity of we."[15] How, in narrating, we search for the you constitutes rhetorical choices of discourse. The phenomenological description of epic mode suggests that the question is one about relationship: how the story is shown and how it is told. The narrative stance takes postures which open up and delimit the world relative to shifts in distance and direction. Is the world disclosed as pointed to or as embodied? If the world is shown and told through external evidence, you and I emerge as impersonal and universal--any reasonable observers who can judge the facts. If the narrative stance shows and tells the world according to evidence which is internal, a personal and particular you and I emerge as participants who also may judge the facts reasonably. Choices in showing and telling the story structure an impersonal or personal narrating of consciousness as the dialogic context in which you and I are reversible communicators. Narrating and reading are co-present rather than causal; and, story is co-narrated in performing.

The structural shifts in narrating constitute you and I to discover different experiences of story within the shared consciousness of communication.

---

[14] Calvin O. Schrag, *Experience and Being: Prolegomena to a Future Ontology* (Evanston: Northwestern University, 1969).

[15] Georges Gusdorf, *Speaking (La Parole)* (Evanston: Northwestern University, 1965), p. 61.

In the movement from phenomenological description to phenomenological reduction, a new experience previously only implicit is explicated as the consciousness of narrating choices for you and I.  In the ecosystem of story, you and I name reversible choices of telling.  Dialogue displaces discourse in the phenomenological reduction as the various modalities of speaking silence.  Narrating offers information <u>and</u> communication as historical and personal meanings. Reversibility makes clear <u>that</u> consciousness of narrating as well as the experience of narration can constitute text.  In narrating, narration is situated in history.

The narrating of information and communication implies judgments about persons in the dialogic context as questions of reliability.  Speaking and silence signify promise-making in the disclosure of world.  The transformation of you and I as we requires trust and risk.  "Risk," writes Natanson, "is established when the affective world of the person is existentially disrupted, and this disruption means that his immediate life of feeling and sensibility is challenged and made open to challenge."[16]  Immediacy claims us in our situation with others which limits and enriches narrative.  In narrating we risk narration and vice versa.  Communication occurs to an extent as we share narrative which is both a structural poetics of story and a rhetoric of telling as they are informed by· phenomenology.

To this point story as narration and telling as narrating constituted different (digital) choices for narrative: your story and my story are articulated as two messages such that either the experience of narration or the consciousness of narrating constitutes narrative.  Either a structural poetics regulates story as context or a rhetoric constitutes story as choices.  Put more directly, in narrative we confront the other's experience and consciousness.  What remains to be explicated in a phenomenology of narrative is that shared history from which story emerges, or that which makes reversibility possible.  Next we turn to a discussion of narrative as the correlation rule which relates narration and narrating, history and you and I as story-telling persons.

## NARRATIVE

The phenomenological description of narrative elucidates narration as discourse structured according to literary and cultural models to interpret story as information.  In performance, story is experienced as lived-world.  The experience of narration constitutes story as the context for choices about telling.  The phenomenological reduction of narrative unfolds as dialogue which discloses narration according to choices in narrating.  In performing, embedded structures of narrating are explicated to constitute story as conscious choices about telling, or as communication.  The experience of a lived-world consciously structured in lived-time and lived-space implies embodiment with others as lived-body.  Reading relates narration and narrating as the conscious experience of narrative.  A phenomenology of narrative offers social roles to play in reading reciprocal within dialogue.  Their reading signifies a history of consciousness already existing in time experienced as immediately read.  The situation of narrative allows the story-teller as social to emerge from within history.

It is lived-body contexted within a social situation in the face of the other which reads.  Neither an object among objects nor a subject among subjects, lived-body is always already social embodiment as narrative.  Analogous

[16]Maurice Natanson, "The Claims of Immediacy" in *Philosophy, Rhetoric, and Argumentation*, ed. Maurice Natanson and Hnery W. Johnstone, Jr. (University Park: Pennsylvania State University, 1965), p. 19.

to the hand, narrative grasps and points to the lived-world. Shifts in narrative relationship correspond to changes in narrative structures in lived-time and lived-space. Embodied in the world, narrative gazes and faces the gaze of the other.[17] In this way, lived-body punctuates text by setting boundaries as the reading person.[18]

Recall the phenomenological description and reduction of narrative as an ecosystem of functions co-present and reversible. That is, in the ecosystem of narrative, terms do not refer to entities within a linear model as discreet, static, causal, and directional, but to relationships in communication. To explicate reading as the conscious experience of narrative, four variations of persona correlative with Merleau-Ponty's system of four terms will be employed.[19] These four terms are persona/hypothetical other, per-sona/visual body, person-a/ introceptive image, and a-person/my psyche. The advantage of this new system is twofold: it avoids the problems of a linear model mentioned above; and, it allows the specification of the relationships between the consciousness and experience of persons. As Lanigan points out, Merleau-Ponty's deliniation of four terms "is not to suppose an intersubjective dualism, but rather to verify the unity of the perceiving person who encounters another."[20]

Persona names narrative as the "hypothetical other" whom I can never know completely, nor conversely. Persona presents another body to me in the narrative situation. As social embodiment, per-sona articulates narrative in the sense of by-sound or sounding-through. Per-sona bodily comprehends narrative through various perspectives as roles. According to Merleau-Ponty, per-sona presents a "visual body"--the body of the other as seen by me from the exterior. Implicit in bodily experience of per-sona is embodied consciousness as person-a which lives narrative sensorily and tensively from the interior. Merleau-Ponty uses the term "introceptive image" to define the image I have of my body, the second self outside of me. Narrative as a-person names the self as that which is known prior to experience of self-as-other or other. "My psyche" as described by Merleau-Ponty is the mass of sensations which occur within my body. A-person is narrative knowable only to me.

The unity of reading person now allows the situation of narration and narrating within narrative and embodiment within reading. The four terms of reading person as embodiment articulate the conscious experience of narrative at two levels analogous to sedimented speech (narration) and existential speaking (narrating).[21] Recall that the phenomenological description and reduction of narrative constitute narration as context for choices about story and narrating as choices of story-telling. The conscious experience of reading person embodied as lived-body reveals two movements as narrative to relate narration and narrating. First, narration suggests a movement from a-person as person-a or per-sona to constitute persona as narrative. That is, reading creates context of choice as the bodily experience or embodied consciousness of story. Narrating illustrates a second movement which takes persona as per-sona and person-a to constitute a-person as narrative. That is, reading creates choices in context as the bodily experience and embodied consciousness of story--which entails a context of choice as persona. Reading person creates

[17] For an application of these narrative relationships in oral interpretation, see the discussion of locus in Wallace A. Bacon, *The Art of Interpretation*, 3rd ed. (New York: Holt, Rinehart, and Winston, 1979), pp. 70-82.

[18] Julia Kristeva, *The System and the Speaking Subject* (Lisse: Peter de Rider, 1975; Atlantic Highlands, N.J.: Humanities, 1976).

[19] Maurice Merleau-Ponty, "The Child's Relation With Others," trans. William Cobb in *The Primacy of Perception* ed. James N. Edie (Evanston: Northwestern University, 1964), p. 115.

[20] Richard L. Lanigan, *Speaking and Semiology: Maurice Merleau-Ponty's Phenomenological Theory of Existential Communication* (The Hague: Mouton, 1972), p. 107.

[21] Richard L. Lanigan, "Phenomenology and Semiotic Communication," Annual Conference of the Society for Phenomenology and Existential Philosophy, Pittsburgh, 4 Nov. 1978, pp. 7-9.

story as <u>choice in context</u> in infinite possibilities within "the binary analog logic thus expressed (Either/Or contexts containing Both/And choice possibilities)"[22]

A phenomenology of narrative describes reading as human communication, the relationship between lived-world and person. Narrative constitutes narration as lived-world and you and I as narrating persons. The essential structure of narrative is the authenticity of embodiment in reading as the movement between finitude of point of view (a-person/person-a) and transcendence through role-taking (per-sona/persona). A-person names the historical story-teller who emerges from persona as choice in context. The conscious experience of narrative creates text as the context for becoming in which the experience of narration and consciousness of narrating are constituted as <u>similar</u> within reading person.

The historical actor alone can perform the shifts between noun and verb to make narration narrate.[23] Reading is a historical performance in which I become who I am able to. A late arrival in phenomenological analysis, "the 'I' appears by means of and through reflection upon phenomenon that in toto are the world."[24] It is in this sense that reading person creates story as history such that we may have narrative in oral interpretation, silent reading, and interpersonal communication. Narrative is the historical moment of narrating narration.

## CONCLUSION

A phenomenology of narrative has emerged in three methodological steps of description, reduction, and interpretation. The phenomenological description of narration discovers story as the experience of a lived-world socially constructed according to cultural models. The phenomenological reduction of narrating structures telling as the consciousness of narrating persons within a rhetorical situation. The relationship between lived-world and person is phenomenologically interpreted as the conscious experience of reading person who constitutes both story and telling as similar within narrative in performance which is historical and personal. The ecosystem thus described defines its boundaries according to the punctuation of reading person who creates text through shifts in performance. What narrative interrogates is the relationship between narration and narrating, system and speaking subject--the coding processes which constitute contexts for choices and choices in contexts as human communication. The phenomenology of narrative undertaken is therefore at once also a semiotic inquiry into the signifying practices of reading person, that play which renews and reshapes the order of his-tory.

Julia Kristeva writes that:

it is only on the basis of a theory of the speaking subject, as subject of a heterogenous process, that semiotics can show that what lies outside its metalinguistic mode of operations--the 'remainder.' the 'waste'--is what, in the process of the speaking subject, represents the moment in which it is set in action, put on trial, put to death . . . .[25]

---

[22]Lanigan, "Phenomenology and Semiotic Communication," p. 9.

[23]Maurice Merleau-Ponty, "On the Phenomenology of Language," trans. Richard C. Cleary in <u>Signs</u> (Evanston: Northwestern University, 1964), pp. 84-97.

[24]Idhe, pp. 50-51.

[25]Kristeva, p. 8.

A phenomenology of narrative can ground the semiotic inquiry into reading person as it informs structural poetics and rhetoric. The reading person at once reads from and usurps history as story. Narrative has the force of continuously calling the reading person into question in the play of his-tory.

Narrative in performance reveals a significant paradigm for the field of speech communication. Narrative as reading names the analog of l'histoire as history--whether oral, silent, or interpersonal. Georges Bataille states it more momentously: "To a greater or lesser extent every man is suspended upon narratives, on novels, which reveal to him the multiplicity of life. Only these narratives, often read in a trance, situate him before his fate."[26]

---

[26]Georges Bataille, foreword to Le Bleu du Ciel, cited in Barthes, S/Z, p. 267.

# 9 / THE SIGNIFICATIVE CONTEXT OF HUMAN BEHAVIOR

CLAIRE ELAINE MCCOY
OHIO UNIVERSITY

Approached with concern for the structures of signification, human behavior in the communicative experience reveals to the scholar a multi-faceted event, a gathering and dispersing, the formation and deformation of experience of world. The study of human communication becomes an interrogation of how the experience as process is given or made present to the one experiencing and of the lines of signification perceived.

A phenomenological-hermeneutic approach to communication varies from the traditional perspectives in several important ways. A critical difference is consideration of the significative context of human behavior. The conventional methodologies fail in their theories and modes of explanation to respect the experiential-communicative process which in fact contextualizes their theories and the events explained by them. Instead, systems are abstractly formulated in an attempt to explain communication phenomena in terms of natural causes and laws without consideration for their meaning implication in experience. These unchanging laws neglect the aspect of continual change in the natural world.[1] By the conception and implementation of such systems, a shaping force often undetected functions in the process of the researcher's understanding. The chosen theoretical framework assumes a "reality." What is sought, is found, and soon experience is interpreted entirely in terms of the perspective employed. For example, thought may be perceived as logic instead of logic being considered as a way of thinking.[2] Also, the subject-object dichotomy which is basic to conventional theory incorrectly delineates the parties experiencing the communicative event, the objective observer or even the communicator as individual, as separate from each other and the communicative world. A third inadequacy of such substantial theories, derived from Aristotelian concepts of space and time used to deploy such substances is their inability to explain the way in which a single substance, sign, or object points to many. It has been shown that there is no one to one coincidence between the substantial things and their meaning. The notion of "non-coincidence" suggests that there is a disassociation of natural events, inclusive of human acts, and the way that they can be deployed in terms of meaning. Various substantial things can "mean" the same while various meanings can be attributed to one thing.

It is precisely such difficulties that a phenomenological-hermeneutic approach to communication explores. The phenomenological approach would require that human behavior be examined within its constituted significative context without which interaction would be incomprehensible. As method, phenomenology

*Phenomenology in Rhetoric and Communication*, ed. Stanley Deetz. Copyright, 1981, The Center for Advanced Research in Phenomenology and the University Press of America.

[1] David Stewart and Algis Mickunas, *Exploring Phenomenology* (Chicago: American Library Association, 1974), p. 20. Also see "The Thesis of the Natural Standpoint and its Suspension," in Edmund Husserl's *Ideas: General Introduction to Pure Phenomenology* (New York: Collier, 1962), pp 91-100. The principle ideas expressed in this paragraph are presented in *Ideas*.

[2] Stewart, p. 19.

requires that conciousness always be related to the experiential world and be expressed in terms of conciousness of its object.  Conciousness intentionality is always an object in its particular situation and the spatio-temporal horizons implied.  Horizon as the context in which one experiences change is present in terms of experiential events.  Conciousness is always conciousness of an object, not as an ontological thing, but as an object experienced in terms of its "how."  Each experienced object "leads on" in that it is more than the present perception.  One side points to other sides, "means" them, and thus establishes a spatial horizon.  At the same time, it "means" the other sides still to be seen and establishes a temporal horizon.  This is at the primary level of experience.  At the secondary level, the object can be and is meant in detachment from its primary spatio-temporal implications.  It may possess a "practical meaning" connecting it with an entire system of objects.  The hammer, for example, points to the nail, the nail to the board, the board to the wall, the wall to the house and then to family and to tradition.  At another level the "meant" objects can assume a process of valuative implications.  The hammer may be good or bad, and, if needing repair, require a replacement and an expenditure.  Meaning exists not in an absolute sense, but in the way that it selects and deploys events, and every event has more meaning than the one that is currently articulated.  Thus, every facet of experience can articulate more and suggest explorablility.

The essential inclusion of the experiential nature of communicative processes is fundamental to a phenomenological study both from the Husserlian concept of the natural attitude and the Heideggerian emphasis on Dasein.  Rather than designing abstract theories, a phenomenological approach seeks to explore the structure of the content of conciousness and to discover how phenomena are given to conciousness.  The presubjective-preobjective nature of the polar ego radically alters the understanding of the event since an individual communicator can no longer be considered apart from the context of his world.  The ego in its act is always correlated to something in the sense that it  "means" that something in a particular way.  The shifting patterns of significative interconnections provided for by the experiential emphasis sustains the pointing function of events, signs, or objects.

The communicative event, then, sketches a context which is traced by human behavior.  Such a description of the communicative process requires the researcher to delimit the communicative region and to identify the structures of signification constituting the experience.  The phenomenon to be considered is the speaking, communicative gesture.  As phenomenon, while it articulates it also constitutes the appearance of the events or things, and provides the modalities of that experience.  This speaking or communication as appearance is transparent with the limits of deployment of things and events.  For example, if one points to a rainbow, the other will look to the rainbow, his eye tracing the arc that the pointing hand sketches across the sky.  Human behavior has traced the lines of signification thus providing a context for the event.  Restructuration happens through the speaking silent gesture as well as through the verbal.

The context of human behavior is a region constituted by the phenomenon of speaking.[3]  Any study of human communication must acknowledge the constitution of the world as significant space and human behavior in communication as manifestation of a world context.  Before the aspect of interaction can by considered, two dimensions of the communicative region need exposition.  The first, the primordial "vital-magical" dimension, will be examined as a

[3]Algis Mickunas, "Transignificative Dimension of Language," Conference on Cross-cultural Phenomenology, Ontario Institute for Studies in Education, Toronto, 1977, p. 2., and Erich Heintel, Einfugrung in die Sprachphilosophie (Darmstadt: Wissenschaftliche Buchgesellschaft, 1972).

source of power, of emergence, and of silence. The second and perhaps more evident, is the dimension of signification which is the <u>verwandtniszusammenhang</u> or unity of interconnected relationships as contextual meaning[4]

## THE VITAL-MAGICAL DIMENSION AND THE SPEAKING SILENCE

A dimension of "speaking" which exists preverbally is presupposed by spoken and written texts. While fundamental to the phenomenon of speaking, this dimension is the vital-magical region of transformation and identification.[5] The designation "vital-magical" suggesting a total immersion of the human in the vegetative and animal world, is one of the origins of language. It is an experience that attempts to master events and vital needs in terms of magical ritual and incantation. The notion of magic can be traced to the Sanskrit root "mag(h)", meaning "to make," "to transform." It functions puncti-formally.

The "puncti-formity" of this dimension is a source of power in that at the vital level every event or object can assume an identity with every other event or object to the extent of their same vital significance. For example, in a hunting ritual in which an animal skin is worn, the performer becomes identical with the "vital" powers of the animal. Taken at the verbal level, the word does not symbolize but assumes the power of or becomes identical with the vital power of what the word announces. There the spatio-temporal distances are abolished. Although a divinity may reside in the sky, during incantation the divinity is present in the ritual and the powers of that divinity are deployed by the ritual.

The "unitary, puncti-formal relationships connecting vitally any point with any other point regardless of spacio-temporal distances or proximities"[6] forms a vital nexus which is the origin of the experience of transformability and the origin of the power of rhetoric. Freed from space-time by the spacio-temporal interchangeability, the vital-magical dimension assumes transformative powers in its pervasive presence to all being-in-the-world and to all phenomena. Through influence, control, and power over other, a "vital" mastery of the world is attained by the identification and transformation of events in terms of their vital role. This power is not lost but is the power of rhetoric. The power of influence, in the transformation of people's minds, their psychological states, can be seen in the power of the word. Such transformative power is assured because the words are not pointing to something but become identical with it. The traditional description of the celebration of the Roman Catholic Mass indicates that the bread and wine are body and blood, not just representative of it. Sanskrit mantras when chanted identify the yogi with the vibration of that which they chant. Many primitive hunting societies identified the hunter with the animal sought. And the power of naming a thing persists over time and across cultural boundaries. The American Indians, often named for animals such as "Sitting Bull" and "Running Bear", were assuming the qualities of the being of the animal with the name.

Human behavior and communication studies must take into consideration this primordial region, this dimension of emergence. The vital nexus as preverbal lacks signification or meaning about somethings, precisely because it does not point to any thing; rather in presenting something it effaces itself. The effacement of the word is its assumption of the power of what it announces.

[4]Martin Heidegger, <u>Being and Time</u> (New York: Harper, 1962), p. 135.

[5]The structure of the vital-magical is derived from Jean Gebser "The Four Mutations of Consciousness," <u>Origin and Presence</u>, m.s., trans. Algis Mickunas and Noel Barnstad.

[6]Algis Mickunas, "Jean Gebser and the Comparative Study of Civilizations," International Society for the Comparative Study of Civilizations, Haverhill College, Mass. 1977, p. 17.

From this dimension speaking as phenomenon emerges. So, the linguistic phenomenon emerges as a capacity to make present, to reveal, to manifest without any space-time location. Silent speaking is the phenomenon of what is spoken about. It reveals irrespective of space or time what is spoken about, whether demons in stories or material objects encountered yesterday. The process is present-making in that things or events appear through the speaking. In ancient times, heroes were sung or they were not heroes. The power of word is originally unique because it is totally identified with the power of the event. The knower of the words is empowered by the very events he conjures up. In the mystery of the vital-magical the birth of configurations occurs in the vibrant speaking silence.

## SIGNIFICATION AS WORLD CONTEXT

The original power which allows the speaker to become identical with or to reveal "as if by magic" what is spoken about is the significative process with its contemporary concern for sign, symbol, and signification in speaking. The power of the story of horror brings terror to the listener, and the power of persuasion such as of political leaders moves and enchants masses to revolt by bringing forth the glories of the future.

Signification is concerned with the "how" of experiencing rather than with substantial things, and it is through the dimension of meaning implication that the dialogical nature of existence is revealed. All articulation manifests a world context. Through a commonality of being everything points to everything else and all that comes to expression in the world has meaning in its context. Inscribed in everything is being together, mit-sein,[7] being with others. Every event or thing presents the other. In books, and cars, and typewriters is the presence of other, mit-sein. The book suggests the bookstore, the publisher, the author, the paper company, the trees. The meaningful totality of references,"[8] the unity of interconnected relationships or verwandtniszusammenhang defines the contextual communicative world in which the other is always present without name and without individuality. An essential unity shows that "understanding is originally attuned and co-originally articulates the meaningful whole of the world."[9]

The implications of such a context effects changes in the discussion of communicative events. "Dyadic" communication would become triadic. Rather than two speakers encountering one another the presence of the world would be indicated. The already present communicative region points toward unspecified although specifiable horizons allowing for the continuity of communication and behavior to occur.[10] The communicative event would have a basis of commonality in the vital and significative dimensions and would therefore lack individuality. Parties would emerge as differing from the experience if the concept of self awareness, of separation arises and immediate restructuring takes place with reflexive consciousness. A communicating party becomes reflexive if, for example, he is thrown back on himself as in determining why differences of viewpoints appeared. In this instance, the dialogical nature of existence reveals itself. Only in the unique separation from others does existence of an individual self emerge. This also reveals the limitations

---

[7]Heidegger, Being and Time, p. 152.

[8]Werner Marx, Heidegger and the Tradition (Evanston: Northwestern University Press, 1971), p. 88.

[9]Marx, p. 91.

[10]Karl-Otto Apel, "The Communicative Community as Transcendental Presupposition of Social Sciences," in Dialog Als Methode, (Gottingen: Reprecht, 1972), p. 9 ff.

of the individual stance, since the other emerges as a challenge, as a different view.[11] The "observer" of the communicative event is participant, interpretor, part of world, influenced, and influences the communicative process. His reflexive involvement contributes to the restructuring or experience of the event. The interpretor's own consciousness intentionality and reflexive awareness of the event alter it by virtue of the variation of significative vectors. For example, a beautiful twilight in the wilderness filled with the scent of mountain laurel and feelings of peace can shift at the growl of a nearby bear. With the new context safety and shelter are a paramont.

This other or world reliance can be seen in the communicative world functioning as a system of signs each pointing to others inexhaustibly. The function of the experienced world in the linguistic process demonstrates this effect. The word is not causally related to meaning but can signify various objects or events within a context which the very speaking process delimits. The linguistic process can symbolize anything, since language in its fundamental sense is phenomenon of something, of an event, of times past and times to come. Recalling the transformation and identification of punctiformity in the vital dimension should be of assistance in grasping this concept. Every aspect of experience reveals world. For instance, fireworks, besides being colorful and forming patterns, point toward celebration, patriotism, freedom, war, death, danger.

Not an abstraction, the communicative event lies within an actual situation which with its immediate concern traces meaning implications constituting the spatio-temporal horizons of the situation; that is, they constitute a global event.[12] A global event is one in which behavior is preinscribed. In the case of a tennis match, a player positions himself in terms of the context of the game. That is, he may move and be prepared with a backhand stroke before the opponent's move is completed. The player is in a sense ahead of himself in time and is moving with a global rhythm of gestures which points to gestures past and those still to come. Environment transcends a given situation as a set of spatio-temporal typological articulations which can be grasped as background structuring human behavior. Socially speaking, the background indicates socially near or remote significance. This nearness or remoteness is not determined by conventional time and space concepts but is structured by the significance of experience. So events are not to be considered in terms of perceived physical space as in the number of feet from desk to door or in time measured by last week versus last year but with regard to their meaningfulness. Lunch scheduled with a friend today may seem significantly remote compared with a job interview in another state in two weeks.

Signification is always contextualized and constitutes the experienced parameters of a situation, environment, and world. The deployment or significative arrangement of interconnections, of humans and events, comprises the world of human behavior.

While world, situation, and environment are interconnected they are not identical and can be distinguished in the following way. Situation is a set of immediate concerns or orientations which are open to concerns from other situations. Any experiential processes which surpass the immediate situation approach environment. Environment is a set of spatio-temporal significations transcending the given situation.[13] Environment is frequently grasped as a background process of inter-relating. While "all situations are within the

---

[11] E. Levinas, _Totality and Infinity_ (Pittsburgh: Duquesne University Press, 1969), p. 16 ff.

[12] Jean-Paul Sartre, _Being and Nothingness_ (New York: Philosophical Library, 1956), p. 303 ff.

[13] Algis Mickunas, "Structuralism of the Environment," North Central Sociological Association, 1977, p. 5.

matrix of the social environment, the movement from a situation toward the environment is the locus where world appears."[14]  The transformation of environment through world restructures the possibilities and yields differing deployment of events and things.  For example, if one notices that it is getting late while he is walking in the forest, he shifts to an immediacy of space and time.  If he then wonders where he is and where he must return, he shifts from the situation to the world and to another environment with spatio-temporal significations.[15]  Significative interconnections "actualize aspects which cover or overlay the situation giving it depth, openness and expansion."[16] Human communication is always in situation, social environment and world.

Human behavior in its gestures reveals the context by tracing the significative deployment of events, of things, and of humans and at the same time reveals the attitudes and loci of communicative parties.  Each behavioral gesture or moment signifies and points to vectors to be traced by other behaviors, by others.  Language as phenomenon is not an object but is the phenomenon by which objects come to presence.  An objective analysis of language will fall short of what language is.

Language as phenomenon would comprise an extension of our fields of experience in terms of the Husserlian notion of phenomenon as the making present of every possible being, objectivity, event, and state of affairs.  This presenting is similar to the activity of judging or perceiving in which such activity constitutes a phenomenon which makes present something other than itself. Therefore, language, as primary phenomenon does not express thoughts, immanent states, or our ideas but rather reveals the world irrespective of space and time.  With the extension of the notion of language as phenomenon it is possible to see the connection between the phenomenological notion of language with a primordial power where one thing, event, or process can be identical with another.  Thus language in its function is the very appearance, the manifestation of the world.

---

[14]Mickunas, "Structuralism," p. 7.

LAWRENCE ROSENFIELD
PENNSYLVANIA STATE UNIVERSITY

Although none did, the authors of these five papers might almost have taken as their common point of departure, Michel Foucault's recent book, The History of Sexuality. Foucault's theme is that sexuality as such does not have ontological status apart from that afforded it by social context and rhetorical need. It is not sexuality per se that deserves our study, anymore than we can properly study crime, madness, or even mankind, but the discourse that reifies it. The universe of discourse becomes the focus for Foucault because in the very rules for textual cohesion promulgated by a given culture will be found that culture's strategies for social control. Thus, a message that purports to be "about" sexuality is simultaneously an instrument which mobilizes, directs, and modifies sexuality in the lived world.

Each author in this section touches upon Foucault's thesis in one fashion or another, testing, elaborating, qualifying it, trying at once to celebrate and to exorcise the powers each, with Foucault, detects in discourse. These are of course apprentice scholars, so their work is raw in spots, filled with murkey allusions, logical slips, gaps in knowledge of the pertinent literature. But because the authors are so uniformly bright, even their flaws prove instructive, delineating a landscape filled with hazards that give pause to the most experienced scholar.

Elaine McCoy seems most closely akin to Foucault. Putting her argument in the most radical terms, she begins to explicate the power language possesses to make phenomena present. Particularly noteworthy are her claims for the primordial or "magical" power of language to transform through the act of naming even as language remains in some sense unspoken, as well as her description of the context of language-connectedness. By this latter she means the "sticky" quality language has that makes it possible for an interrelatedness to be achieved among all significators, both among themselves and they with the entire world of experience. It is out of these dual factors, magic power and language-connectedness, so McCoy claims, that all discourse emerges, as if by miracle. My own belief is that faith in magic of any sort (and I do not believe McCoy is using the term loosely) is the rhetorical stance adopted by those who feel their lack of power to enter into the drama of the cosmos. Rhetorical theorists, who are singularly committed to upholding the possibilities for action in a public realm, are thus not the most likely candidates to harbor language theories incorporating magic. But perhaps I am being too fussy on the matter. And in any event, McCoy's work offers a splendid springboard for developing a rhetoric of human celebration for anyone wishing to extend her thought.

Misses Endress and Bruner would seem, on the surface, to be the most removed from the phenomenological camp and Foucault; but their work is also related in important respects. Primary among these is their effort to also examine the connectedness of discourse, how it is generated, deployed, sent into action. In this they echo contemporary social movement theorists who are concerned to deter-

Phenomenology in Rhetoric and Communication, ed. Stanley Deetz. Copyright, 1981. The Center for Advanced Research in Phenomenology and the University Press of America.

mine how an argument runs as a unifying theme through the sometimes chaotic fabric of social change. While neither phenomenological nor semiotic in the usual sense, their paper does provoke interesting speculation on the character of political power and of symbolic action.

Carol Blair rightly highlights the polarity that separates the critical stances proposed by myself and Professor Gregg. She argues that both positions, the appreciative and the cognitive, are incomplete in themselves. While I am obviously at odds with several of her assertions, it is true that appreciation is pre-political in nature, whereas judgment, which Blair espouses as the end of criticism, consummates the political act in its most profound sense. So in addition to suggesting further needed study on the inherent differences between two critical paradigms, Blair's discussion also points the way toward giving greater thought to the political implications latent in all criticism.

Richard Daniels provides us with a case study of hermeneutics at work; he wishes to explicate certain Christian Fundamentalist tracts phenomenologically. Daniels' undertaking is rather challenging: it is difficult for an intellectual to give a sympathetic reading to the Fundamentalist critique of higher Biblical criticism. His effort is aided by his recognition, often missing from less impartial commentators, that faith in the revelation of sacred text is not the same as credulity or superficial piety. In some respects the Fundamentalists are, in Daniels' view, the most existential of modern men; for they propose to make the manifest manifest in scripture, whereas science contents itself with a rude search for causes (a "working knowledge of reality") begind the veil of appearance. Daniels makes a reasonably convincing case that the Fundamentalist withstands higher criticism by reminding us that the Bible is meant to show us the deity rather than only telling us about him.

The final paper in this section also directs itself to the power of discourse to engage us in the world. Kristen Langellier's paper might more properly be entitled, "A Phenomenology of the Act of Reading." Langellier is trying to restore reading to its oral roots, origins from which it was first torn by Saint Augustine and later rent completely by the invention of printing. As part of her effort, she also continues the modern program of dismantling aesthetic distance as a critical category. Perhaps of most interest to rhetoricians is her treatment of discourse as "show" (em-bodiment or testimonial) and as "tell" (ostensive report), and her claim that rhetoric deals with the former. If she is right (and she makes a strong case), then Kant is correct in claiming that rhetoric has mainly to do with charm, and we need to look afresh at the rhetorical practice of Gorgias.

Hovering around all five papers is a general unease with knowing the world only as an observer. True to phenomenological tenets, these authors all wish their thinking to stem from experiences more intimate than were heretofore deemed seemly among academics. It is a sign of their maturity that they felt less need to defend their inclinations by beating the dead horse of Positivism than they did to declare their allegiance to the newer values. Nevertheless, the contrast between their mode of thought and that of the current leaders of our discipline is unmistakable. The methodology they propose to use emphasizes understanding instead of causal explanation, the search for meaning rather than the need to measure, the participation of the researcher in his subject rather than detachment. Most intriguing is their general disregard for the research ideal of formulating nomic universals (in which mental states are either ignored or defined out of existence--literally ex-communicated--as legitimate subjects of study). This conventional ideal seems to me to be deplorable folly for anyone who professes the serious study of human communication. Historians of rhetoric should applaud the commitment evidenced here to re-search the realm of free human action. That domain can only be enriched by studies such as these.

This is not to overlook the papers' limitations. From the standpoint of original contribution, the papers as a whole suffer from the very scholasticism they all decry. Their main drawback is their hesitance to extend their theoretical inquires into the region of rhetorical theory; all remain preoccupied with learning the vocabulary and the authoritative dogmas of the phenomenological cohort. But such uncertainty is the necessary precondition of all work that aims to synthesize a traditional discipline with a fresh body of literature. When the synthesis fails, the effort comes to be known as a fad and we are left with scholarship that amounts to little more than annotated bibliographies. Such aborted enthusiasms litter the back issues of our journals. I am confident that such will not be the fate with these authors or their efforts. Once they have achieved some mastery over their tools, they give every indication of fulfilling the promise of their titles and of saying fresh things about rhetoric and discourse.

My confidence springs in part from my belief that phenomenology and hermeneutics are by their nature of central interest to speech communication scholars. There are fundamental affinities between rhetoric and these topics. Is not Heideggerian "thinking and discourse," after all, but a provocative reformulation of Roman <u>sapientia et eloquentia</u>? And might the renewed interest in authentic human <u>freedom</u> not also herald the intellectual reversal in academic fashion we have so long been awaiting, in which rhetoric escapes its stereotype as a pantry of <u>ad hoc</u> rubrics for verbal composition and assumes its traditional place as the architectonic discipline? It is unwise to try to anticipate trends in academic taste; but these five papers at the very least reveal serious young authors with fertile minds who have early on in their careers chosen to treat of significant intellectual issues. Such a confluence is always promising.

JAMES AUNE
NORTHWESTERN UNIVERSITY

James M. Edie has written, "Phenomenology must define meaning as an 'open structure,' as a non-fixed, morphological _eidos_ which can be approached perspectivally from an indefinite number of possible viewpoints but which can never be 'possessed' wholly and completely under any one aspect."[1] We all have a certain sense of _meaning_; we know what it is not, but we cannot exhaust the meaning of any experience or experienced object in any one expression. My position in space and time, and my participation in a sedimented cultural heritage, will change meanings--even though some essential structures may appear through the relativities. In fact, we have a sense of meaning as _rational_ when our perspectives blend and our perceptions confirm each other.[2] The purpose of this paper is to consider the meaning of rhetorical utterance phenomenologically. I first will describe a method of phenomenological investigation and apply the method to a well-known piece of rhetoric, in order to attain an intuition of invariant rhetorical structures embedded in a specific rhetorical practice. The final section of the paper will attempt to interpret the findings of the phenomenological investigation in the context of the sedimentations of contemporary rhetorical theory.

## PHENOMENOLOGCIAL METHOD AND APPLICATION

Phenomenology is a rigorous science of experience. Don Ihde summarizes the interpretive (hermeneutic) rules of phenomenology as follows: 1) Attend to the phenomena of experience as they appear. 2) Describe, don't explain. 3) Suspend belief in all existence predicates. 4) Seek out structural or invariant features of the phenomena through the use of free, fantasy variations.[3]

Here is a rhetorical statement: "Ask not what your country can do for you; ask what you can do for your country." A phenomenological analysis of this statement following the above-mentioned hermeneutic rules would proceed through three steps: a description of the sedimentations involved in an initial encounter with the statement, a "making-strange" of the statement through free variation in the imagination,[4] and, finally, a search for invariant structures that appear through the process of free variation.

One could take two approaches toward a description of the natural attitude concerning the phrase being studied. The first would be a careful

_Phenomenology in Rhetoric and Communication_, ed. Stanley Deetz. Copyright, 1981, The Center for Advanced Research in Phenomenology and the University Press of America.

[1] James M. Edie, _Speaking and Meaning: The Phenomenology of Language_ (Bloomington, Ind.: Indiana University Press, 1976), p. 159.

[2] Maurice Merleau-Ponty, _The Prose of the World_, trans. John O'Neill (Evanston: Northwestern University Press, 1973), pp. xxviii-xxix (Translator's introduction).

[3] Don Ihde, _Experimental Phenomenology_ (New York: Putnam, 1977), pp. 32-40.

[4] Cf. Leonard C. Hawes, "Toward a Hermeneutic Phenomenology of Communication," _Communication Quarterly_ 25, 3 (Summer 1977), 39.

description of the experience of the "average" member of the audience in Washington, D.C., on January 20, 1961. As in Marie Hochmuth Nichols' reconstruction of the setting of Lincoln's First Inaugural one would note the weather, the physical structure of the podium, the characteristics of the audience[5]--much as a good reporter or fiction-writer might describe the event, with the exception that no detail would be considered irrelevant in a phenomenological investigation.[6]

My immediate purpose here is not to do a complete phenomenological investigation of the speech, so I will merely sketch what the requirements for such an analysis would be. One would note, for example, that a snowstorm had impeded travel to Washington and cut down attendance at the ceremony, and that smoldering electrical wires in the speaker's stand had interrupted the proceedings.[7] A further step would be to identify the sedimented linguistic meaning of the immediate rhetorical situation. In Alfred Schutz' terms, one might note that the average audience member was embedded in a form of life characterized by the phrase "Cold War," was worried about the possibility of not having successors, and related to most social contemporaries as ideal types portrayed in the mass media, and was inclined to view the inauguration as a kind of sacred event. Into this phenomenological field of the audience Kennedy introduced a set of propositions embodied in the speech:

1) A time of change is here, but we still are committed to defend freedom.

2) We pledge continued loyalty to our old allies.

3) We pledge support for the freedom of emerging nations--allies or not.

4) We pledge support for the struggles of nations suffering from poverty and oppression.

5) We pledge continued support for the United Nations.

6) We ask our enemies to renew the search for peace.

7) We should focus on common problems and possibilities, such as arms control, space exploration, health, the arts, etc.

8) It is important that Americans the rest of the world's citizens accept the responsibilities outlined here, rather that be selfish.

Schutz seems to view speech generally as __monothetic__ (capable of being comprehended as a meaning without living through an original experience of the utterance), but it should be clear from the above reduction that speech must be lived-through __poly__-thetically (as a piece of music must be heard in its entirety) for its meaning to be fully disclosed. Aspects of the speech that are polythetic include delivery, diction, sentence structure, figures of speech, etc.--all the traditional elements of "rhetoric," in addition to the general sense of "growing old together" in a historical situation, to which the rhetoric is a response.[8]

[5]Marie Hochmuth Nichols, "Lincoln's First Inaugural," in Robert L. Scott and Bernard L. Brock, eds., __Methods of Rhetorical Criticism__ (New York: Harper and Row, 1972), pp. 60-100.

[6]Selection, of course, always occurs in a phenomenological description, but as Edie suggests, one can return again and again to the same phenomenon and never exhaust its meaning.

[7]My examples here are drawn from Glenn R. Capp, ed., __Famous Speeches in American History__ (Indianapolis: Bobbs-Merrill, 1963), pp. 231-240.

[8]Cf. Alfred Schutz, "The Dimensions of the Social World," in __Collected Papers II: Studies in Social Theory__ (The Hague: Marinus Nijhoff, 1976), pp. 20-63. For the monothetic/polythetic distinction see Schutz, "Making Music Together," __Collected Papers II__, p. 172.

I have avoided the discussion of Kennedy's purpose in delivering this piece of rhetoric. I would suggest that the speech itself is the noematic correlate of a noetic act of various audiences; as such, one might say that it is partially constituted by its audiences. In any event, my concern here is primarily with meaning for audiences; a worthwhile subject for further investigation would be a phenomenology of speaking-in-public from the speaker's perspective.

There is a second form of description of the sedimented meaning of the speech. Even in attempting a rigorous phenomenological description, the critic (perhaps not the right choice of words here) has a "first reading" peculiar to his own situation in history. A description of one's own prima facie "feelings" about a work may be a useful device for finding more universal meanings and for correcting distortions.

Consider this: in my mind I have an ideal type of a historical object --John F. Kennedy's Inaugural Address--embodied verbally in this phrase which I am able usually freely to recall: "Ask not what your country can do for you; ask what you can do for your country." I can recall no more--except for the brief phrase "A Torch Is Passed" which I see printed in gold on a reddish-brown memorial book about Kennedy which my father bought after the assassination. --Next thought: I do not remember even hearing the speech itself. I was seven years old, and had been warned about the danger of having Roman Catholics in the White House. Associations: courage, idealism, martyred President, youth, ambition, responsibility, patriotism.

From the above two descriptions of sedimented experience two intuitions of invariant structure appear. First, when one attempts to describe sedimentations one seems to choose the sedimentations of socially similar others for description (the experience of audiences in the Soviet Union, for example, almost appears as a free, imaginary variation barely accessible to an untrained conciousness). Second, and most importantly, there appear to be at least two distinct forms of verbal expression: one is the immediate interaction between a speech and its audience, in which a speech plays upon the sedimentations of its audience; the other is the creativity of speechmaking which outlasts its initial performance and becomes a part of the sedimentations of future audiences. Apparently, however--if my memory of the speech provides a clue--the totality of the rhetorical performance is not sedimented, but rather only portions of the performance are thematized in the course of history.

Ihde shows how one may perform "deconstructions" upon various types of perceptual objects to attain a new understanding of those objects beyond the natural attitude. The description of sedimented beliefs concerning Kennedy's phrase dealt with the realm of the natural attitude; an application of the phenomenological attitude to the phrase would require a kind of algorithmic scheme to generate possible audiences and the meanings they could have for the meanings they could have for the phrase. Two caveats would need to be given to such a project: 1) Any phenomenon possesses an internal horizon which limits the possible number of interpretations which may be given (as Ihde says, one cannot see the Necker Cube as a swan flying[9]), 2) Ihde's phenomenology of material objects indicates the presence of a "latent stratum of praxical activity" in each viewing which implies the existence of a uniqueness of each viewing in a particular moment in time and space by a particular body.[10] These two warnings are partially contradictory: the first implies that a basic meaning-structure inheres in the object itself; the second implies that

[9]Ihde, p. 117.
[10]Ihde, p. 127.

there are as many meanings as there are beholders. They are contradictory, but faithfulness to experience requires both positions. We all have had the experience of hearing, "Yeah, I know what you said, but what did you mean?" Or, to approach the problem from another perspective, at times we thematize socially sedimented meaning ("JFK was shot on November 22, 1963, in Dallas, Texas"), at others we thematize idosyncratic responses to a social event("When he was shot I first heard about it in the cloak-room of my fifth-grade class from Pat Travnicek").

Ihde suggests that two forms of deconstruction are possible: one uses stories (hermeneutic) and the other focuses upon transcendent meanings. In the case of deconstructing a linguistic object, I would modify these two deconstructive strategies as follows:  1) For a hermeneutic strategy, think of as many specific audience responses to the object as possible, and describe them as a journalist or novelist would.  2) For a transcendental strategy, consider the potential meanings of the object within the structure of language itself, apart from any lived-historical or potentially lived-historical understanding of the object.

First, here are five imaginary--but not entirely implausible--variations or "stories" concerning Kennedy's audience:

1) A century from now, gangs of youths roam the ruins of Chicago looking for people to rob or maim or rape. In an old school room they find a poster reading, "Ask not what your country can do for you, ask what you can do for your country--JFK." They crumple it into a ball and leave.

2) A Neo-Nazi quotes Kennedy in a speech condemning racial minorities and welfare chiselers, i.e., those who want government to do more for them.

3) A young man, soon to graduate from high school, hears Kennedy's inaugural, decides not to go to college but rather to enlist in the army. He is later killed in Vietnam in 1965. A priest finds a photograph of Kennedy with the phrase "Ask not . . ." printed on it in the young man's missal after he is killed.

4) A graduate student in rhetoric, struggling to meet a paper deadline, searches through a handbook of rhetorical figures in order to find the name of the figure used by Kennedy in his phrase "Ask not. . . ."

5) One of Shakespeare's favorite puns is, "You think I speak of country matters?" playing upon the sameness of sound between the first syllable of "Country" and the Anglo-Saxon term for the vagina. Kennedy, whose extra-marital exploits are now well-known, thus may have addressed (with a wink, perhaps, unrecorded by the camera) a lady-love in the audience: "ask not what your country can do for you" (you're merely using your sexuality to advance your career); "ask what you can do for your country" (instead you should give in to your feelings, let them guide you rather than your ambition--I'll see you after the Inauguration).

The above are just a few deconstructions; clearly there are many more possibilities. They seem arbitrary, but as Ihde writes, "If there is a depth structure of invariance, this is what must be sought through relativities."[11]

---

[11]Ihde, p. 133. If one needs a scholarly precedent for the sexist variation #5, one might consider Kenneth Burke's method of "joycing."

There are fewer possible variations in a transcendental strategy, particularly in this case, since the words themselves have more or less univocal meanings. I can think of four possible meanings of the phrase: 1) No meaning--the hearer is not attentive, is incapacitated, or is not a speaker of the language. 2) The statement is an exhortation against social welfare programs. 3) The statement urges increased social action on behalf of the underprivileged. 4) The statement urges citizens to be ready to bear arms.

Are there any features of the phenomenon which remain constant through the variations I have described? First, there is revealed a possible alternative to Schutz' distinction between monothetic and polythetic phenomena. None of these audiences experienced Kennedy's statement polythetically (except perhaps the young man of #3): all experienced it monothetically as a proposition, but the meaning of the phrase was different for each person. The point here is not to repeat the trivial insight that meanings are in people but to suggest that it is possible to replicate--through phenomenological description--the insights of Austin, Searle, and Frentz and Farrell in distinguishing between the locutionary, illocutionary, perlocutionary, and episodic force of utterances.[12] A project suggested by this brief analysis is the phenomenological description of episodic force. The notion of the "lived-body" and the perspectival nature of perception imply a possible foundation for a theory of episodic force.

Second, the phrase implied a sense of "use" in the field of its perceivers: the phrase could be used to support an ideology, provide meaning for a life, be utterly useless, or be an object of study. The ability of persons to thematize a phrase from a work both increases the work's usefulness and its variety of possible meanings. Such rhetorical/poetical force (perhaps the best term is Longinus' hypsos, "sublime") becomes a phenomenon contradictory to the rhetorical motive: eloquence tends to lead away from the speaker's ability to control the meanings of his words.

Third, there is a horizon of the speaker and of the listener in every rhetorical transaction. Language and cultural similarity are the sedimentations which make meaning possible. An intuitable sense of "distortion" occurs in stories 1, 2, and especially, 5, where aspects of a private horizon are thematized or where cultural sedimentations are not present.

Fourth, in each "meaning" there is present--in addition to the locutionary force of "Ask not . . ."--a kind of formal force: the inherent appeal of the phrase as a figure. In each case, apart from the inherent appeal of the phrase, there is a "felicity" of structure which may be thematized: a musical, polythetic felicity. All utterances, then, might be characterized as occurring in a nexus of opposing forces: polythetic rhetorical form, sedimented monothetic locutionary force, and the horizon of the perceiver. In story #1, for example, the horizon of the gang as a kind of private perceptual structure was sufficient to cancel the effects of form and propositional meaning.

Fifth, I may be unconsciously leading my intuition of invariant structures in a preconceived direction, but there seems to be little insight added by adopting the more transcendental strategy. I would argue that our mental activity involves first constructing a story as a possible experience and second summarizing that possibility in propositional form. James Edie notes that Aristotle, among others, thought "that metaphors are, in fact, nothing other than elliptical similes, that is, comparisons which can be fully clarified if only we can discover their tertium quid, that resemblance which

---

[12]Cf. Thomas S. Frentz and Thomas B. Farrell, "Language-Action: A Paradigm for Communication," Quarterly Journal of Speech 62, 4 (December 1976), 333-349.

makes them look 'like' or appear 'as' one another." Such a position is highly rationalistic, and consistent with the search for a completely clarified and philosophical discourse,

> But the question to know is whether the perception of two events, qualities, functions, or aspects of things and their verbalization in metaphor presupposes the prior existence of a "concept" which we can then thematize, or whether, on the contrary, this experience it-self generates something which we can in later reflection call a "concept," or at least try to explain conceptually, but which is always logically prior to and which always overflows any "concept." Insofar as the metaphorical verbalization of experience itself creates resemblances which could not be seen up to that time and, in that sense, were not there before, it would seem that there are "necessary" metaphors.[13]

I am taking Edie one step further and arguing that every meaning which we have for an object is created by constructing a narrative line around that object. The narrative usually is the rather boring one which is given to us by elite types or by social contemporaries, although we occasionally are more creative. None of my "stories" above are "necessary" stories in Edie's sense, but I wonder if, for example, Kennedy's phrase is not the focal point of an ideological story such as Schlesinger's A Thousand Days or any of the other court histories of the Kennedy Administration.

More variations are possible and more essences may be intuitable from the rhetorical object "Ask not. . . ." There is a sense in which using the phenomenological method commits one to tentativeness. Most important, how-ever, is that it is a tentativeness grounded in the We-relationship con-stituted by willing participants in a dialectic committed to the use of a sharing method.

## INTERPRETATION

The usual method in contemporary social science is deductive-nomethetic --the construction of theories and the testing of them against measurable --usually sedimented--reality. Phenomenology appears to commit one to an alternative position: as Husserl said, zu den Sachen selbst, "to the things themselves." What does our experience of a speech--in this case a fragment of Kennedy's Inaugural--tell us about rhetoric? How do we come to have a sense that something is rhetoric?

Following Schutz one could argue that there are at least three back-ground expectancies which social actors have for social interaction: 1) Should they change places their unique perspectives on the scene before them would be reciprocated, i.e., my "here" would become yours and vice versa. 2) Per-spectival differences originating in the participants' unique biographies are irrelevant for the purpose at hand. 3) There is a possibility of a check on utterances through turn-taking.[14] It would appear that rhetoric violates all three background expectancies, allowing a sense of a different genre of communication to emerge out of the lifeworld. 1) Rather than accepting the reciprocity of "here's" the rhetor insists that his "here" is superior to his audience's "here" by being more real or more true to a common heritage--or at least in calling attention to aspects of the "here" which the audience may be inclined to take for granted. 2) The rhetor has been granted a time and place

---

[13]Edie, pp. 192-193.

[14]Cf. Alexander McHoul, "Ethnomethodology and Literature: Preliminaries to a Sociology of Reading," Poetics 7 (1978), 113-120.

to speak which are his "own." His "unique biography"--whether as an elite type or by his own assertion--allows him to accent his perspectival differences from, or his greater insight into the perspectival similarities with, his audience.[15]
3) Checking out the rhetor's utterances is made problematic by the structure of the situation--hence one of Socrates' objections to rhetoric.

A sense of rhetoric thus seems to emerge in individual consciousness as something other than the usual state of affairs, which may lead to the usual tendency to view rhetoric as nonsense or as endowed with a divine quality. A sense of divinity or legitimacy is given to the speaker by the group story which he creates or upholds. The speaker is, however, held responsible for his interpretation of the outcome of the narrative.

History and child development should be investigated to see if rhetoric emerges in actual experience as I have described it here as an ideal type. The Greeks, for example, initially viewed rhetoric as a divine gift (or, perhaps, as a "knack"), much as a child seems to be astonished when he first "gets" someone to do what the child desires without having to cry or apply physical force.

Viewed in the sense I have described, the contemporary battle between those who argue that not all situations are rhetorical and those who view literally everything as rhetorical needs to be reframed.[16] First, rhetoric emerges out of the life-world and is different from face-to-face communication in terms of the generic expectancies its auditors possess. It is clear that people usually agree to call a situation "rhetorical" only in certain cases. Second, all communicative experience derives from a life-context which is essentially polythetic. Monothetic propositions--whether philosophical or scientific--are abstractions from immediate experience. One might say that the aesthetic is the primary mode of communicative experience--a position which allows for the emphasis upon creativity by the rhetoric-as-epistemic group, while allowing for the reality of sedimentation and, perhaps, false consciousness.

The question of whether philosophy, criticism, and science are rhetorical seems answerable in terms of the background expectancies of the hearers of philosophical, scientific, or critical disourse. When do we agree to call something philosophy? Such a question need not be confined to a contemporary, mundane attitude. Analytic philosophers probably do not consider Plato's dialogues philosophy at all; one wonders what Plato would think of A.J. Ayer. First, there is a taken-for-granted conception of what is real--that which is reducible to logical propositions (universals being more knowable than particulars, for most philosophers), the constraints of critical ideology (critics are usually Marxist, Christians, Jungians, Formalists, or whatever), or that which is quantifiable. Second, in contrast to rhetoric--but perhaps in harmony with good rhetoric--there is a commitment to a structure in which utterances may be compared and corrected through the sharing of perspectives: democracy, the community of scholars, history. Eloquence, then, would appear in virtually every type of communication in which the utterance becomes tied to the force of a unique, personal perspective which creates a new or inten-

[15] I would note, however, that certain types of rhetoric uttered in democratic politcal contexts need not require that the rhetor be innately superior to his audience. In the ancient polis, for example, public discourse was always communication among equals. Only with the resurgence of hierarchically structured political systems did the rhetorician emerge as a kind of "special" communicator. (I am indebted to Lawrence W. Rosenfield for this observation.)

[16] Cf. Walter M. Carleton, "What Is Rhetorical Knowledge? A Response to Farrell--And More," and Thomas B. Farrell, "Social Knowledge II," Quarterly Journal of Speech 64, 3 (October 1978), 313 334, for the latest installment in the "debate."

sifies an old story, but which eventually allows itself to be taken as part of communication of others, and becomes inexhaustible as a meaning. One might then say, with Longinues, that our concern as rhetoricians should not be with rules or genres of discourse, but with constructing a phenomenology of sublime speech of all kinds, in order to understand how the goodness of Being shows itself in language.

CHARLES LAUFERWEILER
UNIVERSITY OF ILLINOIS


In a recent paper comparing various "rules based approaches" to
communication, Donohue, Cushman, and Nofsinger express concern that a
variety of approaches to communication study "characterized by some fundamental conceptual differences . . . will be lumped together and confused,
thereby obscuring the uniqueness and undermining the conceptual and methodological strength of the research."[1] Yet these same authors present the
work of communication scholars involved in conversation analysis--which
they variously refer to as "the interpretive perspective," "the Hawes-
Nofsinger perspective," and "the homogenous rules perspective"--as a unified approach to communication study embracing common assumptions, shared
research goals, and philosophical grounding in the phenomenology of Alfred
Schutz. Their discussion equates the basic conceptual assumptions underlying conversation analysis with those of the ethnomethodologists in
interpretive sociology, whom they similarly present as sharing philosophical
grounding in Schutz's phenomenology.

I want to suggest that this depiction itself lumps together and con-
fuses research which, while sharing the techniques of conversation analysis
as an empirical method, can be seen to embody divergent assumptions concerning the nature of language and meaning. Specifically, not all conversation
analysis is phenomenological in orientation, and not all of that conversation analysis which can be called phenomenological is grounded in the phenomenology of Alfred Schutz.[2]

My discussion will proceed in three stages. First, I will briefly
summarize a system of classification for theoretical approaches to language
and meaning developed by Grossberg.[3] Second, three of the positions in
Grossberg's scheme will be elaborated and exemplified by distinguishing
three "schools" within the ethnomethodology program in sociology--conver-
sation analysis proper, cognitive sociology, and ethnomethodology proper.
Third, these three positions and the corresponding schools of ethnomethodology will be used to distinguish the research programs of Nofsinger,[4]

Phenomenology in Rhetoric and Communication, ed. Stanley Deetz. Copyright, 1981. The Center
for Advanced Research in Phenomenology and the University Press of America.

[1] William Donohue, Donald Cushman, and Robert E. Nofsinger Jr., "Creating and Confronting Social
Order: A Comparison of Rules Perspectives," paper presented at the 64th Annual Meeting of the Speech
Communication Association, Minneapolis, 2-5 Nov. 1978, p. 1.

[2] See Alfred Schutz, The Phenomenology of the Social World, trans. George Walsh and Frederick
Lehnert (Evanston: Northwestern University Press, 1967); Alfred Schutz, Collected Papers I: The
Problem of Social Reality, ed. Maurice Natanson (The Hague: Martinus Nijhoff, 1973).

[3] Lawrence Grossberg, "Language and Theorizing," in Studies in Symbolic Interaction, Vol. 2.,
ed. Norman K. Denzin (Greenwich, Conn.: J. A. I. Press, in press).

[4] Robert E. Nofsinger Jr., "The Demand Ticket: A Conversational Device for Getting the Floor,"
Speech Monographs, 42 (1975), 1-9; Robert E. Nofsinger Jr., "On Answering Questions Indirectly:
Some Rules in the Grammar of Doing Conversation," Human Communication Research, 2 (1976), 172-181.

Jacobs,[5] and Hawes[6] which, while sharing conversation analytic techniques, embody differing assumptions concerning the nature of language and meaning.

## VIEWS OF LANGUAGE AND MEANING

Grossberg has generated a useful classification of the various positions which attempt to move beyond referential views of language and meaning--those which embrace the traditional Cartesian separation of subject and object, knowing mind and external reality. Within such referential views,

> language is considered as an instrument people use--a tool of signifi-
> cation, a functional system for articulation, expression, and repre-
> sentation; and the meaningfulness of language lies in its reference
> to some collection of entities (either subjective mental entities,
> or objective external entities).[7]

Philosophers and social theorists, dissatisfied with referential views as accounts for human experience, have increasingly turned to views in which the meaningfulness of language is constituted, not in reference to subjective or objective entities, but in the properties of language systems or processes. Grossberg maintains that the move to viewing language as either a system or a process involves a conception of language as either a system or a process involves a conception of language as "a relationship between a signifier and a signified, between a material vehicle and its meaning."[8] Within both systems and process views it is possible to privilege either the subjective (meaning as the primacy of the signified) or the objective (material signifier as constitutive of meaning) moment of this relationship.

Systemic views see language as a system of interrelated and interact-ing constituents of which meaning is an epiphenomenal product. Grossberg suggests that "it is the structure of the system--the interactions among its elements--which produces the quality of experience . . . we call meaning."[9] Objective systemic positions view language as a system of con-ventional, "objective", elements (signs) standing in particular relation-ships to one another. Subjective systemic positions, on the other hand, view language as a system of acts of speaking--"acts of a subject within a particular context with other subjects. Meaning arises from and resides in the system of language use. . . ."[10]

Processual views see language as a process of signification which constitutes the subject-object dichotomy as the fundamental structure of human experience in everyday life. "It is out of this process in which neither the subject nor the object are yet differentiated that both are defined and constituted."[11] The objective and subjective positions within process views attempt to radically problematize, respectively, the sub-

[5]Scott Jacobs, "The Practical Management of Conversational Meanings: Notes on the Dynamics of Social Understanding and Interactional Emergence," paper presented at the 63rd Annual Meeting of the Speech Communication Association, Washington, D.C., 1-4 Dec. 1977; Sally Jackson and Scott Jacobs, "Adjacency Pairs and the Sequential Description of Arguments," paper presented at the 64th Annual Meeting of the Speech Communication Association, Minneapolis, 2-5 Nov. 1978.

[6]Leonard C. Hawes, "Conversation and Content," paper presented at the 64th Annual Meeting of the Speech Communication Association, Minneapolis, 2-5 Nov. 1978; Leonard C. Hawes, "A Phenomenology of Conversation," paper presented at the Annual Convention of Society of Phenomenology and Existen-tial Philosophy, Pittsburgh, Nov. 1978.

[7]Grossberg, in press.

[8]Grossberg, in press.

[9]Grossberg, in press.

[10]Grossberg, in press.

[11]Grossberg, in press.

jective and objective moments of the traditional Cartesian separation. As Grossberg suggests,

> Objective processual views make the relationship of the subject to language problematic, thus calling into doubt the very possibility of a transcendental subject. Subjective processual views, on the other hand, attempt to problematize the world in its relation to the subject. Such views, therefore, can be read as explorations of the nature of the transcendental subject. . . .[12]

The application of this classification scheme in an anlysis of social theorizing can reveal sometimes surprising differences in the views of language and meaning held by proponents of seemingly unified positions. As a case in point, three schools of the ethnomethodological program in sociolgy--conversation analysis proper, cognitive sociology, and ethnomethodology proper--can be distinguished as embracing objective systemic, subjective systemic, and subjective processual views of language and meaning respectively.

## CONVERSATION ANALYSIS PROPER

Objective systemic positions are essentially structuralist positions: i.e., they can be read as grounded in Saussure's distinction between langue and parole. Grossberg suggests that

> Objective systemic views see meaning as the epiphenominal consequence of the interactions of the elements constituting language as langue. This system has no real existence apart from the individual acts of speaking (parole) in which it is actualized. Nevertheless, it is this objectively describable structure which gives significance to and makes possible the successful use of language in speaking.[13]

The structuralist views language as an atemporal code, a system of objective signs which is the necessary condition for instances of its actual use. Interest in actual instances of language use by individuals is limited to their illuminative value as manifestations of the workings of this code or system. Stated in another way, objective systemic positions bracket the subject (reject any phenomenological moment) in the interest of generating a structural description of the organization of objective elements in the language system.

The work of sociologists Sack, Schegloff, and Jefferson[14] referred to here as "conversation analysis proper," can best be understood as an objective systemic approach to social interaction. Their focus is on the structural aspects of the sequential organization of utterances in conversation--"the 'systematic form' or 'structure' conversational phenomea exhibit as 'technical objects'."[15] The analyses of these researchers proceed from a foundation of detailed inspection of naturally occurring conversational interaction. Their interest in conversational interaction, however, is not

---

[12]Grossberg, in press.

[13]Grossberg, in press.

[14]Harvey Sacks, Emmanuel Schegloff, and Gail Jefferson, "A Simplest Systematics for the Organization of Turn Taking for Conversation," Language 50 (1974), 696-735; Emmanuel Schegloff, Gail Jefferson, and Harvey Sacks, "The Preference for Self-Correction in the Organization of Repair in Conversation," Language, 53 (1977), 361-382.

[15]Jim Schenkein, "Sketch of an Analytic Mentality for the Study of Conversational Interaction," in Studies in the Organization of Conversational Interaction, ed. Jim Schenkein (New York: Academic Press, 1978), p. 5.

as a sequence of instances of language use or acts of speaking by conversational participants (parole), but as illustrations of the workings of the structural properties of the conversational system itself (langue).  The question of interest becomes "what might be extracted as ordered phenomena from our conversational materials which would not turn out to require reference to one or another aspect of situatedness, identities, peculiarities of content or context."[16]  They argue that in a close examination of an extensive corpus of conversational data (transcripts and tape recordings) a variety of structural preferences in sequential organization is revealed. "Preference" is used as a technical term referring, not to the motivations of conversational participants but rather, to an empirical skewing or predomination of certain sequence- and turn-organizational features of conversation.

Sacks, Schegloff, and Jefferson set themselves the task of exploring "the organizational mechanisms operating within any sequential environment-- which by their case-by-case operation, produce the observed over all skewed distribution."[17]  Further, the authors suggest that "the gross facts which characterize large amounts of conversational data are the product of rules[18] and systems of rules which operate on particular sequential environments."

In the most elaborate example of their project to date, Sacks, Schegloff, and Jefferson detail a structuralist model of conversation as accomplished in and through the organization of turns at talk.  As they suggest, "turn-taking seems to be a basic form of organization for conversation--'basic' in that whatever parties brought to bear in conversation would be accomodated without change in the system."[19]

The turn-taking model is designed to account for a number of empirical festures derived from the analysis of naturally occurring conversational interaction.  Specifically, the authors suggest that in attending to the sequential organization of conversation, the following features can readily be observed--"overwhelmingly, one party talks at a time, though speakers change, and though the size of turns vary; that transitions are finely coordinated; that techniques are used for allocating turns. . . ."[20]  A "simplest systematics" for the organization of turn-taking is presented which is comprised of a system of hierarchically organized and recursively applied rules for turn-construction and turn-allocation and which establishes an economy of structural preferences in sequential organization.  The rules of an objective structural system operate in local conversational contexts and account for the readily observed features of conversational turn-taking.


## COGNITIVE SOCIOLOGY

Subjective systemic positions are essentially interactionist positions. While objective systemic views locate meaning in the relationships among the objective elements of langue, subjective systemic views see meaning as emergently constituted in the acts of speaking subjects (parole). Grossberg suggests that:

within a subjective systemic conception, language is a system of conventions defining and dictating standardized usage.  It has constraining power over individuals.  But the conventionality of

---

[16]Sacks et al., p. 699.
[17]Schegloff et al., p. 362.
[18]Schegloff et al., 362.

[19]Sacks et al., p. 700.
[20]Sacks et al., p. 699.

language is constantly emerging and reemerging in the ongoing process of social interaction and language use. It is not a static
system of overlapping meaning or rules. Only by our continuing
to use language in conventional ways does it function as a system
of conventions. . . . there is no meaning outside of actual use in
interaction.[21]

In locating meaning within the contextual use of an intersubjectively
negotiated conventional system, subjective systemic positions presuppose
intersubjectivity itself, some universal human nature, as ontologically
given. A view of social interaction as negotiation presumes that competent social actors have at their disposal, prior to any particular
interactional setting, a particular set of negotiating processes. Subjective systemic positions see meaning as the structure of relationship
between a conventionally standardized symbolic system and a subject
whose nature is at least partially universal and essentially characteri-
zable. This relationship emerges within the context of particular acts of
language use.

Subjective systemic views are phenomenological in the sense that
they assert "the primacy of consciousness and subjective meaning in the
interpretation of social action."[22] Phenomenological sociologies, such
as those grounded in the social philosophy of Alfred Schutz, are subjective systemic positions. As Heap and Roth suggest "in the phenomenology
of Schutz, intersubjectivity is viewed as an ontologically given feature
of the social world, and analysis is directed toward the constitutive
attitudes and beliefs that make such a viewpoint possible for members of
the social world."[23]

The "cognitive sociology" of Cicourel[24] is such a phenomenological
sociology, and is best understood as a subjective systemic approach to
social interaction. Attewell claims that

the problem for Cicourel . . . is that of social order. This order is
for him, predicated upon members abilities to perceive situations in
such a way that they make meaning of them and act in accordance with
such meanings. . . . What is the essence for Cicourel is the manner
in which members perceive situations in order to then be able to
relate them to normative (appropriate) action.[25]

Cicourel's concerns are best described in contrast to the normative
theory of action employed in most traditional sociological theorizing.
As Mehan and Wood summarize, within such a theory

it is assumed that <u>actors</u> know and follow <u>rules</u> in <u>social situations</u>.
Rules are assumed to exist independently of actors and situations.
They are "external and objective" constraints. . . . These rules

---

[21]Grossberg, in press.

[22]Maurice Natanson, <u>Literature, Philosophy, and the Social Sciences</u>, (The Hague: Martinus
Nijhoff, 1962), p. 157.

[23]James L. Heap and Phillip A. Roth, "On Phenomenological Sociology," <u>American Sociological
Review</u>, 38 (1973), 364.

[24]Aaron V. Cicourel, "Basic and Normative Rules in the Negotiation of Status and Role," in
<u>Studies in Social Interaction</u>, ed. David Sudnow (New York: Free Press, 1972), pp. 229-258; Aaron V.
Cicourel, <u>Cognitive Sociology: Language and Meaning in Social Interaction</u> (New York: Free Press,
1974).

[25]Paul Attewell, "Ethnomethodology Since Garfinkel," <u>Theory and Society</u>, 1 (1974), 196.

take the form of motives, norms, folkways, expectations, et cetera, and are represented as the <u>causes</u> of sociologically relevant actions.[26]

This normative theory leads to a view of social actors as mindless respondents to the demands of rules independently operating in nonproblematic social situations.

Opposed to the normative theory of action is the view that the normative order--actions in accordance with rule--is dependent on the ongoing interpretive activities of persons in the context of particular social situations--"general rules or policies are norms whose meaning in emergent (constructed) action scenes must be negotiated by the actor."[27] Cicourel maintains that an appropriate model of the social actor

> must (1) specify how general rules or norms are invoked to justify or evaluate a course of action, and (2) how innovative constructions in context-bound scenes alter general rules or norms and thus provide the basis of change. Hence the learning and use of general rules or norms . . . always requires more basic interpretive rules for recognizing the relevance of actual, changing scenes, orienting the actor to possible courses of action, the organization of behavioral displays and their reflective evaluation by the actor.[28]

Cicourel is interested in the basic <u>cognitive</u> processes which social actors employ to generate and interpret conventionally normative behaviors in changing social scenes--"how members employ interpretive procedures to recognize the relevance of surface rules and convert them into practiced and enforced behavior."[29] He asserts that an adequate theory of social interaction "would incorporate members use of interpretive procedures to assign a negotiated sense of meaning that becomes a concretized appearance . . . during a specific exchange."[30] The interpretive procedures employed by social actors "provide a sense of social order that is fundamental for normative order (concensus or shared agreement) to be negotiated and constructed."[31] Social actors' interpretive procedures are "invariant properties of practical reasoning necessary for assigning sense to substantive rules."[32] For Cicourel then, social reality is seen as sustained in and through social actors' practical reasoning which incorporates a collection of invariantly shared interpretive procedures concerning how and where to look for meaning in social interaction.

## ETHNOMETHODOLOGY PROPER

The move from subjective systemic to subjective processual views is a move from interactionism and phenomenological sociology, which assume the existence of a transcendental subject as the locus of meaning constituting processes, to a trancendental phenomenology which attempts to explore the nature of this transcendental subject. In subjective processual views the meaningfulness of experience is found in the process of intentionality which is the fundamental structure of transcendental consciousness.

As in subjective systemic views, subjective processual positions see language as a system of use, but conceive of this system as an idealized

[26]Hugh Mehan and Huston Wood, <u>The Reality of Ethnomethodology</u> (New York: Wiley-Interscience, 1975), p. 74.

[27]Cicourel, "Basic and Normative Rules," p. 247.

[28]Cicourel, "Basic and Normative Rules," p. 249.

[29]Cicourel, <u>Cognitive Sociology</u>, p. 53.

[30]Cicourel, <u>Cognitive Sociology</u>, p. 93.

[31]Cicourel, "Basic and Normative Rules," p. 249.

[32]Cicourel, <u>Cognitive Sociology</u>, p. 51.

intended object of the intending acts of transcendental cons'ciousness in which the meaningfulness of experience is constituted. Summarizing Husserl's phenomenology as an instance of subjective processual views, Grossberg suggests that

> although meaningful experience exists only in the process of intention-
> ality, Husserlian reflection allows one to talk about the act of
> intending and the intended object, as if these two moments of the
> process were separable. Subjective processual views emphasize the
> primacy of the subject insofar as meanings only exist for conscious-
> ness. However, meanings are not created by the subject nor are they
> reducible to acts of the mind, mental experiences or personal dis-
> positions. . . . The "intended" objects of this transcendental
> consciousness have an ideal existence. They are not the private
> possessions of particular, individualized consciousnesses.[33]

These distinctions between subjective systemic and subjective processual positions distinguish the work of Garfinkel[34] here referred to as
"ethnomethodology proper", as a subjective processual approach to social
interaction. Subjective systemic social theory, e.g., Cicourel's cognitive
sociology, assumes intersubjectivity in accounting for the production of
shared meaning. In contrast, as Heap and Roth suggest,

> intersubjectivity enters the ethnomethodological domain as the sense
> of intersubjectively contingently accomplished by members situated
> practices. The transformation here involves a shift from the realm
> of the a priori to that of the contingently actual--the a priori be-
> comes a problematic feature of actual accomplishment.[35]

Garfinkel's concern is with those "member practices" by which a sense of
social order is ongoingly accomplished. He argues that

> in exactly the ways that a setting is organized it consists of mem-
> bers' methods for making evident that settings ways as clear, coherent,
> planful, consistent, chosen, knowable, uniform, reproducible connec-
> tions--i.e., rational connections.[36]

The status of ethnomethodology proper as a subjective processual
approach rests upon Garfinkel's peculiar use of the term "member" to refer,
not to persons but rather, to "mastery of natural language."[37] "Natural
language," as Zimmerman warns, "should not be construed in a narrow sense,
e.g., as the syntax and semantics of, say, a specific language; rather the
notion refers to a system of practices. . . ."[38] "Members" are seen, not
as individual biographically constituted psychological subjects but rather,
as agents of the system of natural language practices. As Zimmerman
elaborates,

> ethnomethodology posits a reflexive, or perhaps, a dialectical rela-
> tionship. A widespread, abstract, and general form of social organi-

[33]Grossberg, in press.

[34]Harold Garfinkel, Studies in Ethnomethodology (Englewood Cliffs, N.J.: Prentice-Hall, 1967);
Harold Garfinkel, "Studies in the Routine Grounds of Everyday Activities," in Studies in Social
Interaction, ed. David Sudnow (New York: Free Press, 1967).

[35]Heap and Roth, p. 364.

[36]Garfinkel, Studies in Ethnomethodology, p. 34.

[37]Harold Garfinkel and Harvey Sacks, "On Formal Structures of Practical Actions," in Theoretical
Sociology: Perspectives and Developments, ed., J. C. McKinney and E. A. Tiryakian (New York: Appleton-Century-Crofts, 1970), p. 342.

[38]Don H. Zimmerman, "Ethnomethodology," The American Sociologist, 13 (1978), 9.

zation--the constituent practices of "natural language"--is available as a resource for the accomplishment of society and biography in local contexts; individuals ("members") as agents of this massive socially organized system, do employ these resources; and the activities summarized here are public, observable, controllable events which require no empirically uncontrolled reference to "mind" nor any special modes of access to the private or subjective.[39]

While practices of natural language are not the possession or acts of the psychological subject, they are also not the structures of some objectively describable static system. The system of natural language practices is a system of language activities and usings through the agency of "members". As such, the system of natural language practices can be read as the intended object of intending acts of transcendental consciousness apart from which they have no meaningful existence.

In the last section of this paper I want to apply this discussion of the distinctions between objective systemic, subjective systemic, and subjective processual views to assess Donohue, Cushman, and Nofsinger's presentation of conversation analysis as a unified body of work in communication study.

## CONVERSATION ANALYSIS IN SPEECH COMMUNICATION

Donohue, Cushman, and Nofsinger depict the work in conversation analysis within speech communication as a unified approach to social interaction embracing common assumptions, shared research goals, and philosophical grounding in the phenomenology of Alfred Schutz. However, an examination of the research goals of communication scholars employing the techniques of conversation analysis in investigations of naturally occurring conversational interaction, suggests a divergence in their views on the nature of language and meaning. Specifically, the work of Nofsinger, Jacobs, and Hawes can be read as objective systemic, subjective systemic, and subjective processual approaches to social interaction respectively.

As Nofsinger describes it, the goal of his work is "to contribute to our understanding of the structure of conversation--to contribute to a grammar of doing conversation."[40] Such a grammar if fully articulated would consist of "a complete set of symbols, rules, and metarules--would constitute an explanation of conversation, of the possibility of utterances making sense."[41] Nofsinger hopes to make this contribution through an examination of "the fundamental nature of conversational devices"[42] where the term "device" refers to "a kind of function or role which can be 'played' by a wide variety (perhaps an open or generative class) of utterances."[43]

The substance of Nofsinger's work involves the generation of rules which define or constitute these conversational devices, analogous to Searle's formulation of the constitutive rules which form the foundation of speech acts.[44] One such conversational device is the "demand ticket",

[39]Zimmerman, p. 12.

[40]Nofsinger, "Answering Questions," p. 172.

[41]Nofsinger, "Answering Questions," p. 179.

[42]Nofsinger, "Demand Ticket," p. 1.

[43]Nofsinger, "Demand Ticket," p. 1.

[44]John R. Searle, <u>Speech Acts: An Essay in the Philosophy of Language</u> (London: Cambridge University Press, 1969).

which functions to "begin a sequence of conditionally relevant units which will obligate its initiator to assume the speakers role in conversation. Thus a necessary characteristic of the demand ticket is that it requires a response which will require a response."[45] Nofsinger presents a system of rules which "describe the primary presuppositions which accompany--in fact constitute--the demand ticket itself"[46] as "a conversational function which can be filled by a virtually unlimited set of utterances."[47]

Within speech communication, Nofsinger's work is the closest approximation of the conversation analysis proper of Sacks, Schegloff, and Jefferson. Conversational devices are defined in terms of certain abstract preferences in the sequential structure of conversation--e.g., the demand ticket's series of conditionally relevant units--which function to organize the turn-by-turn talk within local interactional contexts. Nofsinger's conversation analysis is an objective systemic approach to social interaction and is best thought of as structural rather than phenomenological.

The work of Jacobs attempts to blend "a constructivist conception of the communication process and . . . empirical methods which remain sensitive to the content of communication and its organizational structuring."[48] His concern is with "the procedures persons use in constructing and recognizing talk"[49]--"how conversationalists manage the sense of conversation in which they are engaged and . . . how they are able to make sense of conversation in the ways that they do and to organize interaction in the ways that they do."[50] His research explores the relationship between organizational features of conversational structure and the interpretations of the participants.

Jacobs argues that meaning in conversation is an emergent phenomenon which is managed by conversationalists in negotiating the course of their interaction. He contends that "participants in an exchange formulate, display, and confirm their understandings of what is going on within a framework of the practical demands of doing conversation."[51] "The same processes which allow for the production of orderly transactions also result in the continual appearance of interactional emergence."[52] Organizational features of conversation are seen, not as an objective structure making possible particular interactions but rather, as any and every participants knowledge of the practical demands of doing conversation, the strategic possibilities of which are exploited in the management of emergent meanings. As Jacobs suggests,

> the general correspondence between personal motivation and structural preference arises from the ways individuals employ the principles of structural preference as a strategic resource . . . to express what the speaker desires or to meet what the speaker expects the auditor to desire.[53]

It is clear that in his concern with the practices conversationalists employ in the management of emergent meanings, Jacobs is involved in a subjective systemic approach to social interaction. Within his project, "through specimens of naturally occurring talk, the methods by which persons go about managing the sense of that talk is analyzed and illustrated."[54]

[45]Nofsinger, "Demand Ticket," p. 4.
[46]Nofsinger, "Demand Ticket," p. 4
[47]Nofsinger, "Demand Ticket," p. 8.
[48]Jacobs, p. 1.
[49]Jackson and Jacobs, p. 1.

[50]Jacobs, pp. 1-2.
[51]Jacobs, p. 5.
[52]Jacobs, p. 1.
[53]Jackson and Jacobs, 1978, p. 6.
[54]Jacobs, 1977, p. 1.

As such, his approach constitutes a phenomenological conversation analysis analogous to the cognitive sociology of Cicourel, and can be read as grounded in the phenomenology of Alfred Schutz.

The most recent work of Hawes can be read as an attempt to formulate a subjective processual approach to social interaction--an investigation of the nature of the transcendental subject assumed as intersubjectivity by subjective systemic approaches. His project proceeds from a foundation of conversation analysis--"formal description of conversations' performative structures"[55]--to an argument that "conversation is sociality . . . inasmuch as methods generative of sociality are themselves the structural methods generative of conversation."[56] For Hawes, conversation analysis "discloses the persistent, ever present structures of speaking in and through which intersubjective objectivity _is_."[57] As he summarizes,

> the object of analysis is a specimen of conversation making elements of the constitution of sociality available for analysis. Inasmuch as talk is a major element in conversation, the moves are from re-cording talk, to organizing talk as conversation, to the structural description of conversation, to the formal interpretation of the structural description, and, eventually, to questions of sociality.[58]

As one example of such an analysis, Hawes suggests that beginning with Sacks, Schegloff, and Jefferson's structural model of turn-taking for conversation, one can argue that sequentiality as a structural feature of conversation, one can argue that sequentiality as a structural feature of conversations performance, is constitutive of the temporal/spacial order of the intersubjective world. "To take a turn is to orient and attend to a life-word of sociality by inscribing time-space in and through the acoustic/kinesthetic movement of speaking with and for another."[59]

Hawes' conversation analysis is subjective processual in that for him conversational structures are neither objective elements of a system which organizes utterances in local contexts nor, elements of the inter-subjective system utilized in the management of emerging conversational meanings. Rather, it is in and through the performative structures of conversation "that intentionality is disclosed as a form of being-in-the-world."[60] Hawes' project is an investigation of the transcendental subject in which "conversation as a form of speaking can be interrogated for structures constituting and displaying the very phenomenon of intersubjectivity."[61]

## CONCLUSION

This paper has attempted to respond to Donohue, Cushman, and Nofsinger's characterization of conversation analysis as a unified approach to social interaction within communication study. I have tried, through an application of Grossberg's scheme of classification for theoretical views of

[55]Hawes, "Conversation and Content," p. 9.

[56]Hawes, "Phenomenology of Conversation," p. 7.

[57]Hawes, "Conversation and Content," p. 19.

[58]Hawes, "Conversation and Content," p. 16.

[59]Hawes, "Phenomenology of Conversation," p. 4.

[60]Hawes, "Conversation and Content," p. 19.

[61]Hawes, "Phenomenology of Conversation," p. 6.

language and meaning, to demonstrate that although they employ similar empirical methods in the analysis of conversational interaction, Nofsinger, Jacobs, and Hawes can be seen to be engaged in objective systemic (structuralist), subjective systemic (interactionist/phenomenological sociology), and subjective processual (transcendental phenomenology) projects respectively. Such analyses of the implicit positions on language and meaning held by researchers sharing similar empirical methods (conversation analysis) and data sources (naturally occurring conversational interaction) are a necessity if, as Donohue, Cushman, and Nofsinger request, the originality of their individual projects is to be preserved.

# 12 / UNIVERSAL PRAGMATICS, NEW RHETORIC, AND THE EMERGENCE OF RATIONALITY

## ERIC PETERSON
## SOUTHERN ILLINOIS UNIVERSITY

Children often notice discrepancies in their experience of behavior, as in the complaint, "how come it's all right for you but not all right for me?" The problem here is that the proposed reversibility of behaviors by the child does not entitle the child to the other's experiences. Traditionally, common sense names the problem of reconciling personal understanding of the social with personal knowledge of the social in a manner of behavior that is rational. Common sense suggests a rational method by which the ability to be conscious of behavior constitutes the conditions for judgment which regulate specific choices. We behave consciously when the description of our actions is used to generate an interpretation of acceptable instances for a specific act. Likewise, we are conscious of behavior when a specific act by an other (recognized as only part of their experience) is used to generate a rule for appropriate behaviors. Based on these two rule relations, common sense also involves the corresponding relation of our conscious behavior with what we postulate as the conscious behavior of others. Common sense, as method, suggests more than a reflexive manner for rational behavior. Common sense also specifies various modalities of rationality which emerge as structures of relations between the person and the social in the act of speaking.

A philosophy of human communication elucidates two theoretical orientations to the emergence of rationality and the resulatant structures of relations--Information Theory and Communication Theory.[1] Information Theory is typically characterized as a digital logic and is concerned with the transmission of bits of information from a source through a channel to a receiver.[2] Message, in this instance, may be characterized as the correspondence between sign-vehicle and meaning. Communication Theory, on the other hand, is based in analog logic and is concerned with message as text--an empty form which proposes an ambiguous situation and a structure from which to explore that amibiguity.[3] The articulation of these two theoretical orientations within a philosophy of human communication reformulates the emergence of rationality as a meta-theoretical concern.

In this paper I explicate two examples of the meta-theoretical concern with the connection of Information Theory and Communication Theory, and their resultant views of rationality. The viewpoint of universal paragmatics proposed by Jurgen Habermas exemplifies the orientation which grounds rationality in the distinction between Information Theory and Communication Theory.[4] The

Phenomenology in Rhetoric and Communication, ed. Stanley Deetz. Copyright, 1981. The Center for Advanced Research in Phenomenology and the University Press of America.

[1] Richard L. Lanigan, "A Semiotic Metatheory of Human Communication," Semiotica, 27 (1979), 293-305.

[2] Umberto Eco, A Theory of Semiotics (Bloomington: Indiana University, 1976), p. 33; see also Anthony Wilden, "Analog and Digital Communication: On Negation, Signification, and Meaning," in System and Structure: Essays in Communication and Exchange (London: Tavistock, 1972), pp. 155-195.

[3] Eco. pp. 53 and 141; and Wilden, pp. 155-195.

[4] Jurgen Habermas, "Some Distinctions in Universal Pragmatics: A Working Paper," Theory and Society, 3 (1976), 155-167.

viewpoint of new rhetoric proposed by Perelman and Obrechts-Tyteca exemplifies the orientation which grounds rationality in the entailment of Information Theory by Communication Theory.[5]  Finally, I consider aspects of the semiotic base which undergrids both meta-theoretical orientations.

## UNIVERSAL PRAGMATICS

Universal pragmatics, according to Habermas, "should rationally reconstruct the general structures of speech and should thereby exhibit the communicative competence of the adult speaker."[6]  Communicative competence indicates the adult speaker's mastery of the rule systems used to utter sentences. regardless of the natural language or specific context. The rational reconstruction of these rule systems establishes a hierarchy in which the distinction between system elements assigns these elements a position in a series of philosophical pairs. Philosophical pairs are characteristic of systematic thought and emerge from the linking of discontinuous elements. The identification and relating of these philosophical pairs is based in processes of dissociation which are defined by Perelman and Olbrechts-Tyteca as "techniques of separation which have the purpose of dissociating, separating, disuniting elements which are regarded as forming a whole or at least a unified group within some system of thought:  dissociation modifies such a system by modifying certain concepts which make up its essential parts."[7]

Accepting the speech act as the basic unit of analysis, universal pragmatics establishes the dissociation between abstract and concrete as the primary philosophical pair. Habermas specifies this dissociation by stating that "when there is the mention of speech acts below, <u>abstract</u> utterances are always intended; these do not, like <u>concrete</u> utterances, correspond to some contingent context, but solely to a generalized speech-act-typically limited context."[8] The systematic import of this abstract/concrete dissociation is evidenced in the subsequent analysis of abstract utterances. Abstract utterances, to continue Habermas' argument, consist of constative and non-constative speech acts whose propositional component assumes the form of a proposition and a mention, respectively. The identification of the propositional components in speech acts is the necessary condition for the separation of the communication level of states of affairs, which is concerned with the achievement of consensus in terms of communicative roles, and the communication level of intersubjectivity, which is concerned with the establishment of interpersonal relationships. The level of states of affairs reflects the cognitive use of language and the implied validity claim of truth. The level of intersubjectivity, on the other hand, reflects the interactive use of language and the implied validity claim of legitimacy. Thus communication is composed of two distinct levels and the abstract/concrete dissociation is the exemplary philosophical pair in a digital model of communication. The argument for the abstract/concrete digit may be formulated as follows:

|  | constative | proposition | states of affairs |
|---|---|---|---|
| abstract | non-constative | mention | intersubjective |
| concrete |  |  |  |

|  | consensus | cognitive use | truth |
|---|---|---|---|
|  | relationship | interactive use | legitimacy |

[5]Chaim Perelman and L. Olbrechts-teca, *The New Rhetoric: A Treatise on Argumentation*, trans. John Wilkinson and Purcell Weaver (Notre Dame: University of Notre Dame, 1969).

[6]Habermas, p. 155.

[7]Perelman and Olbrechts-Tyteca, p. 190.

[8]Habermas, p. 156.

The above dissociations, however, are always realized within a
concrete context. Any mention of a propostition, for example, occurs as
an utterance. The communicative function of speech unites the two levels
of communication. This function is especially evident, as Habermas notes,
"in expressive language use, where neither the interpersonal relationship
nor the propositional content, but rather the intentions of the speaker as
such become thematic."[9] This mode of communication, concerned with the
expression of intentions, corresponds to the classification of representative speech acts. The expressive attitude of a first person contextualizes
,the performative attitude of a second person and the propositional attitude
of a third person. The abstract/concrete dissociation exemplifies the
formulation of communication as a binary analog:

|  | proposition / mention | propositional content / interpersonal relationship |
|---|---|---|
| abstract | | |
| concrete | | |
| | utterance | expressive intention |

| | constative / regulative | 3 rd person / 2 nd person |
|---|---|---|
| | | |
| | representative | 1 st person |

The abstract/concrete pair further undergrids the analysis of the
relations between the three modes of communication. The previous arguments
are carried over in the analysis of speech acts in the context of semantic
content. This analysis simultaneously raises four validity claims:
propositional truth, norm or value legitimacy, intentional veracity, and
the comprehensibility of semantic content. The four domains which achieve
expression in speech appear in characteristic modes:  external nature
as objectivity, society as normativity, inner nature as subjectivity, and
speech itself as intersubjective communality. The delimitation of four
domains specifies the universal properties of speech as language systems.
Each of the following language systems articulates a specific logical ratio
which allows for the realization of experimental structures. The ability
to identify, classify, or temporalize reality arises within a reference
system. Interpersonal relationships, similarly, are brought about by a
system of personal pronouns and a system of speech acts. Finally, a
system of intentional expression allows for the self-presentation of
subjectivity.[10] The abstract/concrete dissociation constitutes the basis
for a meta-system which specifies the structures of relations among
philosophical pairs. The schematic form of this hierarchy may be expressed
as:

| | proposition / norms/values | truth / legitimacy |
|---|---|---|
| abstract | | |
| concrete | | |
| | intentions / semantic content | veracity / comprehensibility |

[9] Habermas, p. 159.
[10] Habermas, pp. 160-162.

$$\frac{\text{cognitive}}{\text{interactive}} \qquad \frac{\text{external nature}}{\text{society}}$$

$$\frac{\text{expressive}}{\text{(language use)}} \qquad \frac{\text{inner nature}}{\text{speech itself}}$$

$$\frac{\text{objectivity}}{\text{normativity}} \qquad \frac{\text{reference}}{\text{personal pronoun}}$$

$$\frac{\text{subjectivity}}{\text{intersubjectivity}} \qquad \frac{\text{intentional expression}}{\text{reality sui generis}}$$

The generation of a meta-system based on the delimitation of language systems permits the supposition of the various domains (in their giveness or their validity) as modal in regards to hypothesis and negation. Modal, according to Habermas, "means that these regions are experienced or expressed with a view to the possibility of the negation of the form in which they present themselves."[11]   The modalities of being the Habermas identifies correspond roughly to traditional dissociations typical of philosophical inquiry. The distinction between "being" and "appearance," for example, concerns the epistemological problem of judgements of truth about what is known--the objectivity of external nature. Similarly, the distinction between "is" and "ought" concerns the legitimacy of values, as in the axiological problem of the normativity of society. "Essence" and "existence" captures the metaphysical study of reality and, in this instance, the veracity of subjective inner nature. Finally, the distinction between "sign" and "meaning" epitomizes the logical concern with the correctness of reasoning, as in the comprehensibility of the intersubjectivity of language.

The formal model of this meta-system situates the modalities of being in terms of the giveness of domains and the validity claims of corresponding language use. For example:

| | objectivity | normativity | |
|---|---|---|---|
| truth | $\dfrac{\text{being}}{\text{appearance}}$ | $\dfrac{\text{is}}{\text{ought}}$ | legitimacy |
| veracity | $\dfrac{\text{essence}}{\text{existence}}$ | $\dfrac{\text{sign}}{\text{meaning}}$ | comprehensi- bility |
| | subjectivity | intersubjectivity | |

[11] Habermas, p. 165.

The universal pragmatics proposed by Habermas constitutes a heirarchy articulated by the arrangement of philosophical pairs. The following summary of the above progression of three argumentative steps clarifies Habermas' position on human communication. The first step in the rational reconstruction of the general structures of speech begins with the dissociation of abstract and concrete utterances. The adoption of this dissociation as the basis for a universal pragmatics allows for the hypostatization of the rule systems exhibited in the communicative competence of the adult speaker. Utilization of a speech-act-type logic for abstract utterances specifies a digital model of communication, such as that accounted for by Information Theory. A specific example of this movement occurs in Habermas' consideration of the stages of speech acts, Habermas states, "it becomes possible for the propositional content of an utterance to be separated from its relational aspect and for it to become thematized as an utterance in cognitive language use. . . ."[12]

The second step, based in the separation or distinction between the level of states of affairs or objects in the world and the level of intersubjectivity, asserts the possibility of differentiating between three modes of communication: propositional, interpersonal, and expressive language use. A concrete utterance, contextualizes expression and content in the fashion characteristic of the analog status of Communication Theory. At the level of a fully developed system of a fully developed system of speech acts, to continue the above example, Habermas cautions that ". . . the propositional content in this stage remains embedded in action contexts to such an extent that the validity claim raised for it can only naively be accepted or rejected, but cannot be problematized as such."[13] Acceptance and rejection are characteristic of an analog logic as compared to the "not" of negation which is properly digital.[14]

The third step occurs in the delimitation of the four domains of objectivity, normativity, subjectivity, and intersubjectivity which order linguistic universals within a meta-system. This meta-system, in turn, delimits the corresponding validity claims of truth, legitimacy, veracity, and comprehensibility. The meta-system permits the manipulation of both the givenness of domains and validity claims in the modalities of being as either hypothesis/negation or hypostatization/negation. The final result is a formal model which specifies the nature of legitimation through delimitation of language and thereby articulates the function of knowledge as communication. This meta-communicative level establishes Information Theory and Communication Theory as distinct. This distinction is evident with the transition to "discourse" in which, to conclude the above example, Habermas points out that "the validity claim of an assertion or the claim for the legitimacy of a command, _viz._ the underlying norm, can explicitly be questioned and topicalized in speech itself. The propositional content of an assertion, in "discourse," is deprived of its assertive force and is treated as a state of affairs which can either be the case or not (the same goes for the content of a command, _viz._ norm, the validity of which we treat hypothetically.)"[15]

The "rationality" in the rational reconstruction of universal pragmatics legitimates judgments of reality in the validity of states of affairs. This construction constitutes a hierarchy in which the level of objects in the worlds (language) is superior to the level of intersubjectivity. Information Theory achieves ascendancy in the dissociation from Communication Theory. The relation "between objects" is subordinate to the constituting objects. Problems of axiology, for example, are resolved through the manipulation of hypothetical facts ("is") in the negative modality of value ("ought"). Values, in order to

---

[12]Habermas, p. 164.

[13]Habermas, p. 164.

[14]Wilden, pp. 163 and 178-190.

[15]Habermas, p. 164.

be manipulated as negative entities, remain distinct from the facts of reality. As reality dominates value so does rational dominate irrational and, to continue the structure of the hierarchy, so does theory dominate practice. Theory constitutes the philosophical structures within which practice may be located. The meta-theory, therefore, is only theoretically compelling or valid as it establishes the subordinate domain of practice within the arbitrary. The rationality of universal pragmatics is only critical to the extent that reconstruction involves an inquiry into the location of discourse within the structure of language itself. Universal pragmatics does not, as Thomas McCarthy points out, "extricate social theory from the hermeneutic circle in the sense that critique would now take the form of applied theory. . . . the critical interpretation of concrete social phenomena has an irreducibly 'practical' moment."[16]

## NEW RHETORIC

New rhetoric begins with the assumption of audience, of a community of minds, rather than the general structures of speech distinguished by universal pragmatics. The primary philosophical pair derives from the conception audiences form of the real and the preferable. The division between the real and the preferable suggested by Perelman and Olbrechts-Tyteca classifies types of objects of agreement.[17] These objects of agreement are taken as conforming to the agreement of the universal audience. On the other hand, the preferable identifies agreement with a viewpoint specified as a particular audience. These agreements are then examined in relation to the viewpoint of certain audiences (therefore certain agreements) and, finally, in relation to their presentation as regards the state of the discussion. This progression constitutes a digital logic sequence[18] of 1) message:  agreement on the premises as sign presence; 2) context:  choice of the premises as sign absence; 3) code:  presentation of the premises as either sign presence or sign absence. Thus Perelman and Olbrechts-Tyteca suggest a movement from classification to analysis. For example:

| real | universal audience | probability |
|------|--------------------|-------------|
| preferable | particular audience | possibility |

And further subdivided as

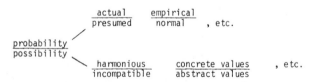

The division of objects of agreement into the real and the preferable articulates the component elements of discourse constituted together as argumentation. As Perelman and Olbrechts-Tyteca state:  "Indeed, contrary to what happens in a proof, where demonstrative processes operate within an isolated system, argumentation is characterized by a constant interaction among all its elements."[19] Examples of discourse are then analyzed as association

[16]Thomas McCarthy, *The Critical Theory of Jurgen Habermas* (Cambridge: MIT, 1978), p. 357.

[17]Perelman and Olbrechts-Tyteca, p. 66.

[18]Lanigan, p. 3.

[19]Perelman and Olbrechts-Tyteca, p. 190.

schemes and then as dissociation schemes. This progression explicates the relation of the real and the preferable within an analog logic sequence[20] of
1) code: both real and preferable as sign presence and sign absence; 2) context:
association schemes as sign presence; 3) message: dissociation schemes as sign
absence. Thus the classification

objects of agreement
———————————————————
techniques of argumentation

dissolves within the context of a specific use. Several choices are possible
since they depend upon context, for choice in context is constituted though
the specific choice is arbitrary.

The distinction between digital and analog logics reveals the inadequacy
of the following formulations:

| judgments of reality | compelling | rational |
|:---:|:---:|:---:|
| value judgments | arbitrary | irrational |

Perelman and Olbrechts-Tyteca argue for a critical rationalism which correlates
with:

| real | objects of agreement | theory |
|:---:|:---:|:---:|
| preferable | techniques of argumentation | practice |

What distinguishes the latter of the two sets of pairs (or new rhetoric from
universal pragmatics) is the dependence upon an audience responsible for the
exercise of choice within a meaningful field of action. The possibility of
freedom is based upon reasonable adherence of a human community through argumentation. If rhetoric is concerned with "discovery of" as well as "the available
means of" then rhetoric embraces decisions in action and in knowledge. Significantly, Perelman and Olbrechts-Tyteca look to a rhetoric which articulates the multiplicity of relations between person, community, and culture according to a logic
of agreement (digital) and argumentation (analog): more precisely, a critical
rationalism in which argumentation entails agreement, a rhetoric construct in use.
Thus, for new rhetoric, Communication Theory entails Information Theory. The reformulation of the traditional dissociation between persuasion and conviction
suggests this logic of entailment. Contrary to the Kantian notion that only conviction (based in the true) can be proved, new rhetoric bases both persuasion and
conviction in the adherence of audience. Whereas persuasive argumentation claims
validity for the universal audience. The difference here depends upon, as Perelman
and Olbrechts-Tyteca state, "the idea the speaker has formed on the incarnation of
reason. Every person believes in a set of facts, of truths, which he thinks must
be accepted by every "normal" person, because they are valid for every rational
being."[21] The rationality of new rhetoric is "critical" as the difference between
persuading and convicting is imprecise and always involves an inquiry into the
constitution of speaker and listener within the context of ongoing discourse.[22]

[20]Lanigan, p. 4.

[21]Perelman and Olbrechts-Tyteca, p. 28.

[22]Maurice Natason, "The Claims of Immediacy" in Philosophy, Rhetoric, and Argumentation, ed.
Maurice Natanson and Henry W. Johnstone, Jr. (University Park: Pennsylvania State University, 1965)
pp. 10-19.

meta-theoretical orientations of universal pragmatics and new rhetoric. Both
orientations conceive the problem as one of meta-communication, that is, recognizing the status of the double articulation of language. Universal pragmatics
specifies this double articulation as the possibility of treating language as an
object of discourse in discourse. New rhetoric, on the other hand, specifies the
double articulation of language in the example of dialogue where even a single
interlocutor exists as a particular yet universal audience. What differentiates
these two orientations is their meta-communicative direction and the resultant
delimitations or boundaries. Universal pragmatics, for example, adopts the explicitly
linguistic model of speech acts proposed by J.L. Austin and elaborated on by
J.R. Searle, thereby incorporating a philosophical meta-system which moves from
linguistically given structures to the location of instances of discourse within
those structures. The articulation of an epistemology, in other words, gives
rise to an ontology within the framework of an axiology.[23] New rhetoric, while
expressing a similar concern with legitimacy, discourse, and epistemology, examines
first the ontological foundation of audience.

At a semiotic level these two view of rationality correlate to what Richard
Lanigan calls an "Ecosystem Model" and a "Phenomenological Model,"[24] and what
Julia Kristeva calls a "semiology of systems" and a "semiology of signifying
practices."[25] Any semiotics which accepts the model of language as a social
code is restricted to being, as Kristeva notes, "a semiotics that records the
systematic, systematizing, or informational aspect of signifying practices."[26]
Universal pragmatics falls subject to this same critique.[27] New rhetoric, by
contrast, continues a dominant rhetorical tradition in recognizing audience as the
beginning point in argumentation. New rhetoric recognizes what a semiology of
signifying practices apprehends as lying "outside" of any semiology of systems--
the process of the speaking subject. Universal pragmatics, in other words, exists
as a semiotic system among other semiotic systems, and the reasons for accepting
a linguistic model of human communication depends upon the adherence of an audience,
adherence which is properly trans-linguistic. New rhetoric situates universal
pragmatics in a continuously renewed critique of rationality through a return to
the speaking subject.[28]

The inability of universal pragmatics to move beyond the limitations of the
linguistic model are revealed in the inadequate attempt to apprehend strategic
forms of communication within a logic of theoretical discourse.[29] Forms such as
lying, manipulating, and playing remain derivative modalities dependent upon
previously established rational structures. What universal pragmatics fails to
account for is how these forms, even as intentional confusion of modalities,
could ever have arisen. Why, if the general structures of speech are pre-given,
should there even be non-intentional confusion?

Play, to take just one example, presupposes mastery of an illusory mechanism
and is post-meaningful rather than co- or pre-meaningful. Habermas states that
"we may . . . regard the understanding of derivative modalities of play . . . as
a test of the stability of ego delimitations."[30] Play, from this perspective,
operates as a transgression against the stability of the system. But the ability

[23]Richard L. Lanigan, <u>Speech Act Phenomenology</u> (The Hague: Martinus Nihjoff, 1977), p. 82.

[24]Lanigan, "Semiotic Metatheory," pp. 9-12.

[25]Julia Kristeva, <u>The System and the Speaking Subject</u> (Lisse: Peter de Ridder; Atlantic Highlands, N.J.: Humanities, 1976).

[26]Kristeva, p. 4.

[27]Charles C. Lemert, <u>Sociology and the Twilight of Man: Homocentrism and Discourse in Sociological Theory</u> (Carbondale: Southern Illinois University, 1979), pp. 215-225.

[28]Eco, pp. 278 and 314-318.

[29]McCarthy, p. 287.

[30]Habermas, p. 167.

to transgress in play (for pleasure or desire) depends upon violation of boundaries, hence the creation of new boundaries and the emergence of punctuation. Rationality, as an epistemological punctuation supposed by culture, emerges from the natural processes of communication, from a non-rational or analog basis.[31] Play facilitates the emergence of the digital from the analog, the rational/irrational from the non-rational, and embraces the "paradox" of punctuation introduced by an analog/digital distinction. The boundary constituted by the analog/digital distinction generates paradox because the digital discontinuity is of a different logical type than the analog continuity it emerges from or transgresses against.[32] Neither the emergence nor the transgressivity of play can be accounted for within a semiology of systems. It is only with the consideration of the speaking subject's capacity to critique the system in which the subject speaks, to transform that system, to repeat certain structures--in short, the apprehension of play is possible only in the identification of a semiotic disposition of the speaking subject.[33]

## CONCLUSION

Rationality cannot emerge from the reconstruction of the general structures of speech alone. Nor can rationality emerge within an enlarged historical reconstruction. Only with the investigation of audience, only with a critique of the speaking subject can the emergence of rationality be explored.[34] Recognizing the status of the speaking subject is to continuously call that subject into question. This critique, Dieter Misgeld contends, "requires that one risk one's preunderstanding as an act of practical discourse, and that one engage in a communicative action denying, in its own accomplishment, its own communal basis. Such a rupture, opening a cleavage in communally shared understandings, cannot be secure of its own groundedness no matter how elaborate the theories instructing it. It remains a practical, situated activity."[35]

A semiotics of signifying practices questions the surplus of the speaking subject, that which remains "unsaid" in discourse but which cannot be left behind. We can never totally return to this historical "silence" because we have never completely left that meaningful field of transaction. We begin speaking amidst the ongoing discourse in a tongue that is familiar and in a style that punctuates and contextualizes. The perspective that emerges from this interaction is not rationally or common sensically pre-determined. In speaking there continues a beginning manner or style of play which moves against both the system of rational relations and the structures of cultural rules. A movement which evolves from a historical horizon and yet transforms that horizon past the reaches of any common sense. If rationality reconstructs possible societal systems, then critical rationality plays them, in a manner of speaking, as the speaking subject who is played goes beyond common sense.

---

[31]Wilden, p. 249.

[32]Wilden, p. 189.

[33]Kristeva, pp. 6-7.

[34]Albrecht Wellmer, "Communication and Emancipation: Reflections on the Linguistic Turn in Critical Theory," in On Critical Theory, ed. John O'Neill (New York: Seabury, 1976), p. 261.

[35]Dieter Misgeld, "Critical Theory and Hermeneutics: The Debate Between Habermas and Gadamer," in On Critical Theory, ed. John O'Neill (New York: Seabury, 1976), p. 182; cf. McCarthy, pp. 354-355.

METATHEORETICAL INCONSISTENCY IN THE
METHODOLOGY OF MARX: AN EXAMINATION
OF PROBLEMS IN THEORY CONSTRUCTION

KENNETH JOHNSON
UNIVERSITY OF MASSACHUSETTS

The phenomenological and analytical philosophical traditions may be viewed as two variations of the same basically anti-Kantian position. Jones suggests that both traditions rejected the nineteenth-century constructivist path out of the Kantian paradigm which failed to distinguish between belief and knowledge.[1] Instead of becoming involved in representative theories of perception and their entanglements, both traditions accepted Brentano's approach to psychology which described consciousness as intentional, a direction, not a state. While the analytical and phenomenological traditions shared this common starting point, they diverged in three significant ways.[2] First, while the analytical tradition viewed the intentionality of consciousness as a reason for ignoring consciousness because of its "transparency", the phenomenological tradition viewed the same intentionality as a justification for concentrating on consciousness. Secondly, the former tradition considered explanation to consist of the analysis of complexes into their constitutive, more simple parts, whereas the latter tradition considered explanation to be irreducible in this sense but rather focused on the interconnectedness of things. Finally, while the analytical tradition focused on logical analysis of language as a means of discovering the relationship between physics and ordinary perception, the phenomenological tradition focused on the "life-world" experience. Although the work of Karl Marx predates both traditions, the issues between the two traditions are evident in his writings.

Marx and Engel's approach toward the study of human organizations and human activity within organizations has often been labelled as straightforward economic determinism. Yet, as Aron has illustrated, Marx is often quite ambiguous in many parts of his writings, e.g., the relation of philosophy to sociology, the relation of economic phenomena to sociology, and the concept of alienation.[3] The present analysis will focus around one of the sources of ambiguity in Marx's thought: the philosophical order concerning the nature of historical law. Marx's conceptualization of history presupposes a meaningful evolution of a supra-individual order. Forms and relations of production are dialectically linked; through a class struggle and the contradiction between the forms and relations of production, capitalism destroys itself. While this conceptualization of historical law appears rather straightforward, the explanatory framework employed by Marx allows different interpretations.

Phenomenology in Rhetoric and Communication, ed. Stanley Deetz. Copyright, 1981. The Center for Advanced Research in Phenomenology and the University Press of America.

[1] W. T. Jones, A History of Western Philosophy (New York: Harcourt, Brace, Jovanovich, 1975), V, pp. 250-363.

[2] Jones, pp. 250-363.

[3] R. Aron, Main Currents in Sociological Thought (Garden City, N.Y.: Doubleday and Company, 1968), I, pp. 145-236.

One interpretation, by those who view Marx as a nineteenth century scientist (e.g., Marxist-Leninist), views this prediction of the historical contradictions leading to the destruction of capitalism and the emergence of a nonantagonistic communist society as fact. On the other hand, an alternative interpretation by those who focus on Marx as a nineteenth century dialectical philosopher (e.g., Parisian left-bank Marxists), views Marx's vision of history as born of a reciprocal action between the historical world and the subject or consciousness that conceives the world. Explicit in this interpretation of history, dialectic is seen as an analytic technique making man's position in capitalist society intelligible. These interpretations of Marx's works raise an interesting question: If Marx's approach to the study of human societies is straight-forward economic determinism, how does one explain the ambiguity at all? The ambiguity in Marx may be viewed as stemming from his unsuccessful attempt to cleanly synthesize two divergent analytical approaches, the scientific method and the dialectical method, within a consistent metatheoretical framework. To state the problem differently, Marx attempted to employ two major analytical devices that emphasized different metatheoretical assumptions and Marx's attempt to reconcile these differences was not consistent. To develop this thesis, four major metatheoretical questions[4] will be posited, the metatheoretical assumptions of each approach (as developed by nineteenth century thought) will be examined, and Marx's attempt to reconcile these differences will be presented. Before proceeding with this analysis, it is necessary to examine the major problem Marx was addressing.

According to Aron, Marx accepted Hegel's assumption that philosophy was complete and that nothing was left but to realize it.[5] However, Marx was keenly aware that while philosophy was complete, the real world was not consistent with the meanings philosophy gave to human existence. This inconsistency generated two problematic questions for which Marx sought answers: 1) How does one explain the inconsistency between the meanings of philosophy and the non-philosophical world?, and 2) How is it possible to provide a means for the masses to realize philosophy? For Marx, the appropriate subject matter for study was society, because within society a mechanism was operating that produced the inconsistency. To study society, Marx employed two analytical tools with inconsistent metatheoretical assumptions about the nature of knowledge.

The first metatheoretical question may be stated as: Should the subject matter for study be conceptualized as subjective or objective definitions of reality? Objectivists assume reality exists quite apart from the knower and is not importantly affected by the act of being known. Conversely, subjectivists assume that the substance of reality is the totality of objects and occurrences as experienced by the common-sense thinking of men.[6] Nineteenth century physical science, heavily influenced by the methods of inductivism and the hypothetico-deductivism of positivism, argued for a more objective or materialistic basis for knowledge of nature.[7] The works of Bacon argue for the discovery of scientific laws through observation of objects and events, and that these observations are the foundation for what is known. Positivism, introduced by Comte, argued that inductivism was only half of a methodology. Based on observations, laws could be induced, however, laws could also be deduced from general premises and then tested empirically. Both influences in nineteenth century science assumed the final arbiter of knowledge to be

[4]W. B. Pearce, "Metatheoretical Concerns in Communication," *Communication Quarterly*, 24 (1977). 3-6.

[5]Aron, pp. 145-236.

[6]A. Schutz, "Concepts and Theory Formation in the Social Sciences," *Journal of Philosophy*, 51 (1954), 257-273.

[7]R. Harre, *The Philosophy of Science* (New York: Oxford University Press, 1972).

through objective definition. Conversely, the dialectic method from Plato to Hegel assumed a more subjective definition of what constituted true knowledge. In particular, Plato viewed dialectic as the proper employment of reasoning toward the attainment of Truth, which is contained in perfect external forms and not in the objects or events surrounding man. Plato distrusted objects perceived through the senses altogether.[8] Aristotle, more of a pragmatist, viewed dialectic not as a means by which man can know Truth in the Platonic sense, but as a method educated people could utilize to help them organize the world.[9] Hence, what is known is to be defined more subjectively than objectively. Hegel's view is consistent with this employment of dialectic as method. Hegel viewed the dialectical method as the self-development of the concept, thus focusing on the self-consciousness of man. According to Hegel, the dialectical development apparent in nature and history is only a copy of the concept going on from eternity, no one knows where, but all events act independently of any thinking of man.[10] Hegel's argument is essentially that while an objective reality probably exists, man's knowledge is limited to the subjective and his knowledge of the objective comes only from subjective experience. To summarize the argument, while the scientific approach assumes that knowledge may be defined objectively, the dialectical method traditionally assumes knowledge must be defined more subjectively.

Marx, early in his career and based on his observation of the difference between philosophical and "real world" meanings, attacked the Hegelian viewpoint of dialectic as a subjective method of analysis and assigned it a "real world" or objective status. According to Engels,

> We, Marx and Engels, comprehended the concepts in our heads once more materialistically--as images of real things instead of regarding the real things as images of this or that stage of the absolute concept. Thus dialectics reduces itself to the science of the general laws of motion, both of the external world and of human thought--two sets of laws which are identical. . . . Thereby the dialectic of concepts itself become merely the conscious reflex of the dialectical motion of the real world, and thus the dialectic of Hegel was placed on its head. . . .[11]

Clearly Marx and Engels in this passage assume dialectic to be material, "real world", and they assign it an objective status subject to the general laws of motion in two identical systems: The external world and the internal world (human thought). Hence, there was no inconsistency for Marx concerning this metatheoretical issue. However, Marx's assignment of dialectic to a real world status produced difficulties for Marx concerning other metatheoretical issues.

A second metatheoretical question may be posited as: What is the appropriate unit of analysis? To answer this question, one must determine whether to select a reductionistic or non-reductionistic conceptualization of the subject matter and whether the subject matter is to be viewed as nomothetic or ideosyncratic. Nineteenth century natural science was also influenced by Corpuscularian philosophy which contained at least two interesting conceptions. First, the properties of individual things and of materials were to be defined for scientific purposes as structural relations among standard elementary in-

[8]R. Demos, ed., <u>Plato: Selections</u> (New York: Scribner's Sons, 1927), pp. 1-25.

[9]Aristotle, <u>Prior and Posterior Analytics in The Works of Aristotle</u> (London: Oxford University Press, 1927).

[10]L. Feuer, ed., Marx and Engels: <u>Basic Writings on Politics and Philosophy</u> (Garden City, N.Y.: Doubleday and Company, 1959), pp. 225-226.

[11]Feuer, p. 226.

dividuals. The presence of a certain mode of organization among the elementary parts of a thing becomes the main feature of the explanation of the powers of individual things and materials to manifest certain qualities to us, and to affect other things. Second, there was a tendency to reduce the number of kinds of individuals to as few as possible, and to reduce as far as possible the multiplicity of materials. The challenge posed for the scientist in Corpuscularian thought was to argue that the multiplicity was nothing but diversity of relations and not the diversity of substance (i.e., of bàsic kinds of materials).[12] In short, the Corpuscularian influence on nineteenth century science was to treat the unit to be analyzed as reductionistically as possible and nomothetically. Conversely, nineteenth century dialectics was basically non-reductionistic and more idiosyncratic in conceptualizing units of analysis. Dialecticians tended in practice to accept the multiplicity of substances as irreducible and to postulate a separate form for every material.[13] In addition, the dialectical method assumed that for every thesis there was an antithesis. A conflict between thesis and antithesis may be resolved in synthesis, however the explanation of synthesis may not be reduced to an explanation of thesis. In sum, the two analytical approaches make quite different metatheoretical assumptions about the unit of analysis. Nineteenth century science assumed that explanations could be reduced to the elements of a unit of analysis and that diversity was due to relations between these simple elements and not due to diversity of materials. Hence, the unit of analysis was nomothetic. On the other hand, the dialectical method assumed a less reductionistic and more ideosyncratic approach to the study of a unit of analysis. Diversity was perceived as a matter of material rather than relations.

The Corpuscularian influence on nineteenth century science was reflected in Marx's unit of analysis--society. Engels wrote in "Socialism: Utopian and Scientific":

> All past history, with the exception of primitive stages, was the history of class struggles; that these warring classes of society were always the products of the modes of production and of exchange--the economic conditions of their time. The economic structure of society always furnishes the real basis, starting from which we can alone work out the ultimate explanation of the whole superstructure of judicial, political, religious, etc. institutions.[14]

For Marx the scientist, the superstructure of society could be reduced to the fewest materials possible (economic, judicial, political, etc.) to be explained structurally by the relations of these materials. Indeed, in going further Marx and Engels claimed that they could explain the form of society by a reduction to a part of its economic structure--the modes of production. While Marx recognized that the modes of production vary from society to society, it was the modes of production that determine every society's form. In addition, Marx assumed all societies' modes of production would evolve in a similar manner. Hence, all history was class struggle. Marx assumed a rather nomothetic approach to his unit of analysis. For Marx, the dialectical philosopher, this economic reductionism was problematic. If the explanation of society was its inherent class struggles (class being based on an economic definition), what were the antithesis and synthesis of his thesis? Having assigned a real world status to the dialectic, Marx needed to answer this question. For Marx, the antithesis of economic reductionism was to be found in his concept of false class consciousness. The present lack of economic

[12]Harre, pp. 140-163.
[13]Harre, pp. 100-139.
[14]Feuer, p. 88.

class struggles was due to the masses not recognizing their true ecomonic interest hence becoming the pawns of bourgeoisie institutions. The synthesis would be when the masses recognized their true class consciousness and revolted to establish the communist society. This attempt to synthesize the two analytical methods suffers from two basic flaws. First, if the society can be explained in terms of the modes of production, then how will the modes of production change in order to allow men to recognize their true class consciousness? How will class consciousness come about? This is never clearly explicated by Marx. On the other hand, if the masses need to be educated to reveal their true class consciousness, then society cannot be reduced to economic modes of production since the revolution can only take place when people are aware of their own economic interest. The ambiguity here in Marx's thought may reflect the incompatibility of his two methods of analysis--one reductionistic, the other non-reductionistic in their assumptions concerning the unit of analysis.

A third metatheoretical question asks: "Is human action different from natural phenomena?" That is, are both natural and social phenomena adequately explained in terms of the same type of necessity and generality? Nineteenth century science, characterized as reductionist, provided the means for nomothetic explanation through the search for the one ultimate cause of physical phenomena--a type of natural necessity. Nineteenth century dialectics also was concerned and interested in finding an ultimate cause, however because of its basic non-reductionistic stance, many forms of causal powers other than natural necessity were perceived to exist.[15] Within the framework of thesis, antithesis and synthesis, dialectics could allow for an ultimate cause (thesis), however other types of causation (antithesis) were possible.

Engels noted three scientific discoveries in the nineteenth century which influenced both he and Marx: 1) the discovery of the cell; 2) the transformation of energy; 3) Darwin's "proof" of the evolution of all organic beings. Each discovery assumed one causal generative mechanism: a form of natural necessity, which was true for all conditions or all "universes" and provided a high degree of generality. For Marx the scientist, the history of human activity, like the history of organic development, came of a natural necessity producing a natural force--evolution. Marx noted,

> Intrinsically, it is not a question of the higher or lower degree of
> development of the social antagonisms that result from the natural
> laws themselves, of the tendencies working with iron necessity towards
> inevitable results.[16]

> For this is quite enough if he proves at the same time, both the necessity
> of the present order of things and the necessity of another order, into
> which the first must inevitably pass over. . . .[17]

With this claim of history as a product of natural necessity, Marx also made the additional claim of universal generality of all history being a class struggle. For Marx the nineteenth century scientist, human activity was solely governed by natural necessity with universal generality. Yet as a nineteenth century dialectical philosopher, who had assigned dialectic to the status of "real world phenomena", such a monocausal explanation was problematic. If the nature of the world was dialectical, there must be an antithesis to natural necessity. To state the problem somewhat differently, if human activity was the product of only one type of necessity, then the dialectic could not be assigned a materialistic status since this required antithesis. While nine-

---

[15] Harre, pp. 100-139.

[16] Feuer, p. 135.

[17] Feuer, p. 143.

teenth century thought, either scientific or dialectic, did not provide a conceptual framework for other types of necessity, Marx recognized another force at work within society but could not give it the status of a force of necessity.

> In one point, however, the history of the development of society proves to be essentially different from that of nature. In the history of society the actors are all endowed with consciousness, are men acting with deliberation or passion, working towards definite goals; nothing happens without a conscious purpose, without an intended aim.[18]

Human beings could initiate action in attmepts to achieve goals, what Achenstein would later argue was a form of necessity--practical necessity with human beings conceptualized as generative mechanism.[19] As a synthesis of the problem of natural necessity, and its antithesis of human purposive action, Marx assumed human purposive action to be secondary:

> But this distinction . . . cannot alter the fact that the course of history is governed by inner general laws. . . . we have seen that the many individual wills active in history for the most part produce results quite other than those intended--often quite the opposite; that their motives, therefore, in relation to the total result are likewise of only secondary importance.[20]

However the problem of inconsistent metatheoretical assumptions concerning human activity persisted. If human motivation is of only secondary importance, then there is only one meaningful type of necessity and no real dialectic in nature. Marx's apparent inconsistency on the inevitability of historical economic evolution produced by natural necessity and that change could be produced by collective purposive human action reflects Marx's inability to synthesize both methodological approaches.

A final metatheoretical question asks: What is the goal of the investigation? For nineteenth century science, the goal of the investigation was the discovery of laws. To explain a fact or an event or other phenomena, a description of all that happened could be logically deduced, in the positivistic framework from a covering law. A general statement or syllogistic major premise containing "all", subject, and predicate functions as a covering law. According to Harré, two important consequences of this covering law and deductivist approach emerged.[21] First, if two explanations could be deduced from a covering law, the simplest of the two was accepted. However, the positivists did not establish simplicity as a criterion of truth. Second, hypothetico-deductivistic positivism implied the symmetry of prediction and explanation: that prediction of at least some new laws and all new particular facts is by deduction. That is, every prediction counted as an explanation after the fact and every explanation counted as a prediction before the fact. Conversely, the major goal of the dialectic method was to discover Truth for Plato, and the laws of thought for Hegel. In dialectic, laws were changeable as truth was discovered. In physical science, however, laws, in the nineteenth century, were for the purpose of prediction, hence not to be amended--although this was seldom practiced.

Marx's employment of the covering law approach is exemplified in the nature of historical law. In syllogistic form, Marx's theory appears as follows:

[18]Feuer, p. 230.
[19]P. Achinstein, _Laws and Explanation_ (London: Oxford University Press, 1971).
[20]Feuer, p. 230.

All forms and relations of production are dialectically linked
(and contradictory) which generates class struggles that destroy
the existing social order.

Capitalism inherently contains contradictory forms and
relations of production.

Capitalism will be destroyed.

This covering law provided both an explanation and prediction within a logical
framework. Marx argued that the goal of the dialectic was to discover laws
subject to the laws of nature, but his conception of laws was more dialectical
than positivist at times. Marx's difficulty to provide an accurate prediction
concerning the destruction of capitalistic societies may have generated this
reconceptualization. As Marx argues in Capital:

A more thorough analysis of phenomena shows that social organisms differ
among themselves as fundamentally as plants and animals. Nay, one and
the same phenomenon falls under quite different laws as a consequence
of the different structure of these organisms as a whole, of the variations of their individual organs, of the different conditions in which
those organisms function, etc. Marx, e.g., denies that the law of population is the same at all times and in all places.[22]

This approach to law is hardly a covering law approach. Instead, it appears
to be more dialectical in that Marx focuses on different structures and functions of social elements that may change the nature of laws operating from
one system to the next, hence a universal prediction on the destruction of
capitalism is not possible, at least specifically. Again, while the metatheoretical assumption of the purpose of investigation may not be inconsistent
between the two methods, laws versus truth, their approaches to the laws are
quite different, which also produces ambiguity in Marx's writings.

An analysis of Marx's approach to the study of human societies by examining his methodology and their implicit metatheoretical assumptions provides
at least three advantages. First, such a study provides an explanatory framework in which to discover the reasons for ambiguity in his writings. As a
scientist, Marx assumed that social phenomena were objective rather than subjective; that the appropriate unit of analysis was reducible and nomothetic;
that human action was the same as natural phenomena; and that the goal of the
investigation was to discover laws. As a dialectical philosopher, Marx assumed
that social phenomena were objective in origin, that the appropriate unit of
analysis could not be reduced to one generative mechanism; that human activity
was different from natural phenomena; and that the goal of inquiry was to
discover laws, not positivistic laws of science. The ambiguity in Marx's
writings may be traced to his attempt to synthesize two methodological approaches that made quite different metatheoretical assumptions.

A second advantage to this approach is pedagogical. Marx provides an
excellent example of the importance in determining a metatheoretical perspective concerning the subject matter prior to the employment of methodological
tools. While Marx cannot be faulted completely on this point since metatheoretical issues were not hotly contested until after the nineteenth century,
the failure to address metatheoretical issues can lead to a number of difficulties at a theoretical level, i.e., ambiguity and inconsistency.

[21]Harre, pp. 55-56.                              [22]Feuer, p. 144.

A third advantage of this analytical approach, from a phenomonological perspective, is that it clearly identifies two major errors in Marx's work. First, Marx's assumption that dialectic was a real world phenomenon and should be viewed as such, did not allow him to dispense with it after its usefulness as a method was no longer valid.  Indeed, Marx placed himself in the position of having to "save" it as a real world phenomenon even when it conflicted with his assumptions as a scientist.  A second error is Marx's assumption that the study of human activity could be conducted in an identical manner as physical or natural phenomena.  Marx spends much time arguing the analogy, and yet seems to recognize that the metaphor doesn't fit.

To Marx's credit, he seems to have exhausted the metaphors and the methods he employed, but appears to have found no way to advance beyond their limitations.  Marx may have taken his metaphors too seriously.

# DISCUSSION / TRANSCENDENTAL AND HISTORICAL COMMUNICATION

## JOSEPH PILOTTA
## OHIO STATE UNIVERSITY

The three papers of concern are dealing with the relationship of speech and social theory. Specifically and succinctly their question is a hermeneutical one: can the doer of science be reduced to the object of science?

Charles Laufersweiler attempts to apply a typology to different research approaches to language and to ascertain which research approach is truthful to the phenomenological enterprise. The classification is to be determined along the lines of the research orientation's theory of language and meaning, yet the theory of subjectivity must be understood in the phenomenological sense of mediation. Subjectivity has a selective and orienting function. Typologies which are employed are given semantically and must be explained in terms of the process of the conjunction between such typologies and the phenomena being typed, as well as the very coming into being of such typologies. In short, without raising the question about the mediation of these typologies in terms of the phenomena investigated and in terms of the "empirical" world to which they relate, then phenomenology is not expressed in the process and reflection is devoid of content. When the question of subjectivity is answered, transcendental subjectivity, which is the fundamental aspect of Husserlian phenomenology and modern hermeneutics, will account for such typologies and comparatives can be determined through the epistemology of difference and identity.

Briefly, we must highlight the previous remarks in terms of the phenomenological enterprise which has been occluded by ethnomethodology and conversational analysis.

The fundamental tenet of phenomenology is consciousness of . . . , or the characteristic of consciousness called intentionality. This is not to be confused with psychological intention which is a causal relationship. Psychologically, there is a relationship between the individual, subjective acts and their objects. For phenomenology intentionality is not a mental relationship to objects, but an ideal imminent activity of consciousness. Intentionality is neither a reproduction of an existing object nor an index of an existent thing. Intentionality is identical with meaning in the sense that the intentional activity of consciousness constitutes meanings.

The concept of consciousness as intentional enables consciousness to relate to itself in a transcendental manner; to posit itself intentionally as an object of investigation. This means if consciousness were not intentional it would not reflect upon itself and know the meaning of its own acts. Intentionality is the condition of transcendental phenomenology. Inasmuch as the transcendental condition is mediated linguistically, language functions transcendentally. Then consciousness is language. Yet, consciousness is consciousness of . . . , hence language is language of. . . . This means that human accomplishment in terms of language presumes the transcendental and cannot be accounted for merely through formal structures or ethnomethodological reflection.

Phenomenology in Rhetoric and Communication, ed. Stanley Deetz. Copyright, 1981, The Center for Advanced Research in Phenomenology and the University Press of America.

James Aune attempts to wed rhetoric to social phenomenology. In the attempt to make this marriage we must remember that every speaking is a mediation of history. Every statement of a speech must assume an organizational thread which is not given in individual statements but is thematically diffused throughout the speech. This is a turn to "vertical" intentionality or the region of internal time constitution. The analysis of internal time constitution grounds the field of rhetoric as "living"speech. Living speech is made available through the notion of "living" <u>present</u> in terms of the contours of protention and retention. The dynamic quality of time or the experience of the "slippage" of the "now" across the homogeneous living present is the experience of the changing yet static interpretation of a speech. The enduring living present can emerge only through the engagement of the human in the world. The speech takes the shape as the "still-to-be-realized" generated in the living presence of the "already-begun-but-still-ongoing" task. This speech becomes manifest with the emergence of the historical moment. The historical moment consists in the inquiry "How has this come about?" This inquiry puts us into the region of transcendental time constitution and history as a communication medium. History becomes the communication of living memory.

In the present case the political speech is the topic of concern. The interpretive understanding is suspended in the tension between the sameness of the transmitted speech and the difference of the current hermeneutical situation. The first task is to appropriate the same message to the times, and thus fuse the horizons of present and past. The application of the speech to the times necessarily takes place in and through language. This translation is achieved through the mediation of interpretive concepts which do not become thematic in the understanding of the text. The interpreting concepts belong to the inner articulation of the topic which is meaning, while at the same time it is a new creation of understanding. Rhetoric thus presupposes the encounter of understanding ( <u>versthen</u> ) and "creation."

The question in Eric Peterson's paper is a problem of sign-pragmatics in general and the theorizing subject. It is assumed in pragmatics that the axiomatics can be correlated to the behavioral (empirical-descriptive). The presupposition is that this correlation can be made. Hence pragmatics claim this is a problem for empirical social science: the understanding of two sign-users. The theorizing subject is a scientific object and thus becomes an object of a specific scientific language; the language of behavior which is then analyzed for its behavioral descriptions. Hence the subject becomes the limit of speaking. Is the limit of the subject chaotic? How is this limit recognized?

This limit is not the province of any objective science nor can it be accounted for within the field of semantics or syntactics. Hermeneutics enters at this point to ask the question of this possibility in terms of history. The question is: If the conditions which give rise to historical processes are interpreted conditions, and if the interpretors are part of the conditions of history, then the hermeneutical process is not identical with the conditions and the historical interpretor. Why? Because the interpretor is already interpreted as a subject. Hermeneutics seeks out this process. It is in this region that the play of interpretation is announced as the derivative of the ego (pragmatically), yet the interpretation is not reducible to the interpretor. The structure of play is the region of interpretation.

Inasmuch as the function of the transcendental subjectivity has come into question during the seminar, we must remind ourselves of its function. The task of transcendental subjectivity (production) is to keep its absolute correlate the world horizon (<u>noema</u>) opened in a way that the transcendental intersubjectivity would be accounted for. The transcendental subjectivity is not in this case an <u>idealistic</u> Ego, but an "Ur-Ego," for which the ground of the pregiven world is not given. In the case of hermeneutics, by the way of the transcendental interpretation of understanding, the problem of hermeneutics gains universal validity. Since the structure of experience is to be found in the situated situation, which is identical to understanding, then we find that this situation consists of the very human history which constitutes the situation and in which understanding finds itself and orients itself. The structure of understanding reaches its concreteness in history through customs, usages and traditions. Experience (meaning) includes in itself the "have-been" of the history as a communicative dimension. In short, any theory of communication based on the pragmatic-behavioral cannot account for the socio-historical and in turn cannot account for communication.

# 14 / INTERCULTURAL COMMUNICATION: AN ETHNOMETHODOLOGICAL PERSPECTIVE

## WILLIAM KENNAN
## UNIVERSITY OF OKLAHOMA

Intercultural communication is a quickly growing interest area which has yet to fully determine its focus, purpose, or goals.[1] The area can be described as performing a highly eclectic brand of descriptivism.[2] Current research seeks to clarify the relationship between culture and communication and the difficulties encountered when members of diverse cultures attempt to communicate. While description is an essential beginning step for any area which purports to be or to become theoretic, the fact is that there exists no perspective from which the wide diversity of current research can be organized. This situation is not unique to intercultural communication; however, it is particularly acute because of foggy notions of culture and its relation to communication, and because of uncertainty as to how communication is used to achieve understanding when communicators represent differing cultures. Consequently, although intercultural communication research is frequently thought provoking and useful in an applied sense, it remains difficult to organinze into meaningful categories which offer the potential for a theory of intercultural communication.

Ethnomethodology affords a useful perspective for exploring social phenomena which should be of particular interest to students of intercultural communication. However, its potential as a philosophical, theoretical, and methodological force has been largely ignored. Although ethnomethodology does not itself necessarily purport to be theoretic it does suggest a descriptive framework which has the potential for the collection and organization of materials which could be viewed as cumulative. Ethnomethodology, with its concern for the structuring aspects of conversation in everday events, suggests a useful point of departure for the study of intercultural communication.

The purpose of this paper is to examine the implications of ethnomethodology for intercultural communication study. Its approach is eclectic in that it draws selected material from a variety of ethnomethodological positions rather than seeking to employ any particular framework. Further, its purpose is not to discourage eclecticism of thought or research, but to suggest some useful ways of conceptualizing and organizing intercultural communication research. The perspective offered here is developed in two sections. The first offers a

Phenomenology in Rhetoric and Communication, ed. Stanley Deetz. Copyright, 1981. The Center for Advanced Research in Phenomenology and the University Press of America.

[1] Fred L. Casmir, International, Inter-cultural Communication: An Annotated Bibliography (New York: Speech Communication Module, 1973). Casmir's work seeks to provide an overview of intercultural communication study. In his discussion of the area he notes that most efforts in intercultural communication "have not yet resulted in definitive works . . . which would assist in developing major theoretical constructs. As a result much of the effort deals with highly diversified, limited, often anecdotal material." p. i.

[2] Peter Caws, The Philosophy of Science (Princeton, New Jersey: Princeton University Press, 1965). Caws notes that description is a useful adjunct to scientific research. He also suggests, however, that description without direction yields results which are difficult to order in any useful fashion.

definition of intercultural communication and develops two central research foci. The second considers three particular areas in which ethnomethodology has relevance for intercultural study.

## INTERCULTURAL COMMUNICATION

The study of intercultural communication focuses on the processes whereby participants from divergent cultures negotiate functional understandings of their their interactive situation.

This definition suggests that meanings are fundamentally interrelated with communication and situation. When meanings are viewed in this manner they become aspects of the communication process rather than things which have been predetermined or learned as a part of socialization. Individuals assign meaning by communicating with others about the topic of interest and how aspects of the topic and the interactive situation are to be understood. Meanings are, thus, rooted in begreifen rather than verstehen; that is, meanings are assigned through the process of interaction among participants rather than existing independently or as a state. In this sense, meanings are situated as features of the communication process.

Participants in intercultural communication "accomplish" situated meanings through negotiation with their fellow participants, and develop a functional basis for pursuing subsequent actions. Communicators establish their understanding of situations by questioning, interjecting, disagreeing, qualifying, etc.; that is, by negotiating the basis for understanding subsequent events. Through negotiation communicators establish tentative guidelines for acting. These guidelines are functional because they allow participants to act in ways consistent with their understanding of the situation while recognizing that functional understandings are always subject to renegotiation.

Situations, thus, reflect the combination of elements, implicit or explicit, at a given moment which contributes to the assignment of meaning by participants. Situations are accomplished through the creation, negotiation, and functional application of meanings. The process of meaning assignation allows participants to actively understand the interactive situation by choosing the basis on which it is to be understood. The selection, organization, and functional understanding of meanings thus becomes an operational definition of a situation.

This definition of intercultural communication study suggests two foci for research. First, intercultural communication requires particular attention to the relationship between culture and communication. The individuals communicative behavior is influenced by cultural membership; that is, cultural aspects of communication mandates basic differences in style, tactics, strategies, and rules. Second, intercultural communication study involves a consideration of the ways in which intercultural communication situations are made meaningful by participants. Communication events are initially constituted from a cultural perspective and can quickly become meaningless for participants. As communication situations become renegotiated through talk they become something that they were not before. The second research focus for intercultural communication involves the analysis of how communication contexts "become." The remainder of this section develops these two considerations into a perspective on intercultural communication research. Before proceeding with that discussion, however, this section offers a definition of culture and outlines some points at which it interrelates with communication.

That communication and culture are reciprocally related seems clear. Kluckhohn's collection of definitions, viewed thematically, points to various facets of this relationship.[3] Walter Ong argues that world view forges the link between culture and communication. Ong's analysis is especially helpful because it makes clear that of key importance to this interrelation is a procedure whereby meanings are assigned to experience. Ong notes that,

> We do not mean simply the world impressing itself upon his passive receptors, sensory or intellectual. A person does not receive a world view, but rather takes or adopts one. A world view is . . . something the individual himself or the culture he shares partly constructs; it is the person's way of organizing from within himself the data of actuality coming without and from within. A world view is an interpretation.[4]

World view, considered as an interpretation, thus, forms the basis for larger and more regular patterns which can be viewed as meaningful features of a culture. Ong's discussion makes it clear that individuals are active participants in the creation of meanings through communication rather than learners of norms, attitudes, beliefs, etc. which are objectively real and distinct from them. Communication is central to the notion of world view because it is the means for accomplishing an interpretation; thus, regular patterns of interpretation, accomplished through communication, give rise to structures recognizable as culture.

Before proceeding further it will be useful to clarify what is meant by culture. Ong's notion of world view leads directly to a useful conceptualization of culture. Ward Goodenough's definition will serve as the basis for discussion. He notes that,

> A society's culture consists of whatever it is one has to know or believe in order to operate in a manner acceptable to its members, and do so in any role that they accept for any one of themselves. Culture must consist of the end product of learning: knowledge, in a most general, if relative, sense of the term.[5]

Culture is not a material phenomenon as some anthropologists claim.[6] Neither are culture and world view equivalent concepts. World view is the interpretation of everyday events, whereas culture, is the interpreted knowledge manifest as meaningful regular patterns of activity.

The definition of culture proposed here can be further refined. Culture can be subdivided into five dimensions. Each dimension represents categories of regularly occuring interpretation accomplished by members of a culture, and each is deeply interrelated with communication. Physicality is the biologic, neural, and genetic aspects of humanness. Personality represents individually generated differences in behavior, sociality is an indication of the tendency toward social organization, and politicality is the organization of social units into larger and larger groups, and the pattern of intergroup relations which develops between them. Finally, symbolicity is an integrative function

---

[3] Clyde Kluckhohn, <u>Culture and Behavior: Collected Essays on Clyde Kluckhohn</u>, ed., by Richard Kluckhohn (New York: Free Press, 1962).

[4] Walter Ong, "World as View and World as Event," in Michael H. Prosser, ed., <u>Intercommunication Among Nations and Peoples</u> (New York: Harper and Row, 1973), p. 28. Also see <u>The Presence of the Word</u> (New Haven: Yale University Press, 1973), p. 27-44; and <u>The Barbarian Within</u> (New York: Macmillan, 1962).

[5] Ward H. Goodenough, "Cultural Anthropology and Linguistics," A paper presented at the Seventh Annual Round Table Meeting, Institute of Languages and Linguistics, Georgetown University, 1956.

[6] John Greenway, "Introduction," <u>The Anthropologist Looks at Myth</u> (Austin: University of Texas Press, 1966), p. xii.

for physical, personal, social, and political considerations. Symbolicity refers to man's symbolic nature, and the tendency to organize experience in terms of some symbolic system.[7]

These dimensions are analytic. They attempt to demonstrate the reciprocal relation between communication and certain aspects of culture. Each is partially a product of the structuring aspects of communication interaction. Even certain aspects of physicality are subject to negotiation among individuals as to their social and biological significance. These dimensions are not intended as theoretic constructs for the analysis of culture or communication. Rather, they highlight the interrelation between culture and communication, and the several ways in which this interrelation occurs. In sum, these dimensions might function as a kind of topical system for the study of certain aspects of intercultural communication. They form a synthetic framework which can assist in the integration of diverse subject areas with a special focus on communication.

It remains in this section to discuss the two foci for intercultural communication study. The final section will integrate this perspective with selected aspects of ethnomethodology.

The first focus for intercultural communication study must be an examination of the reciprocal relation between culture and communication. This activity examines the perspectives from which communication may begin. The ethnomethodologist can begin by assuming that interactants assume a level or common understanding on the part of all participants. Unfortunately, intercultural communication study can not make that kind of assertion because it is at a loss to predict what individuals will presume. If the presumption of common understandings can not be made communicators are likely to begin by applying functional understandings which are employed in their own culture. Thus, cultural diversity adds a confusing dimension for analysis, but it is one which can not be ignored. Research must proceed by first understanding what functional understandings are likely to be employed in intercultural communication. This activity provides a baseline for further analysis of the ways in which individuals develop functional understandings of their interactive situations.

The five dimensions of culture can guide such an analysis. By considering the symbiotic relationship between patterns of interpretation (dimensions) and communication one can begin to tease out the functional understandings which individuals are likely to employ in intercultural situations.

This type of study is largely intracultural in nature. As such it draws heavily from interpersonal communication theory. However, it seems impossible to consider intercultural communication without a careful prior examination of the interrelation between culture and communication and its impact on an individual's approach to intercultural communication.

The second focus of intercultural communication is a consideration of the particular context created by communication between cultures. Much intercultural communication research begins and ends with an activity which examines culture and communication and the difficulties inherent to any intercultural situation. Participants are assumed to communicate on the basis of cultural knowledge, and thus, misconceptions or "breakdowns" in communication occur. Breakdowns of this type presumably give rise to conflict. While a consideration of these issues is a necessary starting point an analysis of this sort by no means completely conceptualizes the study of intercultural communication.

[7]L. Brooks Hill, "Toward a Conceptualization of Cross-Cultural Communication," a forthcoming paper. I am indebted to Dr. Hill for his permission to use these dimensions.

Focus two can be clarified by a consideration of episodes. An episode is, "any sequence of happenings in which humans engage which has some principle of unity."[8] To view communication as episodic is to recognize that individuals segment their experiences into meaningful units. Episodes include events as common as the emergence of a leader, the formation of a clique group, a speech, a play, etc. A description of an episode involves the discovery of the rules through which participants assign functional meanings. As Pearce notes, "A cluster of rules which specify legitimate and expected behaviors and meanings may be considered an operational definition of an episode."[9] Episodes reflect the sense making activity of communicators. Intercultural communication study analyzes the episodes produced by participants of differing cultures.

Pearce describes three episodes which collectively clarify how intercultural communication proceeds. $Episode_1$ consists of patterns of meanings which are culturally sanctioned and which exist independently of any individual or dyad. $Episode_1$, for example,[10] includes social and political entities, social norms, social conventions, etc. $Episode_2$ resembles Ong's world view. It integrates aspects of $Episode_1$ with individual interpretation. Individuals combine aspects of culture with personal characteristics to generate a basis for individual actions. Finally, $Episode_3$ is the interpretation, from the perspective of $Episode_1$ and $Episode_2$, of acts which are observed or those in which an individual participates. $Episode_3$ is a product of communication among participants and represents the process whereby situations are made meaningful.

The notion of episode places focus one and two into perspective. Focus one considers the presuppositions which are required for communication. Focus two assumes focus one as a base point for intercultural communication and then examines the manner in which $Episode_3$ is constituted.

Intercultural communication now can be seen as the interaction between culturally based Episodes as they give rise to Episodes. Thus, to the extent that Episodes and Episodes are compatable, $Episodes_3$ will progress smoothly. In considering intracultural communication Pearce notes, "To the extent that a person's $Episode_2$ resembles a society's $Episode_1$ the person will be able to converse easily . . ."[11] Accordingly, to the extent that $Episodes_2$ are compatable in an intercultural context communication will proceed smoothly. The reality is, however, that $Episodes_2$ rarely resemble each other. Consequently, $Episodes_3$ become a situation in which communication is made meaningful through the negotiation of functional understandings. Focus two suggests that the task of intercultural communication research is to discover the forms which $Episodes_3$ may assume.

This section has offered a perspective on intercultural communication within the broader rubric of human communication study. It has suggested that intercultural communication must begin by better conceptualizing the relation between culture and communication. It has also argued that the area must consider the manner in which intercultural contexts are constituted. Several specific aspects of ethnomethodological thinking have been implicit in this section. Section two more directly addresses these issues and discusses selected aspects of ethnomethodology which have particular relevance for intercultural communication study.

[8]R. Harre and P. F. Secord, The Explanation of Social Behavior (Totowa, New Jersey: Littlefield Adams & Co., 1973).

[9]W. Barnett Pearce, "The Coordinated Management of Meaning: A Rules-Based Theory of Interpersonal Communication," In Explorations in Interpersonal Communication, ed. by Gerald R. Miller (Beverly Hills, California: Sage Publications), p. 21.

[10]See the dimensions of culture discussed above.

[11]Pearce, "The Coordinated Management of Meaning," p. 22.

## ETHNOMETHODOLOGICAL IMPLICATIONS

Richard Schmitt notes that there are as many versions of phenomenology as there are philosophers who purport to be part of the area. He suggests that "Phenomenology is therefore used in two distinct senses. In its wider sense it refers to any descriptive study of a given subject. In the narrower sense it is the name of a philosophical movement."[12] Within this framework are numerous approaches many of whom bear little resemblance to each other. This situation, although applied to phenomenology, also impacts on the work of ethnomethodologists. Research based on the philosophical and methodological perspective offered by Garfinkel, for example, differs in kind from that of Cicourel.[13] Rather than resort to any particular position this section proposes to suggest general issues which are of particular relevance to intercultural communication study.

Ethnomethodology seeks an understanding of the common activities of everyday life. That is, ethnomethodology attempts to describe the ways in which individuals establish functional meanings for everyday events. Circourel, for example views ethnomethodology as being concerned with "how language and meanings are constitutive of the way in which everyday social interaction is assembled and represented."[14] Accordingly, individual participation in a communication event is founded on the presumption of shared and negotiated functional understandings. Such understandings are foundational for an act or set of actions. The arrangement of functional meanings can be analyzed by considering the accounts provided by participants in the communication event. The product of such an analysis is a rule or set of rules which explains the situation, i.e..the rules reveal the organization and creation of functional understandings which serve to make a situation or episode meaningful. For ethnomethodology, the structure of social and cultural reality is reflected in the rules employed by actors to make sense of situations or episodes.

Although a complete discussion of the implications of a rules approach to intercultural communication is beyond the scope of this paper, a clearer understanding of the nature of rules and their relevance for intercultural communication is in order. Cushman and Whiting suggest the significance of rules by noting that they "function as guide posts to direct and indirect shared patterns of expectations."[15] Rules reflect functional understandings to which individuals refer in choosing among alternative actions. Rules do not stand as antecedent conditions (explanans) for subsequent actions (explanandum). Rather, rules are "referred to" in choosing action. An analysis which seeks to discover rules, describes the basis for communication while recognizing that the rules themselves are continually renegotiated.[16]

---

[12]Richard Schmitt, "Phenomenology," in the *Encyclopedia of Philosophy*, ed. by Paul Edwards (New York: Macmillan, 19-7), vol. 8, p. 135-151.

[13]Daniel J. O'Keefe, "Ethnomethodology," to be published in the *Journal for the Theory of Social Behavior*. O'Keefe's analysis highlights the nature of these differences. Also see, Charles J. Laufersweiler, "Diversity and Divergence in Conversation Analysis," A paper presented to the SCA Doctoral Honors Seminar of Phenomenological Research in Speech Communication. Southern Illinois University, April 2-4, 1979; Paul Attewell, "Ethnomethodology Since Garfinkel," *Theory and Society*, 1 (1974), p. 179-210; and Don H. Zimmerman, "Ethnomethodology," *The American Sociologist*, 13 (February, 1978), p. 6-15.

[14]Aaron V. Cicourel, *Cognitive Sociology: Language and Meaning in Social Interaction* (New York: Free Press, 1974), p. 7.

[15]Donald P. Cushman and G. C. Whiting, "An Approach to Communication Theory: Toward Consensus on Rules," *Journal of Communication*, 22 (1972), p. 227.

[16]L. Brooks and William R. Kennan, "Ethnomethodology and Intercultural Communication Study," A paper presented at the Southern Speech Communication Association Convention, Biloxi, Mississippi, April 13, 1979. This paper specifies tentative categories of rules for intercultural communication, and suggests the procedures by which they are negotiated and renegotiated.

It is important to recognize that while the ethnomethodological perspective on rules is similar to both phenomenological and linguistic analysis it employs a focus distinct from either. The phenomenologist, rather than selecting out distinguishing features of a phenomenon or phenomenal set so that they can be integrated into a theoretic structure, "seeks a fuller understanding of the phenomena as a unity. This involves a description of its coherence, durability, and integrity. . ."[17] The phenomenological method proceeds by juxtaposing and comparing elements of a phenomenon to reveal the range of possible meanings. This activity can be distinguished from one which proposes a single explanation as the result of analysis. Further, phenomenology may or may not seek an examination via rules since the role of recording and analyzing data is "to reflect those multiple meanings for the contemplation of the observer."[18]

Sociolinguistic analysis focuses on the discovery of context dependent rules, but with the intention of constructing, at a later time, rules which transcend context and achieve the status of universals. Labov and Fanshel note that we must seek to discover rules which stand free of context. Study must begin, however, by discovering the rules of particular contexts and then by showing that "they apply over and over again in many different contexts."[19] The logical status of these contextual rules imposes on individual actors an "obligation" to act in accordance with them. That is, "the individual speaker has no choice but to interpret a given action in the same way that all members of a society would."[20] This is a rather stringent criterion which is very close to the position that rules stand in an antecedent relation to actions.

By contrast, ethnomethodology focuses on the activities of participants in communication as they order their surroundings. This process proceeds by referring to rules of communication. Rules of this type have single meanings, rather than multiple ones. They are inter-subjectively negotiated by actors through communication, and they are guides for actions rather than "obligations."

Schutz, for example, has advanced the "reciprocity of perspectives" rule as one way of describing the characteristics of face-to-face interaction.[21] The rule can be discussed in two segments. Cicourel gives a clear description of it by saying that,

> The first part instructs the speaker and hearer to assume their mutual experiences of the interaction scene are the same even if they were to change places. The second part of the rule informs each participant to disregard personal differences in how each assigns meaning to everyday activities; thus each can attend the present scene in an identical manner for the practical matter at hand.[22]

Schutz's construction suggests that individuals, even those in an intercultural setting, tend to presume a commonality of experience as an initial basis for making sense of communication (focus one). Accordingly, actors who communicate interculturally might employ this rule, or a similar one, as long as the inter-

[17]Elliot Mishler, "Meaning in Context: Is There Any Other Kind?" Harvard Educational Review, 49 (1979), p. 11.

[18]Ibid. See also, Patricia F. Carini, "Observation and Description: An Alternative Methodology for the Investigation of Human Phenomena," (Grand Forks, North Dakota: North Dakota Study Group on Evaluation, 1975). Carini's work demonstrates the manner in which phenomenological research proceeds.

[19]W. Labov and D. Fansell, Therapeutic Discourse (New York: Academic Press, 1977), p. 73.

[20]Labov and Fansell, p. 75.

[21]Alfred Schutz, Collected Papers, Volume I: The Problem of Social Reality, ed. by Maurice Natanson, (The Hague: Martinus Nijhoff, 1962), p. 11-13.

[22]Aaron V. Cicourel, "Basic and Normative Rules in the Negotiation of Status and Role," In Studies in Social Interaction, ed. by D. Sudnow, (New York: Free Press, 1972), p. 251-252.

action remains meaningful or until it becomes meaningless.  At that point communicators can be expected to renegotiate existing rules in order to make sense
of what has become incoherent (focus two).  Such a renegotiation signals the
development of an intercultural context as described in focus two.  The central
point is, however, that actors make sense of their surroundings by reference to
rules.  Schutz's rule does not obligate an individual to act, rather it provides,
in an intercultural context, a basis for interaction until negotiation becomes
necessary.  It is this referencing as a sense making activity which allows communication to become coherent.

Schutz's rule of reciprocal perspectives points to the importance of situation in relation to rule reference.  While linguists seek universal grammars of
discourse and while phenomenologists    assume that features of a context exhibit
a multiplicity of meanings, the product of an ethnomethodological analysis is a.
focus on the interrelation of an individual and context through communication.
Ethnomethodology views intercultural communication as a situational activity in
which actors actively structure each setting, thus making them, in many respects,
unique.  The rules of such a setting indicate the manner in which it was made
meaningful.

This perspective seems to suggest that theorizing is a difficult, if not
impossible task.  However, a conditional assumption of Labov's notion that the
study of rules must proceed from a consideration of specific context to context
free statements allows the potential for more general statements while retaining
the essential flavor of ethnomethodological thinking.  Although intercultural
communication study seems, at this point, far away from such a construction, research conducted from an ethnomethodological perspective leaves open the potential
for theorizing.[23]

Intercultural communication studies frequently have been maligned by members
of target cultures who argue that only members of the subject population have
the capacity to conduct meaningful research.[24]  Native Americans in particular
have been concerned with this issue largely because they feel that research has
misinterpreted data, and because the subjects themselves are rarely the benefi-
ciaries of such work.  Triandis suggests that such charges can be remedied by
employing members of target cultures as working members of the research team;[25]
unfortunately, this sort of strategy is rarely put into effect.  Research, in
many instances, tends to reflect a cultural perspective, and thus, results may
indicate more about the culture of the researcher than they do about the subject
population.

Ethnomethodology offers two notions which are especially helpful in considering the relation between researcher and subject, and its impact on results:
The first is a realization that analysis must be rooted in the phenomenon, and
second, is bracketing as a particular means of identifying cultural bias.

Ethnomethodology immerses the observer in the event.  In one respect the
observer is a part of the event and serves partially to constitute it.  By
contrast  to operate, from a more traditional perspective requires that an a
priori theory (rooted in a particular culture) be imposed; thus, the observer
is separated from the situation by perspective and by analytic scheme.  Because
ethnomethodology roots the observer in the scene study must begin by operating

[23]Attewell, "Ethnomethodology Since Garfinkel," and O'Keefe, "Ethnomethodology."

[24]Joseph Trimble, "The Sojourner in the American Indian Community: Methodological Issues and
Concerns," *Journal of Social Issues*, 33 (1977), p. 159-174, and Vern L. Bengston, et al., "Relating
Academic Research to Community Concerns: A Case Study in Collaborative Effort," *Journal of Social
Issues*, 33 (1977), p. 75-93.

[25]Harry C. Triandis, *The Analysis of Subjective Culture* (New York: Wiley, 1972).

with common sense assumptions made in the everyday world (focus one). In intercultural communication study, however, those presuppositions differ from those
of many or all members of the subject population. Thus, the negotiation process
(focus two) is confused by applying methods rooted in the observer's culture.
This argument seems to support the complaint lodged by Native Americans; however,
the ethnomethodologist realizes the impossibility of fully sharing an episode$_1$
or episode$_2$ with an interactant. Research conducted from the perspective of
ethnomethodology recognizes that any analysis must reflect the functional understandings generated by participants in a particular situation.

This activity forces a recognition of the tentative nature of all results
pending careful verification. A concern for these issues forces the observer
out of the "natural attitude" and into a careful assessment of assumptions concerning the phenomenon. As Psathas notes, "the observer knows that his scientific findings are themselves provisional truths, contingent upon ways of knowing and modes of understanding which themselves may later be overturned and
changed."[26] An ethnomethodological approach does not impose ways of knowing,
rather it seeks to tease out of interactive situations an understanding of them
for their accurate accounts in intercultural settings.

It is, of course, difficult to accomplish such a description. Thus, data
from intercultural communication study must be carefully validated. First, results are valid only to the extent that they are consistent with the experiences
of participants in interactive settings. That is, research which has little
meaning for subjects reflects inaccurate analysis. A second test of validity
involves the degree to which the explanations allow actors from different cultures to recognize certain actions if confronted with them in the real world.
A third test, suggests that results are valid if they can be applied by non-
cultural members. This test asks: "Can outsiders operate effectively in given
settings based on their understanding of an account?" This test has the potential to draw intercultural training and research into a closer and more profitable relationship.

Bracketing, as an aspect of ethnomethodological analysis, adds to an understanding of the relation between observer and observed and suggests ways in which
researchers may approach data. Bracketing means that, in analyzing and observing
a phenomenon, the observer chooses to hold in abeyance the belief that something
exists or does not exist. As noted above, the intercultural communication researcher must recognize that cultural perspective impacts on the kind of explanation which is possible. By recognizing the impact of culture the researcher
can bracket aspects of it. Bracketing isolates aspects of experience, and then
substitutes and withdraws them until an object or event can be identified as a
particular something. As Schmitt notes,

> Bracketing in this sense means that I become aware of the possibility
> that something which I believe to exist does not exist as I thought it
> did, that a statement which I consider true is not, or that some act which
> I considered right when I did it might have been wrong.[27]

Through bracketing, according to Psathas, the observer, "breaks out of the
natural attitude and examines the very assumptions that structure the experience
of the actors in the world of everyday life."[28] Bracketing forces the observer
to confront particular aspects of a cultural perspective and to see the implications of it for valid analysis. Grounding analysis is phenomenon and brack-

---

[26] George Psathas, "Introduction," in *Phenomenological Sociology: Issues and Applications*, ed.
by George Psathas, (New York: John Wiley, 1973), p. 11.

[27] Schmitt, "Phenomenology," p. 143.

[28] Psathas, "Introduction," p. 14.

eting will not silence critics of intercultural communication research, but together these considerations offer a perspective which has the potential for more valid research.

A third point of correspondence between intercultural communication and ethnomethodology lies in the conception of process.[29] The analysis of process is rooted in the philosophy of Whitehead and manifest in Berlo's interpretation.[30] Whitehead notes that, "The how an actual entity becomes constitutes what that actual entity is. . . . It's being is constituted by its becoming."[31] Although process is central to communication study it is difficult to incorporate into a research method.[32] Ethnomethodological thinking, specifically that regarding indexicality, reflectivity, and intentionality, can assist in more adequately conceptualizing process for intercultural communication study.

Indexicality recognizes that an act of communication occurs within a situation containing events, objects, and rules which are dynamic rather than static. Unquestionably, context adds important information to the interpretation of the utterance. Without knowledge of the "context" of an utterance, the meaning is often misconceived or lost. When one acquires a foreign language, for example, the contextually bound bases of meaning are the last and slowest rules to acquire; without them, however, much of the meaning of interaction is lost.

Indexicality, however, has an additional meaning. As noted above our common sense assumption is that all interaction is highly contextual. This is true in part; however, Garfinkel's interpretation of the term suggests that it is the structuring activity of communication which creates the situation. This is a bit different from presuming that contexts have independent meanings. O'Keefe helps to clarify this difference. He notes that,

> Garfinkel's discussion of indexicality has often been taken to mean simply that all interaction is highly contextual. After all, an 'indexical expression' depends for its sense upon the context in which it is used. . . But Garfinkel's point here goes beyond simply noting the contextual character of interaction. For Garfinkel, it is talk that largely constructs the appearance of an orderly and rational social world; this talk is largely indexical.[33]

This notion is particularly important. Both phenomenology and socio-linguistics recognize actors as standing outside the context, and separate from contextually created meanings. Schutz, for example, argues that rules exist before we are born and we learn them in order to operate as effective social beings. Ethnomethodology suggests that actors, context, and rules become interrelated through communication. Rules, meaning, and context are the products of interaction rather than separate objective entities. The fact that certain rules are

---

[29]For example, David H. Smith, "Communication Research and the Idea of Process," *Speech Monographs*, 29 (August, 1972), p. 174-182 and Leonard C. Hawes, "Elements of a Model for Communication Processes," *Quarterly Journal of Speech*, 59 (Fall, 1973), p. 11-21.

[30]David Berlo, *The Process of Communication* (New York: Holt, Rinehart and Winston, 1960). Despite the linearity of Berlo's "model" of communication, his discussion of communication as process is relevant. He notes, "If we accept the concept of process, we view the events and relationships as dynamic, on-going, ever-changing, continuous. When we label something as a process we also mean that it does not have a beginning, an end, a fixed sequence of events. It is not static, at rest . . . The ingredients within a process interact; each affects all of the others . . . A communication theorist rejects the possibility that nature consists of events or ingredients that are separable from all other events," p. 24.

[31]Alfred North Whitehead, *Process and Reality* (New York: Macmillan, 1929), p. 34-35.

[32]Dean Hewes, "The Sequential Analysis of Social Interaction," *Quarterly Journal of Speech* 65 (1970), p. 56-73. Hewes argues that communication scholars pay lip service to process without developing a research methodology.

[33]O'Keefe, "Ethnomethodology," p. 19.

invariant across situations is not a result of the unity of situations, but rather the accomplishment of persons who order reality in consistent patterns.

Closely related to indexicality, reflexivity deals with the interaction by a member within the context of the utterance. Reflexivity refers to an individual's account of that interaction. As Garfinkel notes,

> Any setting organizes its activities to make its properties an an organized environment of practical activities detectable, countable, recordable, tell-a-story-aboutable, analyzable--in short accountable.[34]

To borrow from Ong, reflexivity is a partial statement of world view by an individual within a particular context. The reflexiveness of a speech act is one significant piece of raw material upon which an understanding of a culture's communication and intercultural communication is founded. As Filmer explains in his discussion of Garfinkel's conception of reflexivity:

> The process of a member accounting for his experience as a process of making unique, specific and individual experiences commonly known, by organizing them in a coherent fashion--such organization (given the typifying properties of everyday language) being an endemic feature of their expression. The result of the expression of their experience by members in all cases is to make the process of accounting-for an essentially (that is, inevitably, necessarily and unavoidably) reflexive one.[35]

The reflexivity of communication, then, is based on the position of the actor as fundamentally interdependent with the setting. Because of this special relationship the individual's account becomes a statement of the basis on which the context was made meaningful. Reflexivity suggests that intercultural communication must draw from the accounts of individuals the categories and data for analysis. Research schemes which are imposed on cultures ignore this important fact.

Finally, intercultural communication is based on an assumed commonality of understanding, which is reflected as an "awareness of" on the part of the participants. This, of course, implies conscious intent on the part of the individual. Hawes clarifies this notion by saying that,

> Speaking, as one mode of communication, is intentional inasmuch as speaking both constitutes and evidences consciousness and consciousness of. That which is spoken about is brought into being in the act of speaking itself; it does not exist independent of the speaking.[36]

Although the determination of intentions is difficult, and according to some writers impossible, we can ascertain from the interactional processes an idea of the necessary, if not sufficient, aspects of intentionality for actions.[37] That, of course, may not totally capture a person's intentions, but it does reveal aspects which may collectively identify broader social patterns.

A consideration of the intent of actors further refines our understanding of the interrelation between individuals and events. To see actors as active

---

[34]Harold Garfinkel, Studies in Phenomenology (Englewood Cliffs, New Jersey: Prentice-Hall, 1967) p. 34.

[35]Paul Filmer, "On Harold Garfinkel's Ethnomethodology," in New Directions in Sociological Theory, ed. by Paul Filmer, Michael Phillipson, David Silverman, and David Walsh (Cambridge: The M.I.T. Press, 1972), p. 215.

[36]Leonard C. Hawes, "Conversation as Sociality," A paper presented at the Speech Communication Association Convention, Washington, D.C., December 4, 1977, p. 2.

[37]H. P. Grice, "Meaning," Philosophical Review, LXVI (1957), p. 377-388.

and aware creates a clearer conceptualization of the sense made of events.  An ethnomethodological perspective allows the student of intercultural communication to consider the motivational factors which come to constitute a particular setting.  A conscious individual makes choices, and in one respect, this is how individuals become interrelated with events.

Viewed collectively indexicality, reflexivity, and intentionality allow a fuller consideration of the dynamic aspects of intercultural communication. To consider data in this manner recognizes the ebb and flow of communication and the centrality of communication as a structuring element in everyday life. As suggested earlier, it is a fundamental task of intercultural communication study to specify the procedures through which such structuring occurs.

## CONCLUSION

The ethnomethodological considerations discussed in this section along with the conceptualization of foci for intercultural communication study suggests a useful way of approaching research.  Although there are additional considerations which are relevant those chosen for inclusion in this paper highlight the special relationship which is possible.  To analyze intercultural communication in this way is difficult, and that may explain why most approaches tend to rely on more traditional perspectives and neglect these issues.

RONALD LEE
UNIVERSITY OF IOWA

Since the time of Homer man has recognized the relationship between language and political power. Book II of the _Iliad_ details "The Debate of the Achaians" and in so doing illustrates the capacity for language to become a vehicle of power. Lewis Carroll in _Alice in Wonderland_ created an example of verbal power:

"When I use a word," Humpty Dumpty said, in a rather scornful tone, "it means just what I choose it to mean. Neither more nor less."

"The question is," said Alice, "whether you can make words mean so many different things."

"The question is," said Humpty Dumpty, "who is to be master. That is all."[1]

In contemporary political discourse, Stokely Carmichael, while addressing the Congress on the Dialectics of Liberation in London, argued that "Those who can define are the masters. And white western society has been able to define, and that's why she has been the master."[2] The political philosopher J. G. A. Pocock has echoed, in part, the analysis of Carmichael when maintaining that "verbalizations act upon people--and so constitute acts of power."[3]

Hannah Arendt, using the term power in a significantly different way, has argued that verbal communication is at the heart of the notion of political power. In _The Human Condition_ she has amplified her view in these words: "Power is actualized only where word and deed have not parted company, where words are not used to violate and destroy but to establish relations and create new realities. Power is what keeps the public realm . . . in existence."[4] Arendt's conception of power rests on the notion of group consensus reached through a process of "unconstrained communication."[5]

Irrespective of various theoretical foundations, many political commentators place language at the center of their conception of power. Clarifying the underlying assumptions of a language based approach to power is the purpose of

---

_Phenomenology in Rhetoric and Communication_, ed. Stanley Deetz. Copyright, 1981. The Center for Advanced Research in Phenomenology and the University Press of America.

[1] Lewis Carrol, _Alice Through the Looking Glass_.

[2] Stokely Carmichael, "Black Power," in _The Rhetoric of No_, ed. Ray Fabrizio, Edith Karas, and Ruth Menmuir (New York: Holt, Rinehart, and Winston, 1974), p. 60.

[3] J. G. A. Pocock, "Verbalizing a Political Act: Toward a Politics of Speech," _Political Theory_, 1 (1973), 30.

[4] Hannah Arendt, _The Human Condition_ (Chicago: University of Chicago Press, 1958), p. 200.

[5] Arendt, p. 200.

this paper. I will argue that this perspective requires a reevaluation of some earlier judgments about radical political discourse. I will address three major issues. (1) What are the phenomenological foundations of a language centered conception of political power? (2) How might a speech act approach to the concept of power be evaluated? (3) Finally, what practical implications does a language centered conception of power have for the understanding of political discourse?

## PHENOMENOLOGICAL FOUNDATIONS

Many students of politics adopt non-linguistic approaches to political power. They equate power with force or the threat of force.[6] As Weber defines it: "Power means every chance within a social relationship to assert one's will even against opposition."[7] David Bell explains that "Behaviorists contend that sanctions (or in Skinner's terminology, "reinforcing consequences") absolutely determine human behavior, and conversely, that all human behavior can and must be explained by analysis of the contingencies of reinforcement that generated it."[8] Power, in this sense, is contingent upon the manipulation of the outside environment in order to reinforce specified modes of behavior.

Although behaviorism is not inherently at odds with a language approach, it does not fully explore or explain the socially constructed nature of political power. The positivist looks for objective features in the external world to explain political phenomena. Conversely, the phenomenologist "examines how the world is experienced. For him or her the important reality is what people imagine it to be."[9] Bogdan and Taylor explain the phenomenological perspective sometimes referred to as "symbolic interactionism" in this way:

> For these theorists, people are constantly in a process of _interpretation_ and _definition_ as they move from one situation to another. Some situations are familiar such as one's home, school, or place of work; others are less familiar and may be one-encounter affairs. All situations consist of the actor, others and their actions, and physical objects. In any case, a situation has _meaning_ only through people's interpretations and definitions of it. Their _actions_, in turn, stem from this meaning. Thus, this process of interpretation acts as the intermediary between any predisposition to act and the action itself.[10]

Language is person defining and perception altering. The power of language to define makes the act of verbalization an act of political power. Pocock has argued that language was power in at least two respects:

> Verbalizations, we now see, act upon people--and so constitute acts of power--in at least two ways: either by informing them and so modifying their perceptions or by defining them and so modifying the ways in which they are perceived by others. Either of these acts of power may be entirely unilateral and arbitrary: performed, that is, by the will of one person only.[11]

---

[6]Arendt uses the term force to refer to the raw power necessary to achieve desired goals. Power, on the other hand, refers to actions taken through reasoned consensus. The approach taken by the behaviorists and Weber fit more compatibly with Arendt's notion of force.

[7]Max Weber, Wirtschaft and Gesellschaft (Tubingen: J. C. B. Mohr, 1925), I, 16.

[8]David Bell, Power, Influence, and Authority: An Essay in Political Linguistics (New York: Oxford University Press, 1975), p. 116.

[9]Robert Bogdan and Steven J. Taylor, Introduction to Qualitative Research Methods: A Phenomenological Approach to the Social Sciences (New York: John Wiley and Sons, 1975), p. 2.

[10]Bogdan and Taylor, p. 14.

[11]Pocock, "Verbalizing a Political Act," p. 30.

Power, then, may act on the speaker as well as the listener. For example, we all formulate intentions in our heads, but the verbalization of those intentions crystallizes and defines them. We listen to ourselves talk in order to change and alter our own perceptions of ourselves and the outside world.

Since language is a shared code of communication, we must use words with common meanings. The power of the word, in this sense, is a borrowed power. Berger and Luckmann comment that: "Language becomes the depository of a large aggregate of collective sedimentations, which can be acquired monothetically, that is, as cohesive wholes and without reconstructing their original process of formation."[12] In this way "language objectivates the shared experiences and makes them available to all within the linguistic community, thus becoming both the basis and the instrument of the collective stock of knowledge."[13] Consequently, the institutionalized meanings of words permit Pocock to argue that: "Language gives me power, but power which I cannot fully control or prevent others from sharing. In performing a verbalized act of power, I enter upon a polity of shared power."[14]

Language is filled with ambiguities. The word can never precisely define us. We use words that have travelled through time and in each new generation have taken on another nuance of meaning. "This much is certain," James Edie commented, "nearly the whole of extant, historical language consists of built up layers of metaphorical expression, and philosophers have been able to claim that they have escaped the hold of metaphorical language only because of their ignorance of the nature of language."[15] Language is a borrowed power which can never fully be commanded because the metaphorical nature of language always leaves some slippage of meaning.

Language has the ability to shape the way we think about the world. It shapes our consciousness because it is the process by which we objectify our experience. Murray Edelman writing in Politics as Symbolic Action notes that "so intimately integrated are language and thought, so completely and subtly do they shape and signal each other, that language can be utilized as a sensitive empirical indicator of values and of social, organizational, and status identification."[16]

The paradox of political power of language can be stated thus: Language has power by fixing meaning, and liberates by keeping meaning ambiguous. The master can define the social reality of the slave by embedding values in his language, but the slave can free himself by reflecting on the ambiguous nature of meaning.

The concept of power is connected necessarily with goals and intentions. Even the traditional approach of Weber takes the "teleological model of action."[17] Power is used for a purpose. A purely descriptive account of power could never explain fully the nuances of the concept. Only through a knowledge of the speaker's intentions and the receiver's perceptions can we understand political power. The fallacy of the behavioristic approach is captured by Searle when he distinguishes between brute and institutional facts. He explains:

---

[12]Peter L. Berger and Thomas Luckmann, The Social Construction of Reality: A Treatise in the Sociology of Knowledge (Garden City: Doubleday, 1966), p. 69.

[13]Berger and Luckmann, p. 68.

[14]Pocock, "Verbalizing a Political Act," p. 33.

[15]James M. Edie, Speaking and Meaning: The Phenomenology of Language (Bloomington: Indiana University Press, 1976), p. 161.

[16]Murray Edelman, Politics as Symbolic Action: Mass Arousal and Quiescence (New York: Academic Press, 1971), pp. 72-73.

[17]Comment of Jurgen Habermas, "Hannah Arendt's Communications Concept of Power," trans Thomas McCarthy, Social Research, 44 (1977), 4.

A marriage ceremony, a baseball game, a trial, and a legislative action involve a variety of physical movements, states, and raw feels, but a specification of one of these events only in such terms is not so far a specification of it as a marriage ceremony, baseball game, a trial, or a legislative action. The physical events and raw feels only count as parts of such events given certain other conditions and against a background of certain kinds of institutions.[18]

·Likewise language has meaning when the meaning has been experienced and not merely when the physical sounds of words are catalogued. David Bell discusses this very point in a critique of B. F. Skinner. Bell uses the concept of influence, which I will argue later is a kind of power, to illustrate the point. Bell contends that influence cannot be explained by a behavioral analysis. He asks, "How can one speak of 'advising' a rat?"[19] One can reinforce behavior through punishment and reward, but cannot explain the process of advising because the adviser has no power to control the contingencies of reinforcement. Influence occurs when one person affects the perceptions, the social reality, of another.[20] The understanding and interpretation of meaning is central to the entire process. J. L. Austin appreciated the distinction Bell is suggesting:

> The sense in which saying something produces effects on other persons, or _causes_ things is a fundamentally different sense of cause from that used in physical causation by pressure, etc. It has to operate through the conventions of language and is a matter of influence exerted by one person on another: this is probably the original sense of cause.[21]

Power, as a cause of events, is institutionalized. Power is not a brute fact, but its meaning and significance lie in the shared and socially constructed meaning understood both by the speaker and the auditor. Power can be understood best from a phenomenological perspective and not through behavioristic analysis.

## SPEECH ACT ANALYSIS AND THE CONCEPT OF POWER

Speech act analysis has become an increasingly popular approach for clarifying important theoretical terminology. In rhetoric, for example, Douglas Ehninger has separated out the meanings of "instructing," "advising," "arguing," "persuading," "ordering," and "forbidding."[22] In a protracted work that parallels Ehninger's in method, David Bell examined the nature of influence, power, and authority. Bell, a political scientist, has used speech act analysis to refine the distinctions between these companion concepts. My concern with his analysis is to examine some theoretical shortcomings, and to explore the possibility of a broader perspective.

Bell is more conservative in his use of speech act analysis than Pocock. For Pocock, the use of language is an act of power. Pocock has remarked that "What has hitherto been rather vaguely termed 'political thought' is now redefined as the exploration and sophistication of political language, and the

[18]John R. Searle, _Speech Acts: An Essay in the Philosophy of Language_ (London: Cambridge University Press, 1969), p. 51.

[19]Bell, p. 117.

[20]The term "social reality" has been much used and abused. I mean by social reality essentially what Mannheim meant by "relationism." All knowledge is knowledge from a particular perspective. See Berger and Luckman, pp. 9-10.

[21]J. L. Austin, _How to Do Things With Words_, 2nd ed. (Cambridge: Harvard University Press, 1962), p. 113, n. 1.

[22]Douglas Ehninger, "Toward a Taxonomy of Prescriptive Discourse," unpublished paper.

connections between language system and political system begin to seem possible to draw."[23]  Bell would not argue with this starting point, but he would not accept Pocock's next move and assume that the use of language is <u>itself</u> an act of political power.  In Pocock's view, language allows people to define their own existence, and to refine their own perceptions as well as the audience's view of the world.  Bell does not deny that language and perception are intimately intertwined, but he is unwilling to use the term "power" to label the connection between language and altered perceptions.  Bell resorts to the methodology of J. L. Austin to clarify and limit the scope of "power."

The controversy at this stage is clear.  To what extent do the concepts of influence, power, and authority outlined by Bell fail to encompass all of the territory Pocock has assigned to power alone?  Bell does maintain that "Comparative study of people in sociocultural settings different from our own yields conclusive confirmation that language shapes perception and thought."[24] And he argues that language and politics are identical phenomena.  "Is all talk political?  Perhaps.  To the extent that talk <u>affects</u> others (and most talk does), it has by definition assumed political overtones."[25]  If one reads carefully Bell's section, "A New Paradigm of Politics," he implies that power, influence, and authority are special branches of language behavior.  The question now becomes, in what sense can language not be an act of power or influence? All talk, in some sense, affects perception.

I want to turn my attention to the concept of influence more specifically. Using the "In saying X, I do Y in context C" format of Austin, influence has been defined by Bell as "If you do X, you will do (feel, experience, etc.) Y (second-person contingent statements)."[26]  One might inquire how the concept of influence can be distinguished from the performatives <u>advising</u> and <u>warning</u>. Certainly advising and warning are subcategories of influence, but in the formulation of Bell, they apparently exhaust the meaning of influence.  The paradigmatic example of influence, according to Bell, is provided in the following passage:  "If you marry that girl, you'll be miserable the rest of your life."[27]  The prediction of an outcome which is not under the control of the speaker is the essence of influence.  In fact Bell mentions the role of adviser in discussing a third-person contingent paradigm of influence.[28]  "The priest serves in effect as an adviser, predicting a whole range of contingencies which will be dispensed by God either in this life or the life to come."[29] Bell portrays influence as a deliberate act.  However, if we separate the concept of influence from advising and warning, influence still has an array of non-deliberate acts within its domain.  For example, I may speak to Jones about having difficulty with my wife.  He may only listen sympathetically, but the conversation may have an influence on his subsequent interaction with his wife.  My communication never took on the predictive form, although Jones may use my story as data for making future marital decisions.  Influence is a subtle and multifaceted process.  Advising and warning, on the other hand, are closer to the analysis suggested by Bell.  Only with a broader conception of influence can one understand how Pocock's general definition of power is compatible with Bell's analysis.

---

[23]J. G. A. Pocock, <u>Politics, Language and Time: Essays on Thought and History</u> (New York: Atheneum, 1971), p. 15.

[24]Bell, p. 5.

[25]Bell, p. 10.

[26]Bell, p. 25.

[27]Bell, p. 25.

[28]The third-person contingent paradigm embraces a situation where the contingencies of reinforcement are in the control of a third-person and not controlled by a second-person or the speaker

[29]Bell, p. 25.

The conception of power in Bell's analysis conforms to the performatives "promise" and "threaten." This would correspond with Hannah Arendt's notion of force.[30] Power is the ability to manipulate outside contingencies; or worded differently, power is the ability to make good on a threat or promise. Power for Bell depends not solely on verbal behavior, but on the manipulation of outside forces. Influence, in contrast, is predicated not on the manipulation of events but on the prediction of coming events. For Pocock language manipulates our view of the world, but in Bell's account some external manipulation of events must occur.

The final subject of Bell's analysis is the concept of "authority." The formula for the expression of authority is the simple imperative, "Do X."[31] The obvious difference between authority and its companion concepts is the absence of any contingent form of communication. As Bell explains, "The mood of authority is distinctive: instead of the hypothetical or contingent form of communication characteristic of power and influence, authority expresses itself in the categorical or imperative."[32] The unique property of authority is transformed into either influence or power. Bell enlarges on this observation in pointing out that: "The distinctive feature of authority is that the categorical form cannot be reduced to a hypothetical equivalent without thereby transforming authority into either power or influence."[33]

Authority is interesting as a rhetorical phenomenon, but for our present purposes cannot help close the gap between the wider conception of language as power and the narrower interpretation of Bell. Authority does not help explain those cases of power, in the broad sense, that fall outside of the three performative formats outlined by Bell.

I subscribe to the broader conception of power embraced by Pocock. This approach to verbalization as a political act opens up a unique and interesting avenue for the analysis of political discourse.

## IMPLICATIONS FOR THE ANALYSIS OF POLITICAL DISCOURSE

Pocock has emphasized the liberating effects of language. More traditional commentators have emphasized the use of language as a dominating force on the population.[34] Those in power, by "fixing" the meaning of language, could control the perceptions and, therefore, the identity of the governed. Mueller has catalogued just such cases of language domination in Eastern Europe.[35] Pocock breaks with this view and asserts that the revolutionary may utilize the ambiguities in language to free himself from the "master-slave" relationship.

In our own field, Gary Woodward has expounded on the dominating force of rhetoric in an article that highlights "mystery [as] a source of social movement."[36] The use of language as a liberating device was explored in Theodore

---

[30]See note 6.

[31]Bell, p. 37.

[32]Bell, p. 37.

[33]Bell, p. 39.

[34]See for Example Jurgen Habermas's discussion of "distorted communication" in Legitimation Crisis, trans. Thomas McCarthy (Boston: Beacon Press, 1975); or Claus Mueller in The Politics of Communication: A Study in the Political Sociology of Language, Socialization, and Legitimation (New York: Oxford University Press, 1975).

[35]See Mueller.

[36]Gary C. Woodward, "Mystifications in the Rhetoric of Cultural Dominance and Colonial Control," Central States Speech Journal, 26 (1975), 298.

Otto Windt's "The Diatribe: Last Resort for Protest."[37] Windt's treatment does not deal with the question of power per se, but instead relates the genre of the diatribe to a philosophical school of Cynicism. As Windt's title suggests, the diatribe from this perspective is viewed as a last resort; but I will argue that it is a necessary first step in any revolutionary movement.

Let me begin by explicating more fully the meaning of the "master-slave" relationship. Pocock defines his terminology in these words, "If the point is reached where I exist, even in my own perceptions, solely as defined in terms set by others, my condition may be called that of the slave."[38] The master is the one who can set the meaning of language. The slave makes the first move toward liberation when he begins to define himself and the world independently of the 'fixed' meanings of the master.

The realization of this "master-slave" relationship is perhaps nowhere as forcefully highlighted as in Stokely Carmichael's and Charles V. Hamilton's book Black Power.

> Black people in the United States must raise hard questions, questions which challenge the very nature of the society itself: its long-standing values, beliefs and institutions.
> To do this, we must redefine ourselves [my emphasis]. Our basic history and our identity from what must be called cultural terrorism, from the depredation of self-justifying white guilt. We shall have to struggle for the right to create our own terms through which to define ourselves and our relationships to society, and to have these terms recognized. This is the first necessity of a free people, and the first right that any oppressor must suspend.[39]

Those familiar with the rhetoric of Stokely Carmichael will recall the central place that definitions held in his arguments for revolutionary change. His analysis centered on the definition of "racism," and the audience's willingness to throw off conventional notions of Western Culture and adopt a perspective outside of the constraints of institutionally imposed language.

The mechanics of redefinition are central to this liberating process. Obviously, redefinition of one's own existence requires intense self-reflection, but objective self-reflection does not come easily after a lifetime of socialization. The task of liberation, specifically cultural liberation, to say the least, is an arduous one. The escape of the "slave" is made possible by the nature of language. The meaning of symbols, of particular words and concepts, cannot be firmly fixed by the "master." Meanings have been formed through a complex of social structures. "Very complex processes of assumption, mediation, and conventionalization have gone on to bring this language to him as a structure of givens, and, as a result, it is usually not possible to say with simple factuality what their authors intended the speech acts originally fed into the language to effect; who meant what by them."[40] Remember that the political power of language is a borrowed power. The meanings of words are fixed over long spans of time and that historical meanings cannot be obliterated in the short term.

The point of all of this is that the historically set meanings, because of the complexity of the process, are not so tightly fixed that large degrees

[37] Theodore Otto Windt, Jr., "The Diatribe: Last Resort for Protest," Quarterly Journal of Speech, 58 (1972), 1-14.

[38] Pocock, "Verbalizing a Political Act," p. 36.

[39] Stokely Carmichael and Charles V. Hamilton, Black Power: The Politics of Liberation in America (New York: Vintage Books, 1967), pp. 34-35.

[40] Pocock, "Verbalizing a Political Act," p. 36.

of ambiguity, large numbers of contradictions and absurdities are still present. It is the use of the slippage of meaning that can liberate the "slave" from the imposed definitions of the "master."

Consider the explanatory power of this kind of language analysis for certain types of radical rhetoric. The strategy of the Youth International Party, or YIPPIES, can be explained rather neatly. If one reads any of the YIPPIE documents, one is immediately struck with the absurdity of style. Rubin and Hoffman play with words. They misspell words intentionally, turn-around traditional meanings, and satirize all that we hold sacred. Everything is held up to ridicule. The YIPPIES self-conciously tried to liberate America from its traditional mind set. Jerry Rubin in his book Do It! explains the YIPPIES goals in the following manner: "There is no such thing as an antiwar movement. That is a concept created by the mass media to guck up our minds. What's happening is energy exploding in thousands of directions and people declaring themselves free. Free from property hang-ups, free from success fixations, free from positions, titles, names, hierarchies, responsibilities, schedules, rules, routines, regular habits."[41] The YIPPIES did not stand for anything other than liberation. They had no ideology or program. "The secret to the yippie myth is that it's nonsense. Its basic informational statement is a blank piece of paper."[42]

The often repeated slogan that the "Revolution is in your head" characterizes this whole approach to protest. Abby Hoffman, writing under the pseudonym Free, explains this concept in the first chapter of his book Revolution for the Hell of It. "Revolution for the hell of it? Why not? It's all a bunch of phony words anyway. Once one has experienced LSD, existential revolution, fought the intellectual game-playing of the individual in society, of one's identity, one realizes that action is the only reality; not only reality but morality as well. One learns reality is a subjective experience. It exists in my head. I am the revolution."[43]

Words are always suspect because they contain the values of a stifling system. Actions are to be trusted and words are to be denigrated. Only through the misuse of language can we be free from its imprisoning power.

A second strategy is possible. Rather than attack the prevailing language the radical/revolutionary may chose to create a separate language or refrain from the use of language altogether. The radical arm of the SDS, for example, created a separate language. One could pick up any radical newspaper of the middle and late 1960's and read Marxist diatribe against capitalism. The Marxist terminology set the radicals outside of the prevailing language paradigm. The SDS made it quite clear that they viewed themselves in the larger context of an "anti-imperialist" movement. They saw their mission as one that transcended current political issues. "Any radical or revolutionary organization that does not recognize this, and does not take the issue of imperialism to the people, is, at this time, working against the interests of the MAJORITY of the American people, and the interests of the oppressed and exploited people of the whole world."[44] By attacking the underlying economic causes of the war, as they saw it, these radicals removed themselves from the mainstream of political rhetoric. They were no longer speaking political language in the American tradition, but a language in which different values were highlighted.

---

[41] Jerry Rubin, Do It: Scenarios of the Revolution (New York: Simon and Schuster, 1970), p. 246.

[42] Rubin, p. 83.

[43] Free, Revolution for the Hell of It (New York: Dial Press, 1968), p. 9.

[44] Students for a Democratic Society, "Bring the War Home," in Mutiny Does Not Happen Lightly: The Literature of the American Resistance to the War, ed. G. Louis Heath (Metuchen: Scarecrow Press 1976), p. 45.

Pocock has argued that "a totally revolutionary politics would be anti-linguistic."[45] The consequence of an "anti-linguistic" revolution is massive destruction. If the revolutionists do not protest through rhetoric they must protest by use of violence. This, of course, is the very line adopted by the Weathermen. Words were no longer sufficient, violence was necessary. As the first comminique from the Weathermen indicates, they no longer were content to follow the precepts of the SDS and merely attempt to educate the masses.

> Ever since SDS became revolutionary, we've been trying to show how it is possible to overcome the frustration and impotence that comes from trying to reform this system. Kids know that the lines are drawn; revolution is touching all of our lives. Tens of thousands have learned that protest and marches don't do it. Revolutionary violence is the only way.[46]

Pocock has characterized the extreme case of the "master-slave" in his analysis. The terminology he uses in discussing this relationship seems strangely foreign in contemporary American politics. Pocock readily admits that "if the ruler is not entirely contained and imprisoned within this or any other categorization of the ruler/ruled relationship, he can act--which includes the performance of speech acts--outside that categorization."[47] For the purpose of analyzing radical rhetoric in America this change of conditions has profound consequences. The American government promotes the impression that shared power already exists and mitigates any image of a master-slave relationship. The denial of the master-slave relationship allows much greater latitude of response to any crises of legitimacy. Lyndon Johnson alluded to this democratic openness to dissent in a 1967 speech on Vietnam: "I think it is the common failing of totalitarian regimes that they cannot really understand the nature of our democracy. They mistake dissent for disloyalty. They mistake restlessness for a rejection of policy. They misjudge individual speeches for public policy."[48] The speech is both an indication of the degree of Johnson's misjudgment about the strength of the peace movement and a statement that indicates his belief that dissent about policy is natural in a democratic society.

Once this less extreme paradigm is operative a wholly different set of theoretical guidelines are necessary for analysis. Pocock suggests that: "From the moment the two of them accept mitigation of the master-slave relationship, the further reversal or transformation of their relationship begins to move from a pattern of dialectical negation toward one of Clausewitzian communication."[49] Pocock adapts Clausewitz's theory of war to a theory of political language. "Essentially this Clausewitzian conception is the chess-playing stage, of seeking to impose strategies on one another by means of symbolic communications which were also acts of power. . . ."[50]

This "chess-playing" paradigm of analysis seems to have limited explanatory power. One is led to believe by this analysis that both parties are working on an equal footing, but this impression is clearly incorrect. The existing power structure still has considerably more leverage than the radical/revolutionary. The revolutionary must polarize himself and his followers from the government. Polarization is essential for two reasons: (1) the revolutionary must

---

[45]Pocock, Politics, Language and Time, p. 281.

[46]Kirkpatrick Sale, sds (New York: Random House, 1973), pp. 631-32.

[47]Pocock, "Verbalizing a Political Act," p. 36.

[48]Lyndon B. Johnson, "American Policy: The Vietnam War," Vital Speeches of the Day, 34 (1967), 4.

[49]Pocock, "Verbalizing a Political Act," p. 38.

[50]Pocock, "Verbalizing a Political Act," p. 35.

define himself outside of the master's language and, therefore, cannot afford
to bargain within the existing and prevailing language paradigm.  (2)  To the
extent that negotiation is possible, the government apparently has shared power
with the people and, consequently, undermined the justification for revolution.

This language based approach to the concept of political power should lead
us to re-evaluate some earlier critical judgments.  For example, Kenneth Burke
addresses the radical American Writers' Congress in 1935 on the topic of
"Revolutionary Symbolism in America."  He argued that the strategy of "identification" was the key to successful propaganda.  "[His] specific job as a propagandist   requires him primarily to wheedle or cajole, to practice the arts of
ingratiation.  As a propagandizer, it is not his work to convince the convinced,
but to plead with the unconvinced, which requires him to use their vocabulary,
their values, their symbols, insofar as this is possible."[51]  Perhaps this is
exactly what the radical should not do.  If the radical adhered to the tenets
of Burke's analysis, the radical would remain within the existing language paradigm.  Language could not be liberating, but would remain a tool of the "master."

Prevalent during the Vietnam War was a scholarly attitude that rejected
the antics of the New Left because they undermined rational debate about the
issues.  This is precisely the position of Eugene Boodheart when he argued that
"militant rhetoric effectively prevents debate.  Or at least, the style makes
it very hard to bring the issue into focus."[52]  Goodheart is particularly critical of the YIPPIES because of their strategy of disruption.  This ethical
condemnation makes little sense once we realize that liberating one's self from
the existing language paradigm is essential in order to create any political
power among the radical element..

This paper is, of course, only an overview of the implications that might
be drawn from a language centered approach to political power, but I hope it
serves to illustrate the potential for this perspective.

[51]Merle E. Brown, Kenneth Burke (Minneapolis: University of Minnesota Press, 1969), p. 21.

[52]Eugene Goodheart, "The Rhetoric of Violence," in Word Politics: Essays on Language and
Politics, ed. Max J. Skidmore (Palo Alto: Freel, 1972), p. 76.

BRENDA BERTELSEN TRUEBLOOD

Mickey Mouse recently "celebrated" his fiftieth "birthday." This celebration extended to a variety of television programs, film festivals, "personal" appearances, and promotional publications. Manufacturers have utilized his image to promote the sales of their products. It is interesting to note that nearly every object that his form has appeared upon has increased the salability of the object. Almost every type of product used some form of his appearance for this reason. His form began as a cartoon drawing that moved silently on the screen, but this is not the Mickey Mouse that is remembered today. What is remembered is the fact that Mickey Mouse was a cartoon image that manifested through a variety of expressions.

Mickey Mouse is a myth. He is a message which is uttered through a form consisting of a certain configuration in cartoon arrangement of circles and tubes. He is not defined by the object of his message. Mickey Mouse, as a form, has a history and a historical relationship; thus he originated contrary to the nature of things. Mickey Mouse takes form through different material manifestations, although his original form was communicated through film.

## WHAT IS MYTH?

Myth is a system of communication. Myth is a message, a mode of signification -- form conveyed through a discourse. Myth is not an idea, object, or concept. Myth is defined by the way in which the message is uttered rather than by the object of its message. Myth is a type of speech chosen by history. It does not evolve from the nature of things. Myth may consist of photography, cinema, reporting, shows, publicity, oral speech, or writing. Myth is comprized of two semiological systems which are staggered in relation to each other. I refer to the first system as the Film Image, and the second system as MYTH. See Figure I below.

FIGURE I

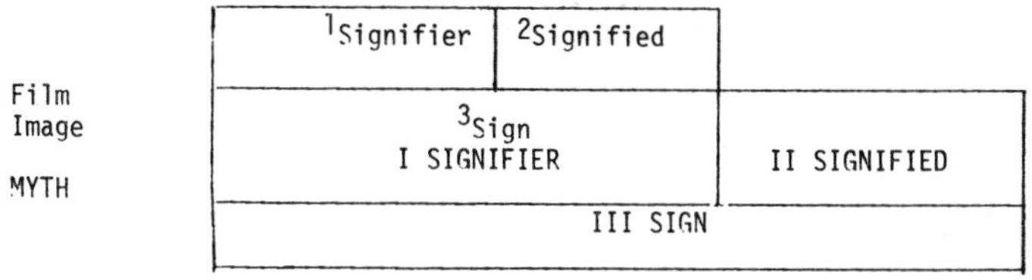

| | $^1$Signifier | $^2$Signified | |
|---|---|---|---|
| Film Image | $^3$Sign I SIGNIFIER | | II SIGNIFIED |
| MYTH | III SIGN | | |

Source:  Roland Barthes, "Myth Today," in Mythologies, trans. Annette
         Lavers (London:  Jonathan Cape, 1972), p. 115.

Phenomenology in Rhetoric and Communication, ed. Stanley Deetz.  Copyright, 1981.  The Center for Advanced Research in Phenomenology and the University Press of America.

Each system contains a signifier and a signified which construct a sign. The sign of the first semiological system, Film Image, becomes the signifier of the second system, MYTH. Myth is a form of meta-language in that the process begins anew at the end of the first semiological system.[1]

## FILM IMAGE SIGNIFIER

In the first semiological system, Film Image, the signifier pertains to the actual message of analysis. It postulates a kind of knowledge that is grasped visually. The signifier is meaning completed and expressed as a system of values containing a history, geography, morality, zoology and literature. The signifier has an equivalence in relationship to the signified, but not an equality. The signifier and the signified act as object-language. In this case, the actual film image of Mickey Mouse is the signifier.

## MICKEY MOUSE AS FORM--SIGNIFIER

Mickey Mouse as a graphic form is relatively simple. He consists mainly of: two large circles which make up the head and trunk, two smaller circles which are appended to one circle representing ears, rubber-hose arms and legs terminate in plump hands (ungloved at this early stage) and large feet (without shoes at this time) for stability. A long skinny tail and short pants decorated with buttons fore and aft were added to the "trunk circle." The head was made expressive by a "mischievous snout", a plum shaped nose and button eyes (minus eyebrows and pupils).[2]

This description does not seem like the cultural or zoological description for a mouse. A mouse might be described as a small rat-like creature that inhabits fields and other dirty places, eats cheese, grain and other seeds, and multiplies very rapidly. Mice have also been described as a "pain in the ass" to get rid of and as dirty animals that live off the garbage of others. Cats seem to be the primary enemy of the mouse with snakes rating a secondary enemy status. This description does not pertain to the image of Mickey. In the films of Mickey Mouse, "all conflict that the animal's real nature might have caused was resolved by an act of creative will: reality was simply ignored. Mickey was a clean mouse right from the start."[3]

The original image that was called "Mickey Mouse" flopped as a silent cartoon.[4] However, when the image began to speak, //Mickey Mouse// began to develop as a complex cultural unit.[5] As production of the cartoon that spoke and sounded continued, the character that had become //Mickey Mouse// changed by public demand from a violent, fun-loving character to a conservative, master of ceremonies. Even his size changed from a small scantily dressed critter to a human-like, large sized, well dressed individual. At one time during the production of the mouse cartoons, Mickey appeared without a tail.[6]

[1] Roland Barthes, "Myth Today," _Mythologies_, trans. Annette Lavers (London: Jonathan Cape, 1972), pp. 109-159.

[2] Christopher Finch, _The Art of Walt Disney: From Mickey Mouse to the Magic Kingdoms_ (New York: Harry N. Abrams, Inc., 1973), p. 50.

[3] Richard Shickel, _The Disney Version: The Life, Times, Art, and Commerce of Walt Disney_ (New York: Simon and Schuster, 1968), p. 95.

[4] Schickel, p. 88.

[5] Umberto Eco, _A Theory of Semiotics_ (Bloomington: Indiana University Press, 1976, 1979), p. xi I am following Umberto Eco's graphic conventions: // will note the cultural unit; / will denote the sign; and    will refer to the content unit.

[6] Irving Wallace, "Mickey Mouse and How He Grew," _Collier's_, 123, no. 15 (9 April 1949), p. 21.

The music that accompanied the mouse in the beginning was public property--
Turkey In The Straw.[7]  As the mouse grew in size and became more humanized, he
acquired his own song--Minnie's Yoo Hoo.[8]  The emphasis on Mickey as the star
changed in the cartoons.  Originally, Mickey dominated the films, but as he
progressed he functioned to introduce or act with another star, who then took
the emphasis away from Mickey.  In fact, even the shape of Mickey changed.
His eyes, hands, mouth and feet became larger, more noticeable and more expressive.  He became less circular and hose shaped and acquired a more human shape.[9]

Mickey's race is ambiguous because his body is black but his face is variously white, yellow, or red at differing stages in his career.  In his cartoons,
he acted as a member of every race, performing every job function, an Everyman
in mouse form.  Even his sexuality was ambiguous because of his high pitched
voice and sudden lack of interest in his female counterpart, Minnie Mouse.  Mickey
and Minnie had a purely platonic relationship which cooled as it progressed.
Each seemed to age to puberty but not much beyond.[10]

From the first cartoon produced, Plane Crazy, to the last, The Simple Things,
Mickey changed dramatically in appearance and in personality.[11]  His form, however, remained the same.  He was always recognized as //Mickey Mouse//.  His
films retained a morality that included protecting females, helping those in
need, doing one's duty without reward, and forgiving an enemy.  All of his
films were farcical, and often political and violent.  Each cartoon followed
in the same tradition as the previous one.  Mickey portrayed a system of values
with all of its ramifications.

## FILM IMAGE SIGNIFIED

The signified is the meaning of the actual film image of Mickey Mouse.
The signified refers to the purified essence of the yielding, shapeless, associations connected to the signifier.  The signified is at once historical
and intentional.  It is the motivation for the utterance.  The signified, unlike the signifier, is in no way abstract.  It is filled with the situation.

## MICKEY MOUSE AS MEANING--SIGNIFIED

Mickey Mouse is interpreted emotionally as a human-like, fun-loving
character actor.  His cartoons are expressed as films of which he is the star.
He is not an intellectual character, although he occasionally appears to think.
Mickey purified the essence of mouse into a cute, lovable, thoughtful creature.  This is not to say that mice have become desirable, but mice are less
desirable to obtain as the purified essence of the American way.  Mickey hid
the political, moral, and violent messages with a farcical, carefree overtone.
His image came to represent an obscure meaning constructed of shapeless yeild-
ing associations with good times, fun and folly.  Thus the cartoon image could
be applied to nearly anything without seeming out of character for Mickey.

---

[7]Finch, p. 70 cited in David Bain and Bruce Harris, ed., Mickey Mouse: Fifty Happy Years (New
York: Harmony Books, 1977), p. 13.

[8]by Carl Stalling of Walt Disney Productions cited in Finch, p. 70.

[9]"Mouse and Man," Time, 30, no 26 (27 December 1937), p. 29.

[10]Ariel Dorfman and Armand Mattelart, How To Read Donald Duck: Imperialist Ideology in the
Disney Comic, trans. David Kunzel (New York: International General, 1975), p. 16.

[11]For a list of films see Finch, Bain, and Leonard Maltin, The Disney Films (New York: Crown
Publishers, Inc., 1973).  A complete list is available from the author.

His image applied to a watch made by the Ingersoll Company saved the business from bankruptcy. After this occurrence, Mickey's image was desirable to the manufacturing world as a salable commodity. In this manner, Mickey came to mean good business. In fact, even in remote areas, Mickey was so recognizable that people refused to accept certain products unless his image was present on it. Certain constraints were placed upon what Mickey's image would and would not appear upon. This was done so that Mickey Mouse would never represent a negative experience in the use of a product. For example, he has never been placed on band-aids, weapons of any kind (unless you consider a squirt gun a weapon), medicine, drug paraphernalia or the like. Mickey has been used to promote all manner of positive experience toys, that is, toys that teach, encourage cleanliness or encourage healthy normal play (as in dolls, dishes, and games of various sorts). His image has also appeared upon Valentines, invitations, and some greeting cards.

Mickey Mouse belongs to everyone regardless of race or creed. Mickey has represented all races and has upheld the morality supported by most religions. His changeable form was always easily identified as Mickey Mouse. Even when the image was three dimensional, Mickey retained his meaning. His films always ended happily, supporting the belief that everything would work out all right if you try. Mickey is an emotional character in his films: he laughs, cries, worries, becomes angry, and is insulted, surprised, excited and frightened. He is shy and bold; he loves and hates; he is bored and capable of fantasy. He partakes in all human needs and desires including sleeping, eating, dreaming, and belonging. In his films he seems to be a real "person" rather than a simple fantasy.

## FILM IMAGE SIGN AND MYTH SIGNIFIER

The sign of the first system and the signifier of the second system results from the relationship between the signifier and the signified, which unites the concept of myth to its meaning. Thus the sign presents value, the meaning presents the form and the form outdistances the meaning. This is to say that the form is presented through the meaning as an incomplete translation and that the form communicates more fully than the meaning. The sign expresses the value of the communication of the form and the meaning.

The signifier of the MYTH system encompasses the value of the Film Image system. The signifier of the MYTH system relates a frozen image complete with a pre-existing values system. The MYTH system is amalagamated into the Film Image system in this manner.

## THE VALUE OF THE FROZEN IMAGE--SIGN AND SIGNIFIER

Even though the image of Mickey Mouse changes, the form of //Mickey Mouse// is frozen. It is recognized as the same because it is a message, a form . This message can be filled out in a variety of ways so long as the form is recognized as //Mickey Mouse//. //Mickey Mouse// is both the signifier and the signified because even though the appearance changes it is still recognized as //Mickey Mouse//. In other words, the sign as a form remains the same, even though it is expressed in different ways, the essential form remains constant. //Mickey Mouse// is an identifiable form even though the presentation varies.

Today, Mickey is rarely seen as a cartoon image or moving picture. His form as a frozen image is seen on cups, trains, pencils, placemats, seed (interesting that a mouse would advertize something a mouse would eat), and three dimensional dolls and toys. He rides on bicycles, flys on airplanes, rides on trains, and is invited to the White House. He even has his own private playgrounds. He has travelled around the world and although he is an American citizen, he speaks almost every language of the earth. He is one of the most seen, remembered, and versitile characters ever created. Today, Mickey almost never speaks, although some toys utilize his recorded voice. In all he is recognized as the one and only //Mickey Mouse//.

The image of Mickey Mouse is frozen at different stages of his career. Few of the toys, pictures, and dolls present the mouse as he originally appeared. The most popular form for Mickey is as he appeared on the Mickey Mouse Watch--complete with shoes, white gloves and tail. The image that includes Mickey in full dress (long pants, hat and tie) is usually reserved for pictures that appear on invitations, stickers, or for specific role/job functions.

## MYTH SIGNIFIED

The signified of the MYTH or second semiological system concerns the message as stolen and restored into a new meaning system. The frozen image of the signifier is stolen and restored into a new meaning context. The image restored is not the same as the image that is stolen. Thus a new relationship between the signifier and the signified develops as meta-communication about the first semiological system, Film Image. What is communicated as sign in the first system is recounted for a new analysis in the second system.

### Mickey Mouse Stolen And Restored--SIGNIFIED

The message as a cartoon image is frozen, stolen and restored for use in a nonmoving form. Even the forms that do move to some degree do not accurately represent the moving image in the complete state. The Mickey Mouse Watch had moving arms and hands but the head and body did not move. The watch did not accurately present Mickey in his original cartoon form as it included white gloved hands and shoes on his feet. The same idea was parodied through a Spiro Agnew watch in which the hands moved backwards. A recent cartoon character, named Snoopy, has also become a watch which is identical in form to the Mickey Mouse Watch with a different content.

Mickey Mouse as a name is also used to denote something other than the cartoon character. It is interesting to note that his name (if the name can be spoken of as his) is often applied to intellectually indulgent organizations such as the institutions of business, government, the armed forces, and education. In fact his image application (e.g., to university t-shirts) is nearly a statement of conclusion ("This university is Mickey Mouse"). The employment of the sign /Mickey Mouse/ allows itself to be identified with //Mickey Mouse//. //Mickey Mouse// (as a cultural unit) signifies a general connotation rather than a cartoon image.

Calling something Mickey Mouse seems to imply a negative judgement, although it is not exactly clear as to why it is negative. It is in the form of an elitist statement. The signifier of Mickey Mouse so dominates that the signified is obscured. What is stolen and frozen is the image as signifier. The meaning (signified) is still present but obscured. The signified is still present but obscured. The signified is distorted so as not to be clearly understandable. So the image from the cartoon is stolen, what is restored is myth.

## MYTH SIGN

The sign for the MYTH system pertains to depoliticized speech. The message as originally uttered is no longer in the same form of values system, rather it is within a new valuing system. The second form refers to the first as a meta-communication. Thus what is frozen and stolen is the film image and what is restored is myth. The sign consistently integrates the signifier and the signified in a purely signifying and a purely imagining consciousness.

### Mickey Mouse As Myth--SIGN

The equation of the image of Mickey Mouse and the term "Mickey Mouse" denotes that a meaning is connected to the image. When the image is applied to an intellectual organization (as in the university t-shirt) the organization seems to take on the meaning of the image/term Mickey Mouse. Mickey Mouse is a farce in that all of his films were farcical and relate to a political intent. Thus the application of the image of Mickey to an intellectual organization is a farce, with political intent.

Hitler attempted to expose and destroy this meaning of Mickey Mouse for his own ideological gains. He attempted to do this by reinstating Mickey as a mouse. His propagandist remarked that Mickey was "the most miserable ideal ever. . . mice are dirty."[12] This exposed the political function of Mickey Mouse as myth. The mouse cartoons were discontinued during the second world war, possibly for this reason. "Mickey Mouse" was used as the code word for the entire operation of D-Day.[13] Thus Mickey Mouse became a warmonger, fighting a battle in which he was never personally involved. Mickey was further condemned as displaying "the people of the capitalistic society under the masks of mice. . . . A definite social satire."[14]

Mickey hid the motives of the political capitalist behind a farcical mask. His innocent image is a powerhouse of meaning. The meaning has been acquired as the progression of the image infiltrated into the culture and language. Mickey is as commonplace as a mouse and as powerful as propaganda. Indeed, Mickey Mouse has become the icon of technological myth. He is an American telephone. The film image which spoke and gave us cultural norms now listens and accepts our personal values.

## CONCLUSION

Because of the disappearance of Mickey as a cartoon character and his simultaneous appearance as an image throughout culture, Mickey has become a myth in the same way Superman has become the ideal human image. Mickey is seen almost everywhere in some form of imagery development taken from his progression of films. It is strange to consider that Mickey never took a breath or walked down a street and yet is so will loved after fifty years. He has become incorporated into our language, culture and lifestyle. The reason he became such an influence and can seem so vital to us is because the cartoon image became a myth. Images of Mickey Mouse no longer refer to the cartoon image, but to the myth of Mickey Mouse.

---

[12]Schickel, p. 159.

[13]"Father Goose," *Time*, 64, no. 26 (27 December 1954), p. 45.

[14]Wallace, p. 36. Cf. Dorfman and Mattelart, p. 19.

# DISCUSSION / PHENOMENOLOGICAL RESEARCH INTO COMMUNICATION: POTENTIAL AND PITFALLS

MICHAEL MCGUIRE
UNIVERSITY OF GEORGIA

Phenomenology offers communication research neither an all-purpose, "cookie-cutter" methodology, nor a consistent set of perspectival assumptions reducible to one paradigm. However, phenomenological research does focus on a delimited substance. Whatever differences the papers in this volume reveal, they share a focus which admits into study questions about human consciousness, or experience, of reality. I believe this is an immensely fruitful focus, and perhaps the only meaningful focus for communication studies. But I harbor some doubts about phenomenological research being able to fulfill its potential, and I want to approach the question of potential by considering how to eliminate these doubts.

An attack on empirical behaviorism lurks in the background of much phenomenological research, and is directly launched in the rest. This attack I regard as a symptom of weakness or confusion. Phenomenology must offer communication theory, not pat answers, but new problems; simply to dismiss empirical methods or findings seems not only uncalled for, but unlikely to advance research. If this attack becomes generalized into an anti-science attitude, relevant research in anthropology, genetics, linguistics, psychology, and other fields may be overlooked to the detriment of communication theory's development. In general we should prefer simple, clear explanations to elaborate obfuscation, and some very powerful explanations of human phenomena are to be found in these other sciences. To ignore them may lead to the reinvention of a wheel which is not even round. Moreover, at the risk of losing any friends I may have left, I hold that phenomenology is inceptionally scientific, and that an anti-science attitude is therefore incompatible with phenomenology. Such an attitude does every phenomenologist a particular disservice when the attack is against an outdated, nineteenth century notion of science, as some have been.

A final pitfall to point out here is the marked possibility for, or susceptibility of, phenomenology to become another realm of nuances expressed in a nuclear language inaccessible to most researchers, and thus unable to fulfill its potential to contribute to communication theory. Perhaps phenomenologists have, as Sigmund Koch suggested once, not only a high tolerance but a positive appetite for the opaque. The firm ground of common language may be only a mask for underlying disagreements or misunderstandings. This problem is not ours alone. Merleau-Ponty's Phenomenology of Perception opens: "What is phenomenology? It may seem strange that this question has still to be asked half a century after the first works of Husserl. The fact remains that it has by no means been answered." Merleau-Ponty overlooks, as do most contemporary phenomenologists writing in France or the United States, the obscure philosopher Hegel's Phenomenology in favor of newer and less German writings. But this further illustrates the significance of the problems confronting phenomenologists in dealing, not only with the uninitiated, but with one another.

Phenomenology in Rhetoric and Communication, ed. Stanley Deetz. Copyright, 1981, The Center for Advanced Research in Phenomenology and the University Press of America.

Now, if phenomenologists can restrain their zeal well enough to accept their own limits and the contributions of other researchers, and to write for the whole field, not just each other, there seems to be tremendous potential for revising many of our theories importantly. How radical a revision this may be, and the direction it may take, will depend largely upon our choices of "authorities" to follow. I believe that the papers collected here abundantly illustrate this point, and I want to elaborate on the issues at stake here.

As I see it, three key issues or topics underlie not only the papers of Mr. Lee, Mr. Kennan, Ms. Trueblood, and Mr. Doyle, but almost all of the papers collected here. First, there is a concern to analyze and explain language and other symbol systems as operations <u>on</u> and <u>of</u> human consciousness. Second, I find the recurrent concept of "social reality" and, even more, so-called "social knowledge," used operationally in phenomenological accounts. Finally, and less noticeably, I think one finds a preference for "rules" over "laws" hiding in the background of papers here. These themes may be considered in turn.

I believe that the scientific study of language and other symbol systems is the very core of our discipline, or, if it is not, should be. Both Mr. Doyle and Mr. Lee are studying language explicitly, though to very different ends and with very different methods. Doyle's paper, which very adeptly pulls tree diagrams out of a variety of language sentences, undertakes establishing the relevance of deep structure analysis to the general criticism of communication. This may be an important possibility, but, if I may offer a value judgment, it is not at all important if it is conducted only at the level of the language sentence. That task linguistics has performed better than we ever will. But to do likewise for an entire discourse or interaction, to follow the lead of structuralist critics, does strike me as a most important direction in which to move the field. And in Mr. Lee's paper I find, I think, an attempt to undertake an explication of the language not of sentences, nor even of a discourse, but of an entire ideological movement. But it is hard to see through the bedfellows Pocock, Searle and Fromm to arrive at the analysis Ron offers. Whereas Doyle's analysis turns inward to the structure of sentences, Lee's turns outward to the functions of language. Yet both papers are trying to look at the ability of <u>parole</u>, speaking, even when in violation of <u>langue</u>, language, to establish and structure the social world.

At this point Ms. Trueblood's paper joins them both. Brenda's application of semiotics to the symbolic universe of Mickey Mouse is working in its own way on the construction of some symbolic or social reality which sometimes is shaped by and other times shapes our communication. I regard her use of the term "myth" to be in error, but I'm picky about that. Her analysis of the semiotic system of Mickey Mouse is interesting in itself, and hers is one of the most focused critical pieces here. Moreover, she blends the looking inward and looking outward which keep the first two mentioned pieces apart. Now, she does not address directly the issue of social knowledge or social reality, but she establishes Mickey's role there very well. Mr. Kennan's paper abruptly fits in right here: he has touched upon an issue so important I feel bad restating it here without his entire paper. That which passes itself off as reality is in a state of very dynamic ongoing Creation during an intercultural communication. The reality which is social--and to this we must nastily return below--clearly cannot transcend cultural borders <u>if</u> it <u>is</u> social, so we have in intercultural communication the situation for our observation in which people are struggling hard to synthesize reality for the moment. What a fascinating possible object for our study!

But we shall make no progress if the sloppy repetition of now too-widely accepted vocabulary merely continues. Terms like "social reality" and "social knowledge" have no meaning unless they contrast specifically along clarified dimensions with other-than-social knowledge and reality. We should aim this criticism where it belongs: our authors are following a dangerously nebulous trend established by authors in our journals carelessly using the terms "social knowledge" and "social reality." Essays in these areas may be very exciting and interesting--perhaps all the more so <u>because</u> they fail to trap themselves in specificity's or precision's web--but diletantism makes a weak basis for theory, and it is now incumbent upon those who champion this vocabulary to make it meaningful. Otherwise, fifty years from now the rest of us, those with simple appetites and vocabularies, will find ourselves rephrasing Merleau-Ponty pondering why Husserl is unclear. The answer is the writing. What <u>is</u> social knowledge/reality? Today it is something badly in need of theoretically adequate definition.

Here again come a potential and pitfall mixed together. In the papers of Doyle, Lee, Kennan, and Trueblood the word or notion "law" is absent, and, at least in the essays by Doyle, Kennan and Lee, one finds instead the notion of "rules" waiting its turn in the background. "And anyone who hears nothing but the will to truth," to paraphrase Nietzsche, "does not have the best of ears!" Here, too, the blame does not fully belong to our authors. The popularity of so-called "rules theory" to fill in gaps to give vague answers where specific questions are needed, is partly a function of current trends of journal publication. Fortunately, the "rules" issue may be addressed here without the intervention of a rules theorist. Speaking from my perspective as a structuralist, I regard rules theory as fundamentally wrong. These theorists attempt to argue that there can be no laws where human behavior and consciousness are concerned. That argument cannot be supported without an approach similar to that of the attack on a concept of science which no scientist holds (a straw man). Here, the mistake consists in linking law to behaviorism as though anyone willing to talk of laws must be a Watsonian or Pavlovian monster. I would suggest that at the very outset, human communication behavior is governed by a law, to wit, that all human beings acquire language. (Had we adequate space, the "exceptions" to the law could be explained by gene damage or brain damage research; the case has been proved if people will but consider it.) Mr. Doyle's paper may be taken as an argument for the existence of other laws in the sphere of language--laws about how language has meaning. Mr. Kennan's paper, as I pointed out at the conference, could open the door to another area in which certain laws operate. To reformulate his question, "Are there laws governing the invention of communication 'rules' when two persons become conscious that they are communicating across cultural barriers?" I believe there are such laws, though I will defer to Kennan to find them. As for Mr. Lee's paper, it may be that laws limit the ability of language to construct reality; such laws would elaborate what facts other than communication are of importance equal to or greater than language in this specific context. Ms. Trueblood's paper relies on Barthes's scientifically oriented semiology as presented in <u>Mythologies</u>, and may be said to offer us an application of Barthes's law of the so-called mythical signification system, a law which establishes a difference of kind between signifying systems. No researcher should be embarrassed to speak of laws which yet admit exceptions: geneticists can use their laws to structure life, but genetic mutation--the breaking of laws--continues to operate outside of the predictions of genetic laws. Few competent scientists, however, would therefore urge a rules perspective for genetics.

The discussion of these and all the papers at the seminar left me feeling I was being treated to a glimpse of our field's future. Phenomenological research on speech communication is well out of the stage of hiding on the backstreets in the darkness on the edge of town. By asking some new and important questions about the jungleland of conscious experience, phenomenologists within our field have much to contribute to our appreciation and understanding of that which communicates. Abandoning the categories of studying communication used

by other approaches may lead to an assessment of how our known world is constructed which has the value of beginning at the end point--people's phenomenal
worlds--instead of with arbitrarily presupposed beginnings which one reasons
"should" be sources of influence.  I, for one, would welcome such rethinking.

(Ed. note:  Doyle's paper was not included in this volume.)

DAVID BRANCO
NORTHERN ILLINOIS UNIVERSITY

Maurice Natanson's introduction to the first volume of Alfred Schutz's
Collected Papers points out that "the fil conducteur" of Schutz's intellectual
life was "a concern for the meaningful structure of the world of daily life,
the everyday working world into which each of us is born, within whose limits
our existence unfolds, and which we transcend only in death."[1]  Natanson also
noted that Schutz took as his "central task" the "realization of a philosophy
of mundane reality, or, in more formal language, of a phenomenology of the
natural attitude."[2] · This natural attitude is, according to Natanson, the foundation of "the taken for granted everyday world of living and working," a world
which is "the nuclear presupposition of all other strata of man's reality."[3]
Finally, the natural attitude means that "the essential foundation of mundane
existence remains unrecognized by common-sense men whose lives are nevertheless
structured and built upon the matrix of daily life."[4]  [italics mine]

This paper begins from the premise that there is substantial potential for
confusion and convolution among a number of these world/life/reality terms and
concepts that Natanson notes from Schutz.  For example:  "the world of daily
life," "the everyday world," "mundane reality," "the taken for granted everyday world," and "the matrix of daily life" all also are intimated as equivalent,
at least by implication.  This paper argues that this state of affairs is an
issue for phenomenological analysis, and one that is not well clarified by
Schutz's terms (via his "kind of a junior author,"[5] Thomas Luckmann) in The
Structures of the Life-World, the book considered the exemplification of
Schutz's opus.  In this book the emphasis is on the term "the everyday life-
world," whose "unexamined ground" equates with the natural attitude.  Schutz
explains that:

> The everyday life-world is the region of reality in which man can engage
> himself and which he can change while he operates in it by means of his
> animate organism.  At the same time, the objectivities and events which
> are already found in this realm (including the acts and the results of
> actions of other men) limit his free possibilities of action.  They place
> him up against obstacles that can be surmounted, as well as barriers that
> are insurmountable.  Furthermore, only within this realm can one be under-
> stood by his fellow-men, and only in it can he work together with them.

Phenomenology in Rhetoric and Communication, ed. Stanley Deetz.  Copyright, 1981.  The Center
for Advanced Research in Phenomenology and the University Press of America.

[1] Alfred Schutz, Collected Papers, Vol. I: The Problem of Social Reality." Ed. and intro. by
Maurice Natanson (The Hague: Martinus Mijhoff, 1962), p. xxv.

[2] Schutz, p. xxv.

[3] Schutz, p. xxvi.

[4] Schutz, p. xxv.

[5] Alfred Schutz and Thomas Luckmann, The Structures of the Everyday Life-World.  Trans. by
Richard M. Zaner and H. Tristam Engelhardt, Jr.  (Evanston: Northwestern University Press, 1973),
p. xxvii.

Only in the world of everyday life can a common, communicative surrounding world be constituted. The world of everyday life is consequently man's fundamental and paramount reality.

By the everyday life-world is to be understood that province of reality which the wide-awake and normal adult simply takes for granted in the attitude of common sense. By this taken-for-grantedness, we designate everything which we experience as unquestionable: every state of affairs is for us unproblematic until further notice.[6]

Now, if the "everyday life-world" is meant to subsume the terms Natanson earlier had ascribed to the sphere of Schutz's primary conceptual concern--as Luckmann alleges it is[7]--then it too is open to some confusion. That this is so is verified not only by Schutz's admission of the chance of "further notice," but also by his description of the "stock of knowledge" that is said to "guide" persons in the everyday life-world.[8] For example, a stock of knowledge is "opaque" and, among other things, includes "gaps," and allows for "problematic matters.[9] "Routine" explications of socially transmitted (and habitualized) "recipes" provide directions for the individual's operating in the face of such problematic matters. As Schutz says, there is a "pragmatic motive" that makes daily life [emphasis mine] practicable-goal-minded and motivated. Now, not only does Schutz find it necessary to admit of the everyday life-world that it has "gaps" and that its pragmatic motivation pertains specifically to "daily life," but also he later attempts to explicate life-world "stratifications" in the forms of "provinces of reality," of "zones of operation," and of "temporal arrangement."[10] Later, Schutz also works to distinguish among "horizons" within which the individual can operate in the life-world,[11] and to distinguish between "typical" and "atypical" kinds of experience.[12]

In the Preface to The Structures of the Life-World, Luckmann admits that the circumstances of Schutz's death required that Luckmann had to revise and rework the originally proposed organizational structure of the book. Perhaps this is pertinent to the project this paper intends to proceed with. It may be that Luckmann has assumed, for example, that the various distinguishings within Schutz's characterization of the everyday life-world presume foreknowledge of and are codetermined by the distinctions Schutz earlier had made regarding "multiple realities." For instance, Schutz noted in his 1945 essay, "On Multiple Realities," that "there are several, probably an infinite number of various orders of realities, each with its own special and separate style of existence."[13] In that essay Schutz painted pictures of five particular orders of reality; and, significant to this paper, he noted that:

All these worlds--the world of dreams, of imageries and phantasms, especially the world of art, the world of religious experience, the world of scientific contemplation . . . and the world of the insane--are finite provinces of meaning. . . . This finiteness implies that there is no possibility of referring one of these provinces to the other by introducing a formula of transformation.[14]

But the explication of these worlds of reality appears neither completed nor related to the everyday life-world by Schutz. It is this sort of radical analysis towards which this paper attends itself.

---

[6]Schutz and Luckman, pp. 3-4.

[7]Schutz and Luckman, p. xiii.

[8]See, especially, Schutz and Luckman, pp. 15-17.

[9]Schutz and Luckman, p. 15.

[10]Schutz and Luckman, pp. 28-53.

[11]Schutz and Luckman, pp. 137-40.

[12]Schutz and Luckman, pp. 235-41.

[13]In Schutz, Collected Papers, Vol. I., p. 207.

[14]Schutz, p. 232.

Specifically, the project assumed here is an attempt to begin to delineate "levels," or "arenas," or categorizations, for and of the everyday life-world. This categorization is founded on the phenomenological opus Schutz has provided, but it also takes a sociological turn that Schutz evidently never came to authorize. This does not mean, of course, that this paper will pretend to provide a sociological-theoretical analysis or critique of Schutz's work, a task assumed by far more able scholars to varying degrees of success.[15] What is contended here is only that there is easy opportunity to convolve the elements of Schutz's everyday life-world; what is attempted here is a categorization of those elements--largely rhetorically considered and perhaps only idiosyncratically seen--into sociologically grounded levels.

Taking the contemporary sociological notion of "everyday life"--particularly as it is conceived dramaturgically by Erving Goffman[16]--as grounding and starting point, this paper argues for a notion of a phenomenological life-world that, "experientially oriented, is divided into four levels or arenas:  (A) "daily life;" (B) "everyday life;" (C) "anyday life;" and (D) "someday life." Except for level (B)--"everyday life"--none of these seems to have earned substantial exposition or explication by scholars of any kind, including sociologists.[17] But such a categorization does seem to make pertinent distinctions within the Schutzian usage of "everyday life-world:" (A) "daily life" and (B) "everyday life" at least are terms Schutz uses outright; (C) "anyday life" seems at least to correspond closely with Schutz's notions of "gaps" in stocks of knowledge and with the idea of "further notice;" and (D) "someday life" at least seems to correspond well with both ideas of further notice and of "obstacles that can be surmounted, as well as barriers that are insurmountable."

These four levels will be distinguished from each other in five areas of "artistic" (not statistical, certainly) "Factor analysis" (see Appendix, Tables I-V):  in terms of their "occurrence," their "experiential" nature, the nature of their "horizons," their appropriate "perspectival (methodological) bearing, and their comparative "communicational" elements.[18]  It can be assumed--as it

---

[15]See, for instance and especially, Nathaniel Lawrence and Daniel O'Connor, eds. Readings in Existential Phenomenology (Englewood Cliffs, N.J.: Prentice-Hall, Inc., 1967); Jack D. Douglas and John M. Johnson, eds., Existential Sociology (Cambridge, Eng.: Cambridge University Press, 1977); George Psathas, ed., Phenomenological Sociology: Issues and Applications (New York: John Wiley and Sons, 1973); Maurice Natanson, Phenomenology, Role, and Reason (Springfield, Ill.: Luckman, The Social Construction of Reality: A Treatise in the Sociology of Knowledge (Garden City, N.J.: Doubleday Anchor Books, 1967).

[16]The dramaturgical perspective is perhaps particularly relevant as a starting point in light of Schutz's characterization of the everyday life-world as the world of "working" as well as living, and as the "everyday working world." The Greek ourgos base for "dramaturgy" refers to the etymological base of "work." And, as Smart notes, it is "indeed likely that the everyday life-world will constitute the primary province of meaning, from which other finite provinces of meaning may appear only to be quasi-realities, /and/ it is also the case that from the perspective of the world of science the everyday life-world at times appears to be only a quasi-reality." See Barry Smart, Sociology, Phenomenology and Marxian Analysis: A Critical Discussion of the Theory and Practice of a Science of Society. (London: Routledge and Kegan Paul, 1976), p. 98. The dramaturgical perspective is derived primarily from Erving Goffman, The Presentation of Self in Everyday Life (Garden City, N.J.: Anchor Books, 1959); Encounters: Two Studies in the Sociology of Interaction (Indianapolis: Bobbs-Merrill Co., Inc., 1961); Interaction Ritual: Essays on Face-to-Face Behavior (Garden City, N.J.: Anchor Books, 1967); Relations in Public: Micro-studies of the Public Order (New York: Harper Colophon Books, 1971); and Strategic Interaction (Philadelphia: University of Pennsylvania Press, 1969).

[17]There are, of course, numerous attempts to investigate the psychological manifestations of lived-experience levels of the levels dealt with in this paper, but sociological treatises of this type do not, when they approach the issue at all, integrate various levels of lived-experience with the phenomenological notion of the everyday life-world. And, of course, philosophers often have waxed rubically about what here is termed "someday life."

[18]As a prolegomenon, this paper only partially pretends to begin to explicate in its fifth factor (Table V) a "communicational" exegis of the sort evidently prospective in the collaborative work of Schutz and Luckmann, about which the latter reports that a volume to follow The Structures will include "two chapters on social action and on signs, symbols, and communication." Schutz and Luckman, p. xx.

will be shown--that the four levels generally are characterizable--in phenom-
enological/existential, or "experiential," terms, that is--as lesseningly taken-
for-granted and increasingly atypical in their elements and within factor lines,
as one moves from the daily, through the everyday, through the anyday, to the
someday life-levels.

It must be emphasized somewhat fervently that many of the distinctions
within the systematization developed here are somewhat gross--there are profuse cases, of course, of nuances between and among the life-levels, within
many of the factors considered. Also, it must further--and perhaps even more
fervently--be emphasized that the systematization proffered here is, only, a
prolegomenon--and one succinct and perhaps too succinct--a potential and plausible starting point for such an endeavor.

The experiential perspective employed in this paper refers to the individual's cognitive or mental habitation at a, or any, given moment in the course
of the subjective experience of his life. This may be a somewhat awkward usage
or phrasing, but such a determination and predisposition are needed for any
adequate understanding of the usages of other phrasing that will occur frequently in the following text--such as, "world," "realm," "meaning," and others
that may soon become apparent to the reader.

## "LIFE-WORLD" LEVELS

### Daily Life[19]

This is the part of the experienced life-world habituel, or d'ordinaire--
the dramaturgical "daily round," and only such. It is the exemplar of Schutz's
ideas of taken-for-grantedness and of typicality. It comprises an almost mechanistic state-of-being, of consciousness, in which the individual can be
viewed essentially as a body-in-activity, present in the life-world in no re-
markable sense and going about fulfilling scheduled, impersonal matters on a
redundant, coincidental round. This level, idealized, can be termed the traffic
model, wherein the individual follows the "dotted line" or the "bouncing ball,"
and wherein he is cottled in a world he is imposed in and imposed on--he trods
among the horde, acting within a realm of persistent recurrence. This level is
most generously "explained" by the ethnomethodological model--straightforward
behaviorism is perhaps more appropriate, however--in which the individual, al-
lowed only to (only) describe his activity, would be able only to give reports
of events relatively equivalent to other events enacted in essentially similar
manner at some programmatically previous time. This level is spawned by the
prevailing economic institutional structure, and the individual thereby operates primarily according to the first two strata in Maslow's "prepotent hierarchy
of needs"[20]--the physiological and safety strata. Events are happenchancely
received or perceived, and there are clear-cut recipes for determining actions.
The individual communicationally only exudes a sense of his "self" by his biological or bio-social presence, which with his " contemporaries"[21] is limited
to a "trusting"[22]state of meaningfulness and mutuality and which, rhetorically,
amounts only to profuse mutual presence. "Linguistically," the level's upper
analytic limit is primarily "phonetic"--its discursive exemplification lies in
the form of chatter, prattle, twaddle, and the like. Statistically or numer-
ically speaking, this perhaps is the predominant sphere of events in the life-
world.

[20]Abraham Maslow, *Motivation and Personality* (New York: Harper, 1954). See Chapter 5,
especially.

[21]This, of course, is the Schutzian use of the term--as are the others within the factor. See
Schutz and Luckmann, pp. 68-92.

[22]See Huston Smith, *Condemned to Meaning*. Foreword by Arthur G. Wirth (New York: Harper and
Row, 1965).

Everyday Life
    This is the part of the life-world determinatif. It is most appropriately
viewed from the dramaturgical sociological model, wherein experience is primarily composed by and for the individual, who conscribes to ideologically grounded
rules of conduct via (moral) expectations and obligations. It is the "working"
model of business and ritual-participation, in which the individual travails in
teams of consociates, all of whom likewise are best pictured in terms of dramaturgical "roles" or "personalities or "identities." Individuals paradoxically
operate collusively in terms of (generally personal and pragmatic) expedience
and calculation to achieve (Maslow's) "Belongingness" and "love" needs. This
is the realm of Endeavor (Smith), wherein the individual can be characterized
as operating along a presumably unending horizontal line into the future, in a
pervasively perceived, yet tentative and fragile, sense of the present. It also
is the realm of action, in which events occur in a sense of incidence and thor-
oughness--thus it is, in its evident whelmingness, "paramount" in being linguistically envisioned as syntactical-structural. Communicationally, the individual
expresses or presents his "self" in interpersonal situations of mutual co-pres-
ence that suffer disruption or maintenance via (social) interactional contingencies. Rhetorically, collusive participation is the primary arena, and, thus,
locutions are exemplified in forms such as jargon and circumlocution. Events
occur--are expected and obliged to do so--as they "should." In terms of human
energy consumption, this surely is the predominant realm of experience in the
life-world.

Anyday Life
    This is the life-level esperance, or echapée. It is the realm of personal
contingency wherein the individual (at least potentially) can traipse within
a motile and future-conditional world supposed by and for him. Geometrically
described, it follows an angular "line" of extrication--of change or outlet,
rejuvenation or provocation--and of departure from everyday "rules." It is
the world of self-conception, of release, of potentiality, and of expectancy
and batedness. It is illusory (in its "eventual" achievement it is itself consumed or destroyed), constituted of Hope and aiming in anxious anticipation
(always as long as it maintained) at esteem. It is grounded on cultural terms
which allow for "novel" occurrence; and it is best viewed, therefore, from a
social-psychological perspective. This level is comprised of events or experiences which the individual inscribes into the life-world--they are thus dramatic and temporary and, in a sense, their possibility of actualization is
predetermined by one's "predecessors." Events or experiences "could" or "might"
occur, in this life-level--it is an area of incipience, of (potential) exigence.
Communicationally, the individual conceives or perceives a potential "self,"
one he assigns to himself in a sphere of exclusion (from the more "typical"
life-levels). Relationally, or intersubjectively, this is the purely personal
realm, in which boasts, daydream narratives, and the like (expressed aloud or
not) comprise the exemplification of the locutional factor. This also is the
area of "semantic" linguistic representation--where fundamental, bottom-line
appresentations of meaning are located. In terms of artistic or creative cog-
nition, this probably is the predominant life-level; in terms of diffuseness,
via the inviolability of our minds insofar as it yet exists, this probably
more-than-probably is the predominant realm.

Someday Life
    This is the life-level terme, or conclure, or inevitable. Geometrically
pictured, it is a vertical line separating everyday horizontal lines from unknown markers. It is comprised of events that will, or at least very likely
will, occur at sometime--manifestations of events or experiences of which it
is composed include, ultimately, those such as death, insanity, enlightenment,
or other forms of expiation, all of them matters of singular incurrence. This

realm is bound to "necessary" contingencies.  Its arena of awareness is psycho-philosophical or, perhaps more appropriately, metaphysical.  It institutionally is maintained within and by the mythological sphere to which the individual ascribes himself; thus, intersubjectively it is logically non-regulative, it relates the individual to the world of his "successors," and it is primarily achieved in contemplation, or meditation, or intuition.  It is a world in the present, but of the future; thus, it is experienced either as momentariness or as permanence.  The realm of imminence, it (ideally) is approached and encoun-tered with reticence:  communicationally, the individual seeks or encounters the Self, and rhetorically he pronounces resignation or designation in and of his seclusion.  Locutionally, this realm of the "lost" into which the individual trips is exemplified by non-verbality or silence or, perhaps, prayer; it is the intrapersonal realm of contemplation, apprehension, or reckoning in the face of Trouble and/or Mystery, and towards the aim of fulfilled self-actualization. The world of imminence, in and through which the individual is disposed, it is most appropriately studied from the dramatistic perspective.[23]  In this level, the individual thoroughly or completely alludes to his mutable Self and accepts its elimination from the other life-levels, so that a "syntacticsemantic" lin-guistic apprgsentation--realization or recognition of the Ineffable--results in resignation.[24]

## CONCLUSION

Obviously, this paper has assumed a too-ambitious task.  The caution that it has been intended only as a prolegomenon to a further-elaborated project cannot be over-emphasized.  But, as a beginning, it does intend to explore and expose fruitful grounds for further explication.  These grounds cannot be in-dicated solely by the text of this paper--the appended tables are meant more as explicative than as supplemental to the text.[25]  In their explicative func-tion, the tables are more likely to help show the distinctions made, hopefully, between and among the various levels, than they are to characterize very fully any given level.  Unfortunately, a delineation of the "natures" of the factor-areas each table means to represent is beyond the limits of this paper, and must remain somewhat vague:  hopefully, readers can glean some intuitive under-standing of the factor areas from the collection of factors within them.  This paper obviously cannot be a "factor analysis" of the everyday life-world.

This paper also is not intended as an "article of faith."  Though the text's succinctness amounts to something of an inadequacy for such a project, the paper as-a-whole is meant to stand as a substantial beginning towards what is con-tended to be a readily available exposition and explication of the evident short-comings of the phenomenological notion of an everyday life-world.

[23]Perhaps one illustrative sense of this approach is expressed by Kenneth Burke in an attempt to clarify what he means by the "principle of oxymoron."  For instance, he says: "The sublime resides in moral and intellectual 'immenisities.'  And even when the sublimities are represented by physical objects, like plains, sea, sky, and mountains, they are 'moral' because the contrast between us and their might and proportion is forcefully hierarchic.  Next, insofar as sensory order and social order affect each other, awed and delighted identification with physical power can call forth a transcendent feeling of personal freedom.  That is, by the paradox of substance, one can imaginatively identify oneself with the mountain's massive assertiveness while at the same time thinking of one's comparative futility."  Kenneth Burke, *A Rhetoric of Motives* (Berkeley: University of California Press, 1969), p. 325.

[24]Perhaps I. A. Richards, *Practical Criticism: A Study of Literary Judgment* (New York: Harcourt, Brace and World, Inc., 1929), p. 273, best makes this clear: "Such are the feelings that may be aroused by contemplation of the following:
  i.   Man's loneliness (the isolation of the human situation).
  ii.  The facts of birth, and of death, in their inexplicable oddity.
  iii. The inconceivable immensity of the Universe.
  iv.  Man's place in the perspective of time.
  v.   The enormity of his ignorance."

| LEVEL | DAILY | EVERYDAY | ANYDAY | SOMEDAY |
|---|---|---|---|---|
| **FACTOR** | | | | |
| Ordinary-language terms of expression | X "did" (today as it did yesterday, or last week/year . . .) occur. . . | X "does" (as it's supposed to/should) occur. . . | X "could" (or might/may) occur (sometime). . . | X "will" or very likely will, at least, occur some-time |
| Regularity | persistent recurrence | pervasive occurrence | novel occurrence | singular incurrence |
| "Temporal" nature | redundance | thoroughness | temporariness | momentariness, or permanence |
| Relative temporal relevance | coincidence | incidence | exigence | reticence |
| Atypicality/Startlingness | activity | action | incipience | imminence |

TABLE I

NATURE OF <u>OCCURRENCE</u> AMONG "LEVELS" OF EVERYDAY LIFE-WORLD

| LEVEL<br>FACTOR | DAILY | EVERYDAY | ANYDAY | SOMEDAY |
|---|---|---|---|---|
| Self-Objectifi-cation | bodies | roles, personalities, identities | self-concept(ions) | self (mutability) |
| Mutuality | presence (assumed, given) | co-presence (pre-sumed) | release, "vacation" (allowed for) | elimination (accepted) |
| "Sense" of Action | unremarkableness | expectation-and-obligation | potentiality | inevitability, eventuality |
| Operational Activ-ity, nature of | scheduling, organiz-ing . . . | expedience, calcu-lation, prospects | expectancy, bated-ness | contemplation, apprehension, reckoning . . . |
| Emotive immediacy | (routine/oblivious) happen chance | (prevasive-moral) expectation | (anxious) antici-pation | resignation |
| "Play" form (self-others) | delusion | collusion | illusion | allusion |
| Maslow's "prepotent hierarchy of needs | (1) physiological, and (2) safety | (3) belongingness/love | (4) esteem | (5) self-actu-alization |
| Smith's "categories of meaning" | (D) Trust | (C) Endeavor | (B) Hope | (A) Trouble, and (E) Mystery |

TABLE II

NATURE OF "EXPERIENTIAL" FACTORS AMONG "LEVELS" OF EVERYDAY LIFE-WORLD

| LEVEL FACTOR | DAILY | EVERYDAY | ANYDAY | SOMEDAY |
|---|---|---|---|---|
| "Existential" manifestations, illustrations | following "dotted line" or "bouncing ball;" traffic . . . | work; business; projects; ritual-participation . . . | extrication (change or outlet); rejuvenation/ provocation . . . | death/insanity/ enlightenment-satori/ expiation . . . |
| Degrees/types of Contingency | routine (unobjectionable) contingencies | (social) interactional contingencies | potential (personal) contingencies | necessary contingencies |
| "Step/style" re: Membership | trods (among) horde | travails (in) team(s) | traipses (as) individual | trips (collapses) (into/onto) "lost" |
| Self:Others (Schutz) | contemporaries | consociates | predecessors | successors |
| Intersubjective "Logistics" | traffic | moral expectations and obligations | personal "motility" | contemplation, intuition, meditation |
| "Geometric-- spatial/temporal-form" | "round"/ circular | horizontal "line" | angular/ oblique)-acute) | vertical "line" separating horizontal line from unknown markers |
| Tensiveness | past in present (and future?) | pervasive (and tentative/fragile) present | future conditional (in present) | future-present (?) |

TABLE III

NATURE OF "HORIZONS" AMONG "LEVELS" OF EVERYDAY-LIFE-WORLD

| LEVEL<br>FACTOR | DAILY | EVERYDAY | ANYDAY | SOMEDAY |
|---|---|---|---|---|
| (Phenomeno-logical) Realms of awareness | biological/bio-social | sociological | social-psychological | psycho-philosophical/metaphysical |
| Appropriate "model" of study/analysis | behavioral-ethno-methodological | dramaturgical | dramatic | dramatistic |
| Selves: Life-world | imposed on and in . . . | composed by and for . . . | supposed by and for | disposed in and through |
| "intersubjective logic" | recipes | rules | exceptions to rules | non-regulative |
| Institutional-ity (enforcement, maintenance...) | economic | ideological | cultural | mythological |
| Self-World Notational Scheme | description | conscription | inscription | ascription |

TABLE IV

NATURE OF "PERSPECTIVITIES" AMONG "LEVELS" OF EVERYDAY LIFE-WORLD

| LEVEL / FACTOR | DAILY | EVERYDAY | ANYDAY | SOMEDAY |
|---|---|---|---|---|
| Individual Communicationally | exudes "self" | expresses-presents (social) "self" | conceives/perceives (potential) "self" | seeks/encounters Self |
| Rhetorically, "self" exhibits (actively and/or passively)... | presence in profusion | participation in collusion | assignation in exclusion | resignation (or designation) in seclusion |
| Locutional illustration-exemplification | chatter, prattle, twaddle . . . | jargon, circumlocution . . . | boasts, daydream narratives | non-verbal/silence; or some prayer . . . |
| Linguistic appresentation | phonetic level | syntactic (structural) level | semantic (effability) component | syntactic-semantic (re: ineffability) sphere |
| Relationality | impersonal | interpersonal | personal | intrapersonal |

TABLE V

NATURE OF <u>COMMUNICATIONAL</u> ELEMENTS AMONG "LEVELS" OF EVERYDAY LIFE-WORLD

MICHAEL PRESNELL
SOUTHERN ILLINOIS UNIVERSITY

Derrida points out that the history of Western civilization has been dominated by the metaphysical notion of being as a presence. Pure being is a perfectly present being. The idea, taken as perfectly present to consciousness, is
the perfect example of the Western metaphysical tendency. The idea as expressed
risks becoming defiled being, a being which is no longer perfectly present but
which is mediated through a communicative act.

Husserl claimed that there are two kinds of signs: an indicative sign
which has a communicative function, and an expressive sign which is always involved in an indicative sign, but which may exist by itself in "solitary mental
life." Consciousness, for Husserl, does not communicate to itself, and therefore need not involve itself in indicative signs. Expressive signs are irreducible to communicative interaction and hence serve as an irreducible foundation of meaning.

Derrida locates Husserl in the classical Western metaphysical tradition.
If consciousness is transparently present to itself as pure expression, consciousness is pure being. Expression as the irreducible foundation of meaning
hides nothing from consciousness.

For this classical metaphysical position to maintain the notion of consciousness as being and posit pure being as communicatable, a medium of expression which is simultaneous and absolutely proximate with being must be
assumed. This medium is the voice. The voice and the spoken thought have been
held to be the synthesis of being and being's expression. Thought is immediately present to itself in speaking. Phonetic writing carries on this tradition
by re-presenting the voice, hence uniting the voice and the concept in a materiality which is the sign of a sign of pure being. The voice as the sign of
pure being thus rests in the center of meaning, an absolute presence. Thus
Western culture has been phonocentric, i.e., taking the voice as being's pure
expression. The intuitive presence of being in the voice dominates any indication of being in writing. Writing is a presence which is merely indicated,
that is, an absent presence. The life of being is itself absent and writing
needs to be spoken to revitalize it. Writing thus takes on the significance
of the murder of life, the killing of spirit. Writing indicates death as the
absence of life, the absence of the voice.

Saussure suggested that, instead of positing a sign as one undifferentiated
whole, the sign be considered composed of two inseparable but distinguishable
elements: the signifier and the signified. He defines the signifier as the
sound-image and the signified as a concept. From the point of view of phonocentric culture, the signifier as the indicative function is constantly being
repressed, since the more transparent it becomes the more the concept is revealed in its purity. The signifier stands as the body of the sign and the
signified part as its spirit. Body/mind, object/subject, ontology/epistemology

Phenomenology in Rhetoric and Communication, ed. Stanley Deetz. Copyright, 1981. The Center
for Advanced Research in Phenomenology and the University Press of America.

dualisms are represented as the signifier/signified dualism. The domination of idealism (the domination of meaning as the signified) over materialism (the signifier as a trace) is revealed as part of the underlying structure of Western metaphysics. The material, the worldly, the contingent, can be seen throughout Western thought as corrupting the spiritual, the heavenly, the universal.

But Saussureian linguistics also revealed that meaning is generated not out of the signified but from the chain of signifiers. Saussureian linguistics thus presents the opportunity to critique phonocentrism, but only if the sign as signifier/signified can be understood as itself breaking with phonocentrism. If the new science of semiology which Saussure proposed is to take into account its own theoretical foundations, the sign must be problematized.

Derrida has shown the Husserl's transcendental subjectivity is really a transcendental signified, i.e., a transcendental foundation of meaning. But if meaning is generated out of the chain of signifiers, what needs to be demonstrated is how the subject is positioned within the signifying chain. A materialist account of the subject is in order.

Saussure contended that a sign is generated out of a system of differences and has no positive content outside of this system of differences. The phenomenological notion of intersubjectivity can be seen as an attempt to take into account the relational characteristics of meaning. Instead of positing the voice as the origin of meaning, conversation is posited as its dialectical foundation. But the metaphysical notion of presence still remains. Even though being as presence is invoked through the movements of conversation as dialectic, being is still revealed as a presence which takes as its source of validity the ideality of meaning--structures rather than the materiality of a chain of signifiers. The <u>material</u> pre-conditions of meaning have not been elucidated.

The notion of the sign as produced through a system of differences does not allow the sign to be taken as having a positive content. Instead of being centered, the source of meaning must be dispersed throughout the system of differences which conditions it. Jakobson demonstrated this on the level of phonemes, and Derrida makes use of these findings.

There is no purely and strictly phonetic writing.

If, then, there is no purely phonetic writing, it is because there is no purely phonetic phone. The difference that brings out phones and lets them be heard and understood itself remains inaudible.[1]

If consciousness is a sign for Husserl (expression) it must have been produced out of a system of differences. This system of differences in not consciousness itself, located in the subject, but is dispersed. The conditions of consciousness are not conscious but unconscious. The movements of consciousness, therefore, have been marked out already. A prior writing lies at the heart of the voice and at the heart of the sign. This writing disrupts the continuity of speech as self-presence and the sign as an isolatable unit, since the system of differences is non-locatable and non-specifiable as a positivity. The system of differences "allows for the dissonant emergence of writing inside of speech, thus disorganizing all the received order and invading the whole sphere of speech."[2] Writing, then, is that which is always already inhabited by the traces of other signs. The sign is always written and always an implicit text.

[1] Jacques Derrida, <u>Speech and Phenomena: And Other Essays on Husserl's Theory of Signs</u>, trans. David B. Allison, (Evanston: Northwestern University Press, 1973), p. 133.

[2] Jacques Derrida, <u>Positions</u>, (Paris, 1972), as trans. and quoted in the Translator's Preface in Jacques Derrida, <u>Of Grammatology</u>, trans. Gayatri Chakravorty Spivak, (Baltimore: The John Hopkins University Press, 1976), p. lxxvii.

Eco explicitly agrees that a sign is also a text, that is, it "conveys many intertwined contents" and as a text, "represents the result of the coexistence of many codes."[3] On the other hand, Eco seems to fall victim to the phonocentrism of Husserl.

Eco accepts phenomenology as potentially disclosing the intuitive, original source of meaning. He suggests that "semiotic meaning is simply the socialized codification of a perceptual experience which the phenomenological epoché should restore to us in its original form."[4] Eco takes ideas to be signs of perceptual experience and names to be the signs of ideas. Thus, ideas are cultural units which, as such, concern semiotics. Perceptual experience, on the other hand, represents one of the boundaries of semiotics as a field of study. Eco acknowledges that perceptual experiences exist in a social context which conditions their codification. Yet he dismisses the examination of these conditions, implying that they are not of interest to the semiotician because they do not involve communication but rather the "mechanisms of human intelligence."[5] This is similar to the argument that Husserl makes when he claims that expression can be grasped only intuitively since it is only indication which communicates, and consciousness does not communicate to itself. Eco has extended this issue a bit by pointing out that ideas as cultural units do enter into communication, and hence the possibility of "intrapsychic" communication is suggested as available to a materialist analysis. But the idealistic nature of Eco's theory of semiotics is revealed, since ideas, for Eco no less than for Husserl, have an intuitive origin.

> Phenomenology undertakes to rebuild from the beginning the conditions necessary for the formation of cultural units which semiotics instead accepts as data because communication functions on the basis of them. The phenomenological epoché would therefore refer perception back to a stage where referents are no longer confronted as explicit messages but as extremely ambiguous texts akin to aesthetic ones.[6]

As I will argue later, the subject can be considered an aesthetic text in Eco's sense of the term. But Eco himself has closed off the possibility of analyzing this text by positing the formation of the perception as a process outside of the domain of semiotics.

The voice for Eco stands in an unproblematic relationship with perceptual experiences. In describing the process of mentioning (the process of using indexical devices as pointers to a cultural unit) Eco uses the example of seeing a //cat// in the dark and slowly recognizing that it is a //cat//. He reminds us that what pointers mention are not objects in the world taken as physical events, but cultural units. "[B]oth the word /cat/ and ... the ... token _perceptum_ //cat// culturally stand for the same sememe."[7] The process of coming to recognize a //cat// as the cultural unit⟪cat⟫is the process of

> perception as interpretation of sensory disconnected data . . . organized through complex transactional process by a cognitive hypotheses based on previous experiences.

Thus I apply to an imprecise field of sensory stimuli the cultural unit ⟪cat⟫. I can even translate the experience into a verbal interpretant (/I saw a cat/).[8]

[3] Umberto Derrida, A Theory of Semiotics, (Bloomington: Indiana University Press, 1976), p. 57.

[4] Eco, p. 167.

[5] Eco, p. 248.

[6] Eco, p. 167.

[7] Eco, p. 164.

[8] Eco, p. 165.

Note that Eco apparently means that the <u>sensory experience</u> is translated into speech, as if the guarantee of having grasped a cultural unit is our ability to speak it (". . . I can even . . ."). Eco is apparently a nominalist in the Lockean sense. He is satisfied with disclaiming a referential theory of signs, and replacing it with the idea as a cultural unit. As Eco himself summarizes it:

> The procedure leading from a bunch of experiences to a name is the same as that which leads from the experience of things to that <u>sign</u> of things, the idea. Ideas are already a semiotic product.[9]

The implication seems to be that to name a "bunch of experiences" is to experience things. Eco quotes Husserl as if he is in agreement when Husserl says

> that to <u>name</u> an object as /red/ and to recognize it as red are the same process, or at least that the manifestation of the <u>name</u> and the intuition of the <u>named</u> are not clearly distinguishable.[10]

No wonder Eco is interested in the epoché of the phenomenological method, and re-marks that, "It would be worth ascertaining to what extent the idea of 'meaning' found in the phenomenology of perception agrees with the semiotic notion of a cultural unit."[11] Eco interprets phenomenology as a nominalism, and sees in this interpretation of phenomenology a similarity to his own view. The voice simply re-presents the cultural unit (the idea) as already accomplished by a process which is beyond the scope of semiotics. As a cultural unit which is different than an idea, the spoken word enters into different semiotic systems. But the word and the idea are, for the speaker, in absolute proximity.

And how does this apply to proper names? Are persons as self-reflective coincident with their name as an index of their self-reflection? If they are, then the subject can only be considered a unitary, homogenous subject. Eco says that proper names which refer to someone we know denote that person in a way similar to an iconic sign. Proper names of unknown persons connote but do not denote.[12]

But what about self-reference? If I say "My name is Mick", /My/ cannot be taken as an indexical pointer which locates the perceptum //Mick//. /Name/ is a cultural unit which denotes a type of indexical device. /Is/ roughly means that the semantic properties of /my name/ are to be assigned to /Mick/. This is different than saying /I am Mick/ in which case I have <u>mentioned</u> myself by assigning a cultural unit to myself as a perceptum. As soon as someone else utters my name the special nature of proper names is revealed. I may hear my name as a connotation for someone else even thogh I only intend to give my name as a denotation. A proper name always carries with it a connotation (such as sex, cultural affiliation, status, informality or formality, etc.). A name al-ways positions the individual within a semantic universe, even if that universe is not very rich at first, as in the case of the name of an unknown person. It is the purpose of names to allow us to enter into a symbolic exchange. It is the experience of the other which reveals to me the connotative aspects of my own name, assuring me that I have indeed entered into symbolic discourse rather than simply having been mentioned.

Lacan describes how we enter into symbolic discourse through the dialec-tical interaction of self and other. The self and other are constituted through this dialectic and owe their existence to it. As in language as a semiotic sy-stem, there is no original sign. In Lacanian psychoanalysis there is no origi-nal self or other. The subject is created out of a system of differences.

[9]Eco, p. 166
[10]Eco, p. 167.
[11]Eco, p. 167.
[12]Eco. pp. 84-5.

Since our desires arise out of the interaction of self and other, they are always desires for a satisfaction which cannot be located entirely on the side of the self. Desire is generated out of the gap which separates self and other, and it is only an imaginary object which pretends to satisfy this desire.

Hence, the Lacanian notion of desire is born from a sense of lack as the basic structure of psychic processes. The tension between need and its articulation generates desire as a lack. Desire is produced when needs are expressed through the necessarily frustrating articulations of language. It is the nature of language to turn homogenous experience of need into discrete expressions which bind these experiences into semantic units. Taking up the linguistic world within which the subject is born, the subject is inserted into a chain of signifiers. It is the signifying chain which makes meaning possible. The signified always remains a possibility rather than a completion. Signifiers "insist" upon an indeterminate range of interpretations. Thus, to focus on the meaning of discourse only is to ignore the pre-conditions for meaning. What needs to be examined is the positionality of the subject as marked out by the signifying chain. The signifying chain is other than myself.

The subject as signifier is brought into the signifying chain by being given a name. In Western culture the name that is given is the name of the father. Subjection to the will of the Father taken as the symbol of symbolic culture, is manifested as being given a name. The power of the Father is the power of giving names: the power to create an identity and to control it through knowing its name (its essence). I can never gain my complete independence since speaking about myself is always a speaking about a prior writing: the writing of the Father who has positioned me within symbolic discourse, within the chain of signifiers. I wish to be my own origin (the Father) and my own completion (which is death). My desire is the desire to write myself out of existence by writing myself into it. Instead, a text is produced, i.e., an elaborated subject which was written by my hand only after my hand had been written.

Anxiety in the face of the other is the result of realizing that I do not own myself because I can refer to myself. This kind of anxiety reveals that I am the other (a system of connotations which I can neither escape nor control but which nonetheless establishes my position within symbolic discourse). The other is inscribed in my name as I speak it. Personal identity is a self-focusing message, an aesthetic text.

Eco points out that it is the nature of the aesthetic text as invention to be able to "perform any or all productive functions (being composed of various types of judgement and acting as a meta-semiotic statement) and it can require any kind of productive labor."[13] The ambiguity of personal existence produces the person as an aesthetic text. The constant flux between my name as a denotation and as a connotation violates norms that I set for myself as the result of my own self-typification, and the norms that others have for me as their typification of me.

> A violation of norms on both the expression and the content plane obliges one to reconsider their correlation, which can no longer be the same as that foreseen by the usual code. In this way the text becomes self-focusing: it directs the attention of the addressee primarily to its own shape.[14]

This passage from Eco adequately describes the basic code conditions (extra-coding) involved in self-reflection as transformative. The more I take myself to be donotable, i.e., defined by a particular sign-function within a sign

[13]Eco, p. 261.

[14]Eco, p. 264.

system, the less I am an aesthetic text and the more my name simply denotes. I am part of a system of signifiers which have obscured (repressed) their signifieds. The more I take myself as a connotation the more my name connotes a dispersed semantic quality which enters into an infinite matrix of semantic fields. Neurotic repetition of behavior is the result of the former case and schizophrenia is the result of the latter case. In the case of the neurotic it can be seen why the body (as a signifier) becomes the object of attention, e.g., hypochondria. The ambiguity of the aesthetic text (person) has been solved through the fascination with denotative signs. In the case of the schizophrenic, the body becomes divorced from the sense of being a person because the aesthetic text has been dis-ambiguated by ignoring its denotative value. Surrealist art re-presents schizophrenic experience because it destroys the usual denotative values of objects by allowing their connotative significance to dominate, the code-switching taking place as the result of contextual displacement.

But, returning to the subject as an aesthetic text, the subject is a text which is produced. Only subsequently is the subject a text which produces. The modes of sign production available to the subject (which Eco suggests is unlimited theoretically) is limited by the position of the subject as produced. Narcissism has its equivalent in art for art's sake. The position of the subject as an aesthetic text is limiting because the subject is closed off from the production which initially gave rise to the subject. The aesthetic text is an aesthetic text because it no longer enters into the production system which produced it. The de-construction of the aesthetic text requires that the aesthetic text speak not to itself but explodes the sign system which gave rise to it.

This, of course, cannot occur if the subject as an aesthetic text is taken either as a transcendental signified which guarantees meaning by grounding it in intuition (Husserl), nor can the deconstruction of the subject occur if the subject is a transcendental signifier which can stand as a substitute for any other signifier (Lacan). While writing does have a certain priority over speaking since writing is always already inhabited by the traces of other signs, while speaking obscures the signifiers by dominating signifieds, it will not do to simply replace one kind of domination with another. Neither can we obliterate the distinction between the signifier and the signified. The signifier as the trace of a presence which is now absent and which can never be made completely present, must be written. But we must also take into account its repression and its inaccessibility to us as a meaning, since its full meaning is precisely what is absent for us. The signifier must be written, erased, and read. We must read through its erasure. Derrida proposes the graphic convention of crossing out a word while leaving it legible to signify this written-erased-read movement, e.g., si̶g̶n̶i̶f̶ier.

Hawes asks a very interesting question: "How are written documents used in talk about these documents."[15] The situation examined is a verbal briefing of a written document. Thus, the relationship between speaking and writing is examined in a practical circumstance. Hawes considers speech the vitalization of writing. "The written documents are passive, inert objects . . . until some organization member uses them (or parts of them) to actually do the clarifying, reprimanding, covering up, and forecasting."[16] Hawes says that the objects of talk and/or writing "have a prior existence" to the talking or writing. He relies on the Schutzian contention that even events in the future are talked about as if they have already happened, i.e., they are constituted as objects which have an existence prior to the talking or writing by referring to them in the

[15]Leonard C. Hawes, "How Writing is Used in Talk: A Study of Communicative Logic-in-Use," *Quarterly Journal of Speech*, 62 (December, 1976), 350-60.
[16]Hawes, p. 352.

future perfect tense. Had Hawes posited the objects of talk and/or writing as cultural units taken as signs, he could have avoided making a priori claims about time indexing. As it is, he has to implicitly claim that talking vitalizes all objects of discourse. "A past activity categorized in present talking becomes an object. Stated another way, present talking functions to transform past talking and writing from activities in one's memory into objects in one's talk."[17] It is as if our memory of a past document fails us until we speak about it. The writing alone does not make the ideas present. The metaphysics of presence has such a sway that the significance of writing is nearly denied completely.

What Hawes asks is "How does . . . the logic of written documents differ from the logic of talk <u>about</u> these documents?"[18] The use of as denotative is analyzed by comparing their relationships as establishing categories. In the written document, words are analyzed to form categories of objects referred to as "report" and "recipient", where "report" refers to another document which supposedly was sent to "recipients". The talk about the written document was analyzed to form two categories of objects referred to as "member" (of a committee) and "work" (of committee members). Verbs were listed in a third category in both cases called "linking activities". Hawes observes that:

> Unlike what is being done in the writing, in which nonhuman object categories are seen to be in a simple object-activity-object relation to one another ("tabulations" present "results" and "copy" was sent to "contacts"), in talking, both human and nonhuman objects are heard as causal agents.[19]

Hawes concludes that talking tends to be personalized, treats people as causal agents, and serves to particularize the objects referred to in the written document. Writing, on the other hand, tends to be impersonal and rarely refers to people as causal agents. Hawes has discovered the results of phonocentric culture. He further notes that: "people most adept at personalizing . . . impersonal objects written documents . . . are people of high status in the speech community."[20] Speaking about the document carried more status than either speaking without referring to the document or simply presenting the document. A machine inhabited by a ghost is more powerful than a ghost or a machine alone.

From an examination of the issues it seems that a theory of semiotics should include: 1) a metatheoretical understanding of the sign to clarify its idealistic and materialistic underpinnings (supplied by Derrida), 2) a theoretical clarification of the affective grounding of the sign (provided by Lacan), and 3) a theory of codes which can serve to guide research (provided by Eco). Hawes provides an example of how research into the nature of sign systems can verify or explicate the workings of semiotic systems hypothesized by theories and metatheories of semiotics.

None of the above mentioned theoreticians and researchers have provided a comprehensive theory of semiotics. The theoretical activity of semiotics itself cannot allow the generation of a theory which provides closure. Semiotics should remain an activity rather than become a position in the system of the history of ideas. Semiotics can remain a viable critical activity so long as it realizes itself as a dialectical materialism.

[17] Hawes, p. 354.
[18] Hawes, p. 354.
[19] Hawes, p. 358.
[20] Hawes, p. 360.

## 19 / AN EXPLORATION OF A PHENOMENOLOGICAL APPROACH TO UNDERSTANDING: AN ANALYSIS OF THE CONVERSATION AND TEACHINGS OF DON JUAN

MARK SHAW
PENNSYLVANIA STATE UNIVERSITY

The subject of this paper is understanding. More specifically it is concerned with how individuals come to experience a common understanding-- a common sense. By common sense I intend more than loosely tied or inade- quately arrived at beliefs and opinions. Arendt states that common sense is the very opposite of "private feelings." Rather, common sense "is that virtue by which we and our five individual senses are fitted into a single world common to us all and by the aid of which we move about in it."[1] There are two key elements in Arendt's conception of common sense which will be the focus of this study of understanding. One is that common sense involves a shared framework by which we see and understand a common world. The other is that this shared framework is arrived at through talk.

Common sense is that shared framework with which we "know" the world common to us all. Implicitly, common sense means that individuals abandon their ideosyncratic assumptions about the world and participate publicly in creating a shared understanding of the world. In this paper, an under- standing of how individuals "see" a common world is considered phenomenologically.

In his examination of Husserl, Spiegelberg explains that phenomenology is the, "study of the essential structures of the acts and contents of con- sciousness, a study to be based not on mere empirical generalization but on the intuitive grasping of the essences of the phenomena. . . ."[2] For the purposes of this study, the key element of Speigelberg's discussion is the notion of "essential structures." Briefly, the phenomenologist brackets or suspends the taken-for-granted assumptions in order to understand the "Phen- omena" for what it is and not what the person brings to the situation. The ability to see the world phenomenologically seems especially important in terms of our present concern with common sense. In order to obtain a common world, individuals must learn to "see" without confounding the world with their own ideosyncratic presuppositions. Yet the ability to suspend basic assumptions does not mean necessarily that the researcher extract all apriori assumptions about the world. Rather, according to Spiegelberg, phenomenological method implies "freedom from presuppositions that have not been thoroughly examined, or, at least in principle, been presented for such

Phenomenology in Rhetoric and Communication, ed. Stanley Deetz. Copyright, 1981. The Center for Advanced Research in Phenomenology and the University Press of America.

[1] Hanna Arendt, Between Past and Future: Eight Essays in Political Thought (New York: The Viking Press, 1968), p. 178.

[2] Herbert Spieleburg, The Phenomenological Movement: A Historical Introduction, 2nd ed., Vol. 1 (The Hague: Martinus Nijhoff 1969), p. 118.

examination."[3] Hence, this paper is concerned with how presuppositions and experiences are transformed from privately held opinions to a common under-standing.

In order to appreciate and explain common sense, we need to examine how our ideosyncratic conception or framework of the world becomes common. Arendt's discussion of common sense implicitly suggests that it is achieved through talk.[4] A world is common to us all in that it is discussed and implicitly or explicitly agreed upon. In effect, we "know" because we can discuss it with one another. Things are only arbitrary and subjective when we hold them pri-vately without discussion. Hence, one way to examine and describe how people come to understand one another is to examine their talk and the presuppositions implied by it. There is some evidence to suggest that talk is an illustrator of an individual's understanding of the world.

In previous studies, language analysis has been used as a method for examining style and meanings that enrich our talk. Historically, language analysis has been used for authenticating authorship. There are many **subtle** facets of style that emerge in an author's writing which may be detected through analysis. Language analysis procedures may be useful to the purposes of this study. Morton suggested that writers have unconscious pat-terns and choices of words.[5] This is born out by Tallentire, Fortier and McConell, Berry-Rogghe, and Burton who have all contributed to the analysis of style.[6] Basically their findings suggest that style is unique to the individ-ual and that it can be detected through language analysis.

Aside from authorship studies, the analysis of language may be helpful for identifying the meanings individuals hold. For instance, Bradac, Desmond, and Murdock reported that lexical studies may be useful for understanding the attributed credibility of the speaker.[7] They examine the effect of diverse messages upon learning and attitudes of the listener. These results imply that language analysis may be helpful for uncovering the attitudes and beliefs held by individuals. In an analysis of a therapy session, Greene found that over time the patient's language style began to converge with the style of the therapist.[8] His analysis of style had uncovered evidence of the progress-ing improvement of the clients in the session. Johnson and Hopper found that individuals can accurately identify the relevant factors in a conversation after hearing only a small portion of the dialogue.[9] Possibly, individuals can identify communication structures from a small sample. In addition, the analysis of theme words and pronoun usage enables investigators to examine an individual's meanings. Speier notes that "topics is but another element of conversational structure around which participants organize their concerted

[3]Spieleburg, p. 83.

[4]Arendt, p. 220-223.

[5]A. Q. Morton and A. D. Winspear, "The Computer and Plato's Seventh Letter." _Computer and the Humanities_, 1 (1966), 72-73.

[6]D. R. Tallentire, "Towards Archive of Lexical Norms: A Proposal," _The Computer and Literary Studies_, A. J. Aitken, R. W. Bailey and N. Hamilton-Smith (eds.), (Chicago: Aldne Atherton Inc., 1973), pp. 39-60; P. A. Fortier and J. C. McConnell, "Computer Aided Thematic Analysis of French Prose Fiction." _The Computer and Literary Studies_, pp. 167; Godelieve L. M., Berry-Rogghe, "The Compilation of Collactions and their Relevance in Lexical Studies," _The Computer and Literary Studies_, pp. 39-60; Dolores M. Burton, "Some uses of Grammatical Concor-dance, _Computer and the Humanities_, 2 (1967), pp. 145-154.

[7]James J. Bradac, Roger J. Desmond, and Johnny I. Murdock, "Diversity and Density: Lexically Determined Evaluative and Informational Consequences of Linguistic Complexity," _Communication Monographs_, 44 (4,1977), 273-283.

[8]John Greene, "An Inquiry Jnto the Relationships Between Changing Relationships and Word Size." An unpublished manuscript, 1977.

[9]Bonnie Johnson and Robert Hopper, "Gender, Task, and Relationship: A Study of Generative Mechanisms in Dyadic Interaction," Presented at the SCA convention, 1978.

interactions. Accordingly, we are led to ask: 'What does a topic do in a conversation rather than what are the topics?'"[10] Here Speier is pointing to a phenomena occuring in natural talk which does more than describe, it explains the direction of a conversation based on the way themes are raised and used in conversations.

Another conversational structure I will discuss is pronoun reference. Speier states that pronouns are "important principles for conversationalists to use competently because they permit them to show how they hear and understand each other's conversational contributions."[11] What Speier is saying is that the use of pronouns says something about how the actors see and understand each other during the interaction. For example, Speier says that the use of pronouns points out how interactants in the conversation include and exclude members through their use of pronoun reference. Here again, the conversationalist should look for pronoun usage, and like the other methods mentioned, go beyond the mere description and find how the usage affects the flow and meaning of the conversation. In sum, language analysis empowers the researcher to examine an individual's style and meanings even though these may operate on some tacit level of understanding. Assuming that our presuppositions and taken-for-granted assumptions are reflected in our talk, it should be possible to detect them through an analysis of language.

In this study, I examine style, theme words, and pronoun usage in conversations between a participant observer and his subject. There are several reasons why focusing on a participant observer's attempts to understand a culture are particularly relevant for examining how individuals understand one another.

In sociological studies, participant observers must be able to understand the culture which they are studying as a native understands it. A usual procedure for the researcher is to find experiences which the two cultures share in common in order to build a foundation for understanding. Bryun states that the participant observer must, "describe particular events or experiences that insiders and outsiders have in common."[12] Moreover, the participant observer not only must understand the culture as the members of that culture understands it but must also maintain an impartial perspective and report findings that colleagues will accept and understand. This issue presents the researcher with an interesting problem: Can the meanings of one culture be translated and understood by members of another culture who have not shared the common experiences.

This review suggests the following research questions:

1. Can differences in the taken-for-granted assumptions be inferred from differences in language usage by the participant observer and the subject?

2. Over time, can a convergence of linguistic style between the two be detected that suggests increasing understanding?

3. In what direction does the convergence occur?

[10] Matthew Speier, How to Observe Face-to-Face Communication: A Sociological Introduction (Pacific Palisades, California: Goodyear Publishing Co., Inc., 1973), p. 92.

[11] Speier, p. 89.

[12] Severyn T. Bruyn, The Human Perspective in Sociology: The Methodology of Participant Observation (Englewood Cliffs, New Jersey: Prentice-Hall Inc., 1966), p. 29.

For this study, I will use portions of dialogue from the books written by Carlos Castaneda about the teachings of don Juan.[13] Although the three books have not been written for the scholarly community, and some controversy exists as to their authenticity, I am using these books in this study because they present an exciting illustration of the issues which I am discussing in this paper.[14] Moreover, they traverse over ten years of Castaneda's acquaintance and apprenticeship with don Juan; 2) don Juan's culture sharply contrasts with Castaneda's; and 3) the books are widely read, thus documenting their appeal.

Upon reading about Castaneda's experiences with don Juan, issues of taken-for-granted assumptions become evident. Early in the dialogue the reader is struck immediately by the fact that don Juan's notion of logic and reason bears little resemblence to the norms held by Castaneda. There are innumeral instances in which a strange experience is rationally explained by Castaneda only to be later refuted by don Juan. Don Juan and Castaneda argue continually over the structure of their respective world. For example, one issue occurring throughout is Castaneda's note taking. Castaneda tries his best to learn about don Juan's culture in ways that his own culture deems best--note taking and learning through talk. On the other hand don Juan asserts that one learns through doing. Notes will not help Castaneda understand experience.

### PROCEDURE

To answer the questions and issues posed above, I used the CLAS program for analyzing a selected portion of three books written by Castaneda during his years as an apprentice with don Juan.[15] CLAS is useful for this analysis for several reasons. First, it is able to "read" from the text, theme words and examine their usage over time. Second, it can provide information important for determining style by measuring and comparing: word length, sentence length, type token rations, and word frequencies. Overall, the following routines will be performed with CLAS:

1. elicit a theme list to compare the usage and choice or words

2. examine selected pronouns

3. compare the mean number of words

4. compare the mean number of words per sentence

5. compare the type token ratios

For this analysis, I will use selected portions of three books by Castaneda: Journey to Ixtlan (Journey) Separate Reality (Reality); and Tales of Power (Tales). The possibility of using the complete text was not an option because of constraints in time. The use of these portions may produce fragmentary

[13]Carlos Castaneda, A Separate Reality: Further Conversations With Don Juan (New York: Pocket Books, 1971); Journey to Ixtlan: The Lessons of Don Juan (New York: Pocket Books, 1972); Tales of Power (New York: Pocket Books, 1974).

[14]There is some controversy about the authenticity of these works. The language analysis provided in this study suggests that the conversations reported do represent two individuals. However, it is not my purpose to make a definitive decision on that issue. Further analysis of style would be needed.

[15]CLAS: A Computerized Language Analysis System. George A. Borden and James J. Watts. CLAS is a computerized language analysis system which performs standard statistical analyses on all input, plus giving the user the option of outputting a concordance or an index of all the words of the input text or a selected subset of these words. It is written in PL/1 for an IBM system 360/65.

pictures of what occurred but may also justify extending the study into other areas or even spending the amount of time necessary to translate the remainder of the texts into language readable by CLAS.

The portions that were used in this analysis focused on the theme of "warrior." The decision to use this theme preceded the decision to use the particular procedures of this study. The theme of warriors is found throughout the texts and touches on most of the important teachings of don Juan. Only those portions of the texts dealing with the theme "warrior" were used in this analysis. Records as small as 112 words and as large as 2600 words were kept as data. Once the theme was selected a theme list was also created in order to elicit how much the themes were used in their talk. This list contained words found in a thesaurus. Words were included under the heading of "warrior" or other related words. The following theme list was created:

> alert, aware, do, effort, struggle, victory, challenge confronting, face, encounter, brave, decision, action, conflicts, match, contended contests, strive, quarrel, farce, wrestle, agonize, combat, choose, will, battles.

There are two methodological problems which should be raised before preceding with the results. First, the dialogue is really not an accurate transcription of don Juan's words. It has been obtained by notes and memory. The accuracy of those notes may be spurious--especially when one considers how subtle stylistic nuances are. However, the following analysis on style differences provides some evidence for accuracy of Castaneda's notes. Secondly, this analysis relies upon Castaneda's narrative form in many instances to compare against a reportedly spoken form. Yet this may not provide as much problem as it initially suggests. Blankenship has reported that there was little difference between written and oral style and that the most significant difference would be found between authors.[16]

In this analysis I decided not to use statistical inferential tests. Basically this is an exploratory study. Random sampling of data required for such tests are not appropriate to the issues being explored in this paper. The goal of this paper is not to test reality in a population, but to suggest procedures for examining the phenomenology of understanding. Therefore I use only descriptive statistics of the samples I studied.

## RESULTS

### Theme Words
The analysis of the theme list is shown in Table 1. Overall, only .1% separates don Juan from Castaneda in the use of theme words but the closeness of the two means is misleading. The three segments representing the three books written at different times will be considered independently. In the earliest segment, Journey, .6% of all the words used by don Juan were from the theme list, as compared to .154% for Castaneda. In Reality, the difference between them shrank. Four of every 1000 words used by don Juan were from the list compared to 7 from a 1000 for Castaneda. In Tales, both persons decreased the theme usage and the difference again converges. Don Juan uses .229 and Castaneda comprises only .101%. When these results are taken together we see immediately that the two people cross twice during the time period. There are differences and there is evidence of convergence. The direction and import of this convergence is considered in the discussion section.

[16]Jane Blankenship, "A Linguistic Analysis of Oral and Written Style," *Quarterly Journal of Speech*, 48 (1966), 419-422.

Pronoun Usage
    There is also difference and convergence in the use of pronouns.  "I" comprised only 1.35% of total tokens used by don Juan while over 6.7% of Castaneda's tokens were "I".  Table 2 shows the trend of difference and convergence over the three works.  In Journey, "I" accounts for nearly 9% of Castaneda's tokens though "I" comprises only 1.35% of don Juan's.  In the Reality segment, "I" accounts for only 6.39% of the tokens used by Castaneda; don Juan's remains stable at about 1.43%.  In the final segment Tales, "I" accounts for 4.76% of the tokens used by Castaneda and 1.27% of those used by don Juan.

    The pattern of usage of the pronoun "you" provides an interesting contrast.  "You" represents over 3% of the tokens used by don Juan but only 1.24% of the tokens used by Castaneda.  Moreover, as the graph of Table 3 shows, don Juan's use remained fairly stable over time while Castaneda's flucuates.  There is substantial difference in the use of "you", but in the middle segment there is some convergence in the direction of don Juan.

Function Words
    Function words are used to identify subtle stylistic differences between the two people in the conversation.  The results of the use of function words is reported in Table 4.  Overall a slight difference was found between them.  Function words accounted for just under 1% of the tokens used by don Juan and nearly 1.5% used by Castaneda.  As with pronoun usage, don Juan appears to be more stable than Castaneda across works.  There are differences and some convergence at the end.

Word and Sentence Length
    The mean number of letters in the words used by each person are reported in Table 5.  There seems to be no difference of any importance between them.  The scores for sentence length are reported in Table 6.  Overall, there is a difference suggesting a difference in style; don Juan uses more words in his sentences than Castaneda--nearly 3 words per sentence separate the two.  There is also an interesting pattern of difference.  The difference is greater in the second work, Reality than in Journey.  In Tales, they begin to converge toward Castaneda.

Type Token Ratio
    A type token ratio is a figure derived from taking the total number of different words used (types) divided into the total number of words (tokens).  However, the size of the text has the effect of reducing the score of the ratio.  Since the text included more lines of Castaneda's than don Juan's a statistic was used to account for the variation in text size.  This is the Carroll Type Token Ratio.  Table 7 shows the variety of words used by don Juan and Castaneda after the size of text had been accounted for.  There is a difference between the two and some convergence in the third work, Tales.


                                DISCUSSION


    The results of this study provide some provocative answers to the research questions posed above.  Recall that these questions were:

    1.  Can differences in the taken-for-granted assumptions be inferred from the difference in linguistic usage by the participant observer and the subject?

    2.  Over time, can a convergence of linguistic style between the two cultures be detected which suggests increasing understanding?

    3.  In what direction does the convergence occur?

Clearly there are differences in language style. Only in word length were there no differences. And for most of the measures of language style, there was some "convergence", some narrowing of the size of difference over time represented by the three books. But are the differences recorded above reflecting the differences in the taken-for-granted assumptions? In addition, can the convergence of language style recorded above provided some answers to our orginal concern with understanding. The following discussion provides some evidence that differences in meanings did exist between don Juan and Castaneda and that a convergence of meaning occurred between them over time.

In the results, three indicators suggest that the differences in Castaneda's style and don Juan's corresponds to the initial difference and eventual convergence in understanding. These are: Theme words; pronouns; and the Type Token Ratios.

The striking result of this study is not simply the difference in language style between Castaneda and don Juan, but the fluctuating patterns of these differences. Notice that early in his association with don Juan, Castaneda uses a comparatively low level of theme words. By the middle years he has not only changed that style of talk but surpasses the level reported by don Juan. One explanation for the direction and shape of this change is that don Juan, as any teacher would, introduced early in the education of Castaneda, the terms of his culture. As a student of this culture, Castaneda learned quickly the terms and ways of don Juan. He mimicked the terms used by his teacher. Gradually he depends less upon direct imitation as the meanings of the concepts became clearer to him. This would not be unlike situations in our culture in which students first exposed to the canons of a discipline must rely heavily upon the jargon while they gain some understanding of the issues. The use of pronouns supports this inference.

Notice the use of the pronoun "you" by Castaneda. At first he rarely uses the term as evidenced by the low percentage. But by the middle of his apprenticeship, "you" statements increase to its highest recorded level--a jump of over 200% from his previous score. Castaneda appears to be doing a lot of "reality checking" with don Juan during this time. In other words, "you" statements are used to seek clarification from don Juan on various issues of the culture which lends support to the "learning student" metaphor used to explain the differences in theme words.

A check of the concordances provided by CLAS for the pronoun "you" supports this inference. In the concordance of uses for "you" in the middle segment Reality, one finds sentences such as: "What would you do?", "What shields?", "What are you talking about?", "What do you mean by selecting the items of my world?", "But you said that I am not a warrior, so how can I choose . . .?", "What do you mean?", "I really don't understand you.", and "What do you call the world?" Notice that all of these statements are seeking verification of the world as don Juan sees it. This lends support for the explanation that Castaneda is trying to understand the world of don Juan and is seeking understanding by relying mostly upon the explanations of don Juan rather that translating them back into his own personal culture.

Contrast these concordances with those found previously and after these middle conversations. In Journey, "you" is found in sentences such as: "Has it ever occurred to you, don Juan, that I may not want to change?", "I get scare when you say that.", "Can you describe them?". "No, I don't see what you mean at all." Although some of these early statements reflect some probing of don Juan's culture they seem not to reflect an eagerness to know don Juan's world. Two of the statements hint at rejection of don Juan's teachings and the others present a subtle challenge that is not present in the statements found in the Reality segment.  In the final segment, Tales, the number of "you" statements has dropped and the usage has changed once again:  ". . . because I haven't dared come to see you and I. . . .", "I see what you mean.", and "I would rather be with you in the desert."  These concordances show that Castaneda is begining to learn and understand the teachings of don Juan.  Moreover they show that he is beginning to "see" his teacher differently that before. By the final stages of his apprenticeship Castaneda not only seems concerned with learning the ways of his teacher, but of his relationship with him as well. This is important because it suggests that the pronouns reflect some subtle changes in Castaneda's relationship with don Juan over the years.

The differences in the use of "you" shows that Castaneda was attempting to learn and understand the culture.  His use of "I" statements suggests that he did achieve an understanding of don Juan's world.  Changes in his use of "I" reflect Castaneda's subconscious acceptance and understanding of the teachings.  Throughout the book, don Juan continually tells Castaneda that he is too indulgent and dwells upon himself.  When the "I" statements are considered, it is clear that don Juan was right.  The concordances of Castaneda's "I" statements reads:  "I said art.  I had always wanted to be an artist and for years I had tried my hand at that.", "I vehemently asserted that his insistence about changing my way of life was frightening and arbitrary.", "I contended that I was aware of my impending death. . . ." and so on.  In these statements there is a particular sense of self-pity and failure that had been a focus of don Juan's teachings throughout the years.

The change in focus away from self-indulging evidenced by the reduction of "I" statements lend the greatest support for the issue of understanding and the change in taken-for-granted assumptions.  Interestingly, the issue of "I" statements was never made explicit by either, yet it emerged through the content analysis as a sharp indicator of the symptom of indulgence and its improvement.  They are unconscious indicators of his understanding of the lessons. Castaneda consciously attempted to understand don Juan's world and the use of "I" indicates that over time he began to act accordingly.

Not only does the use of pronouns in this study provide evidence of understanding but of convergence as well.  With the concordances above we can see that Castaneda consciously and unconsciously attempted to learn the ways of don Juan.  Hence, Castaneda changed more than don Juan.  The various stylistic differences that were detected between the two people also support this inference.  However, the direction of convergence is equivocal.  Most of the results suggest more changes were made in Castaneda's language style, yet in two measures of style and word choice, the pattern reverses.  First, over time both don Juan and Castaneda relied less upon theme words.  This result may be due to the teaching method of don Juan.  During the years of his acquaintance with Castaneda, he relied less upon using the terms of his culture.  Incidently, the reduction of that reliance corresponds to Castaneda's increasing understanding of the culture.  As for function words, the convergence is symetrical.  Function words are  considered subtle indicators of style and these results indicate that the style of both began to merge over time.  But for the most part the indicators of style seems to add little to our knowledge of the phenomenology of understanding.  One reason for this is that the concordances obtained from function word do not reveal the richness of the dialogue found with pronouns and themes words.

## CONCLUSION

The purpose of this study was to examine the phenomenology of understanding. I argued that individuals experience understanding.  I argued that individuals experience understanding by suspending or bracketing their own ideosyncratic conceptions of the world and seeking a common understanding. Two facets were explored. One considered understanding as a phenomenological experience in that common sense required the examination of presuppositions. The other facet posited that the presuppositions individuals hold may be detected in their talk. These issues were explored through a language analysis of Castaneda's conversations with don Juan. Though no statistical procedures were used, the results suggests that a language analysis is useful for examining these issues of understanding.

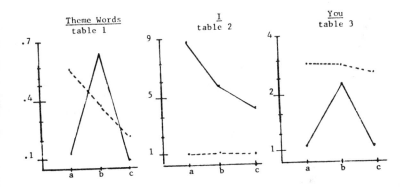

Don Juan　　　-----------
Castaneda　　　_____

a -- Journey
b -- Reality
c -- Tales

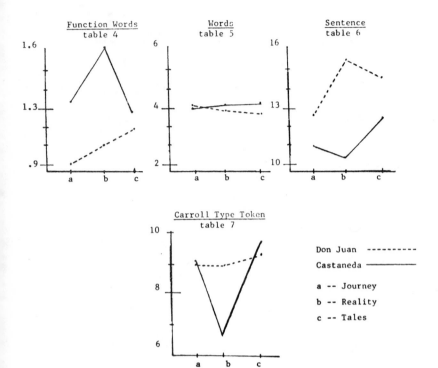

# DISCUSSION / IDEA AND TECHNIQUE

## Leonard Hawes
## University of Utah

My task is to characterize three manuscripts, different in almost every respect except, perhaps, one; the three authors take the constitution of a text to be problematic, albeit for very different reasons. Mr. Presnell makes an argument for semiology as a critique of the more phonocentric conceptions of language and conversation, such a phenomenology. Mr. Branco argues that some of the terms in Luckmann's editing and compiling of Schutz's more recently published texts are convoluted, and he proposed four features of four life-worlds to clarify this textual ambiguity. Mr. Shaw does a rough cut stylistic analysis of selected portions of three of the four known Castaneda books. Shaw's main concern is to make a phenomenological argument for how individuals "see" a common world from descriptive statistical evidences of selected texts.

I shall proceed by addressing each manuscript in some detail; which is only another way of saying that I shall characterize these texts--just as the authors did their's--to serve the practical problem at hand--which, you no doubt recall, was to write a critical commentary.

Mr. Presnell, rather than assuming voice to be simultaneous and absolutely proximate with being, argues instead that speaking only discloses a prior text-- a prior writing. The text, not the person, is the subject of study. To execute his argument he first attacks phonocentrism, particularly phonocentrism's assumption that writing is merely a signifier for an absent presence. The presence, absent in writing, is the voice. In short, Presnell's argument is against the domination of meaning as the signified--the idealist position-- and for the signifier being conceived as a trace--the materialist position.

Presnell is highlighting some implications of semiology as a materialistic science. First, semiology is not concerned with a science of the social if the social is taken to be some constellation of people(s). Rather, semiology is concerned with a system of differences generative of signs differentiated according to funciton; i.e., signifier and signified. The system of differences has no positive identity--it is only apparent relative to its own absence--that is, in writing. Writing is the positive rendering of the system of differences semioticians see when looking at a language of any kind.

Second, if writing, as text, is the proper subject of semiotics, then the source of meaning is not centered in the individual as subject but rather is decentered and dispersed throughout the system of differences. Such a position hardly squares with our more cherished bromides such as, "meanings are in people not in messages." For semiotics, the source of validity is not the structure of the message or the structure of the person's internal apparatus but rather is the materiality of a chain of signifiers. It is a person's situatedness within this chain of signifiers that limits one's ability to influence the very conditions which made its production possible. Presnell's

Phenomenology in Rhetoric and Communication, ed. Stanley Deetz. Copyright, 1981, The Center for Advanced Research in Phenomenology and the University Press of America.

argument is that writing has a priority over speaking inasmuch as writing is always already inhabited by the traces of other signs. The signifier, as the trace of a presence now absent and which can never be made completely present, must be written.

Mr. Branco sets for himself the task of clarifying ambiguities evidenced in the text of another; specifically in the edited/co-authored/compiled The Structure of the Life-World--the joint work of Schutz and Luckmann. For example, "the world of daily life," "the everyday world," "mundane reality," "the taken for granted everyday world" and "the matrix of daily life" are terms of Schutz's philosophy of natural attitude but are not properly defined and differentiated. To remedy this ambiguity, Branco elaborates four categories of phenomenological life-worlds in accord with four features of each. The resulting graphic representation is a four-by-four matrix the cells of which contain descriptive features of each of the four life-worlds thereby explicated. The four phenomenological life-worlds Branco proposes are (a) daily life, (b) everyday life, (c) anyday life, and (d) someday life.

"Daily Life" is the predominant sphere of social events in which individuals are bodies-in-activity and behavior is that of the mechanistic daily rounds. "Everyday life" is the working model of business institutions and ritual participations; the behavior is ceremonious in the ritual sense and individuals occupy roles and positions in an unfolding social drama. "Anyday life" is the life-world of personal contingency; it is a motile and future conditional world supposed by and for him. It is a world in which there are gaps in one's stock of knowledge and one anticipates awaiting further notice on many occasions. Finally, "someday life" involves matters of singular or infrequent incurrence; it is the life-world of the possible, plausible, implausible, and impossible.

Mr. Shaw's project is rather eclectic. In his words, he seeks "an understanding of how individuals 'see' a common world" and "is concerned with how presuppositions and experiences are transformed from privately held opinions to a common understanding." Shaw proposes a language analysis of three of the four known Castaneda texts. More specifically, Shaw selects material pertinent to the theme of warrior, feeds this material into a CLAS program which outputs a (1) theme list, (2) frequencies of selected pronouns, (3) mean number of words, (4) mean number of words per sentence, and (5) type/token ratios. These descriptive statistics are then used to construct affirmative answers for two of his three research questions:

1.  Can differences in the taken-for-granted assumptions be inferred from differences in language usage by the participant observer (Carlos Castaneda) and the subject (don Juan Matus)?

2.  Over time, can a convergence of linguistic style between the two be detected that suggests increasing understanding?

As one might suspect from the outset, and as one critic has noted already, the papers display some weaknesses--both procedurally and conceptually. These papers are the work of our most promising apprentices in the arts and crafts of practicing the rituals communication research. Mistakes warrant noticing but not preoccupation. It is the promise of original insight which is to be nutured here. Too much attention to procedures, at this stage of development, risks insufficient attention to what the authors' projects are becoming.

First, consider the following weaknesses. Shaw doesn't define such crucial terms as "style," "language analysis," "conversation" and "presupposition;" he dismisses the authenticity controversy cavalierly and prematurely--particularly in light of his use of a method grounded historically in the work of authenticating texts; one of the four Castaneda books is arbitrarily excluded; the "complete text" is never specified; and the descriptive statistics and their use in the construction of answers are completely superfluous to the project. Nevertheless, Shaw makes a nice conceptual linkage between the study of style and the study of conversation--a marriage, if you will, of Hymes' most recent version of his project on speech communities and the two camps currently describing conversion from very different points of view (i.e., the group of Sacks, Schegloff, Jefferson, Schenkein, Pomerantz, etc., and the group of S. Duncan, Allen, Guy, Jaffee and Feldstein, all following in the tradition of Chapple).

Although I am not optimistic about the prospect of describing conversation in terms of quantitative ratios ever getting us to a generative epistemology of conversation, Shaw's work clearly displays such a quantitative influence. The interpretive ground to be covered in the journey from descriptive statistics to hermeneutic claims is too great to argue for more than remote correspondences, however.

Perhaps the most obvious weakness in Branco's paper is its increasing vagueness and its rather abrupt termination. Although the phenomenological life-worlds of "anyday life" and "someday life" are described more rhapsodically than are the life-worlds of "daily life" and "everyday life," making the six-way contrasts is a bit like apples and whatever. Nevertheless, the four categories of life-worlds do have phenomenological groundings and do appear to add precision to Schutzian terminology.

The projects of "Occurrence," "Experimential nature," "Nature of horizons" and "Perspectival bearings" appear deceptively simple. What Branco has done, in a surprisingly understated fashion, is to systematize a variety of projects which, if completed, would detail his four categories of life-world. The most significant contribution of Branco's paper is the scope of the work required to systematically explicate the convolved terms Schutz and Luckmann use to articulate a philosophy of the natural attitude.

In a curious way, Mr. Presnell accomplishes more than Mr. Shaw or Mr. Branco because his project is not as ambitious--it risks less. But he is quite successful in what he set out to do--i.e., critique phonocentric conceptions of language and propose a Derrida-inspired conception of the text as the proper subject and as the de-centered source of meaning. It is the level at which the argument is constructed and the care with which the construction is executed that is most impressive. For example, there is a rather minor section of the paper--it could as easily have been relegated to the status of a content footnote--it locates phenomenology as clearly idealistic and thereby semiology as clearly materialistic. There are ontological questions hiding in the backstreet of Mr. Presnell's paper; in the darkness, near the edge. But these questions are visible only in light of the questions of "text as subject" and "de-centered meaning."

For phenomenology and communication to enjoin horizons, several fundamental questions must be recognized. These three papers are concerned, directly or indirectly, with some of these questions. For example, "what is voice and where is it located in speaking and in writing?" "What are the generative differences between phenomenology and semiology"? "Is a materialist science of speaking possible"? These are not the old familiar questions for which trusty cliches can be passed off as answers. Many such questions have an odd ring to them insofar as the question itself escapes our ready understanding.  Certainly technique and conclusion are inseparable, but technique improves with practice.  This is not necessarily the case with our ability to formulate worthy questions.  The authors all managed to at least broach some of these questions.  Hard work is all it takes to become a technician.

# BIBLIOGRAPHY

WORKS CITED AND SELECTED BIBLIOGRAPHY
OF WORKS IN ENGLISH ON COMMUNICATION
AND CONTINENTAL THOUGHT

ACHINSTEIN, P. Laws and Explanation. London: Oxford University Press, 1971.

ADORNO, T.W., ed., et al. The Positivist Dispute in German Sociology. London: Heinemann, 1976.

AHLSTROM, SYDNEY E. A Religious History of the American People. New Haven: Yale University Press, 1972.

ALLEN, JEFFNER. "Husserl's Overcoming of the Problem of Intersubjectivity." Modern Schoolman, 55 (1978), 261-271.

ALTHUSSER, LOUIS. For Marx, trans. Ben Brewster. New York: Vintage, 1970.

ANDREWS, JAMES R. "The Passionate Negation: The Chartist Movement in Rhetorical Perspective." The Quarterly Journal of Speech, 59 (April 1973).

APEL, KARL OTTO. "The Communicative Community as Transcendental Presupposition of Social Sciences." Dialog Als Mehtode. Gottingen: Reprecht, 1972.

----------. "The Common Presuppositions of Hermeneutics and Ethics." Research in Phenomenology, 9 (1979) 35-53.

----------. "Towards a Reconstruction of Critical Theory." Philosophical Disputes in the Social Sciences. Ed., S.C. Brown. Sussex: Harvester Press, 1979, pp. 127-139.

----------. Towards a Transformation of Philosophy. London: Routledge and Kegan Paul, 1980.

ARATO, A. & GEBHARDT, E., eds. The Essential Frankfurt School Reader. New York: Urizen Books, 1978.

ARENDT, HANNAH. The Human Condition. Chicago: University of Chicago Press, 1958.

----------. Between Past and Future: Eight Essays in Political Thought. New York: The Viking Press, 1968.

ARISTOTLE. Prior and Posterior Analytics in the Works of Aristotle. London: Oxford University Press, 1927.

Phenomenology in Rhetoric and Communication, ed. Stanley Deetz. Copyright, 1981, The Center for Advanced Research in Phenomenology and the University Press of America.

ARNOLD, CARROLL C.  Criticism of Oral Rhetoric.  Columbus, Ohio:  Charles E. Merrill, 1974.

----------.  "Rhetorical and Communication Studies:  Two Worlds or One?"  Western Speech, 36 (1972), 75-81.

ARON, R.  Main Currents in Sociological Thought.  Garden City, New York: Doubleday and Company, 1968.

ATTWELL, PAUL.  "Ethnomethodology Since Garfinkel."  Theory and Society, 1 (1974).

AUSTIN, J.L.  How to Do Things With Words.  2d Ed.  Cambridge:  Harvard University Press, 1962.

BACON, WALLACE A.  The Art of Interpretation.  3d Ed.  New York:  Holt, Rinehart, and Winston, 1979.

BALES, ROBERT F.  Interaction Process Analysis.  Cambridge:  Addison-Wesley, 1950.

BAIN, DAVID & HARRIS, BRUCE, eds.  Mickey Mouse:  Fifty Happy Years.  New York:  Harmony Books, 1977.

BARTHES, ROLAND.  Writing Degree Zero, trans. Annette Lavers and Colin Smith. Boston:  Beacon, 1970.

----------.  S/Z, trans. Richard Miller.  New York:  Farrar, Straus and Giroux, 1974.

----------.  "Myth Today."  Mythologies, trans. Annette Lavers.  London: Jonathan Cape, 1972.

BAUMAN, Z.  Hermeneutics and Social Science.  New York:  Columbia University Press, 1978.

BELL, DAVID.  Power, Influence, and Authority:  An Essay in Political Linguistics.  New York:  Oxford University Press, 1975.

BENGSTON, VERN L., et al.  "Relating Academic Research to Community Concerns: A Case Study in Collaborative Effort."  Journal of Social Issues, 33 (1977), 75-93.

BERGER, PETER L. & LUCKMANN, THOMAS.  The Social Construction of Reality:  A Treatise in the Sociology of Knowledge.  Garden City:  Doubleday, 1966.

BERLO, DAVID.  The Process of Communication.  New York:  Holt, Rinehart and Winston, 1960.

BLACK, EDWIN.  Rhetorical Criticism:  A Study in Method.  New York:  Macmillan, 1965.

BLALOCK, H.  Theory Construction:  From Verbal to Mathematical Formulations. Englewood Cliffs, New Jersey:  Prentice-Hall, 1969.

BLANKENSHIP, JANE.  "A Linguistic Analysis of Oral and Written Style."  The Quarterly Journal of Speech, 48 (1966), 419-422.

BOCHNER, A. "On Taking Ourselves Seriously: An Analysis of Some Persistent Problems and Promising Directions in Interpersonal Research." Human Communication Research, 4 (1978), 179-191.

BOGDAN, ROBERT & TAYLOR, STEVEN J. Introduction to Qualitative Research Methods: A Phenomenological Approach to the Social Sciences. New York: John Wiley and Sons, 1975.

BOLLNOW, OTTO FRIEDRICH. "What Does it Mean to Understand a Writer Better Than He Understood Himself?" Philosophy Today, 23 (1979), 16-28.

BOOTH, WAYNE C. The Rhetoric of Fiction. Chicago: University of Chicago, 1961.

BOURDIEU, P. & PASSERON, J. Reproduction in Education, Society, and Culture, trans. Richard Nice. London: SAGE Publications, 1977.

BREEN, ROBERT S. Chamber Theatre. Englewood Cliffs, New Jersey: Prentice-Hall, 1978.

BRETALL, ROBERT, ed. A Keirkegaard Anthology. Princeton: Princeton University Press, 1946.

BRADAC, JAMES J., DESMOND, ROGER J., & MURDOCK, JOHNNY I. "Diversity and Density: Lexically Determined Evaluative and Informational Consequences of Linguistic Complexity." Communication Monographs, 44 (1977), 273-283.

BURKE, KENNETH. Language as Symbolic Action: Essays on Life, Literature, and Method. Berkeley, California: University of California Press, 1966.

----------. A Rhetoric of Motives. Berkeley: University of California Press, 1969.

BURLESON, BRANT R. & KLINE, SUSAN. "Habermas' Theory of Communication: A Critical Explication." Quarterly Journal of Speech, 65 (1979), 412-428.

BURTON, DELORES M. "Some uses of Grammatical Concordance." Computer and the Humanities, 2 (1967), 145-154.

BRUNS, GERALD. "Intention, Authority and Meaning." Critical Inquiry, 7 (1980), 297-309.

BRUYN, SEVERYN T. The Human Perspective in Sociology: The Methodology of Participant Observation. Englewood Cliffs, New Jersey: Prentice-Hall, 1966.

BRYANT, DONALD C. Rhetorical Dimensions in Criticism. Baton Rouge: Louisiana State University Press, 1973.

BURRELL, GIBSON & MORGAN, GARETH. Sociological Paradigms and Organizational Analysis. London: Heinemann, 1979.

CARLETON, WALTER M. "What Is Rhetorical Knowledge? A Response to Farrell--And More." Quarterly Journal of Speech, 64 (October 1978), 313-334.

CAMPBELL, D. & STANLEY, J. Experimental and Quasi-Experimental Designs for Research. Chicago: Rand McNally, 1963.

CAMPBELL, KARLYN KOHRS.  "The Ontological Foundations of Rhetorical Inquiry."
    Philosophy and Rhetoric, 3 (1970), 97-108.

----------.  Critiques of Contemporary Rhetoric.  Belmont, California:
    Wadsworth, 1972.

CAPP, GLENN R., ed.  Famous Speeches in American History.  Indianapolis, India-
    na: Bobbs-Merrill, 1963.

CARROLL, J.M. & BEVER, T.G.  "Segmentation in Cinema Perception."  Science,
    191 (12 March 1976), 1053-1055.

CASTENEDA, CARLOS.  A Seperate Reality:  Further Conversations With Don Juan.
    New York:  Pocket Books, 1971.

----------.  Journey to Ixtlan:  The Lessons of Don Juan.  New York:  Pocket
    Books, 1972.

----------.  Tales of Power.  New York:  Pocket Books, 1974.

CATHCART, ROBERT.  "New Approaches to the Study of Movements:  Defining
    Movements Rhetorically."  Western Speech, 36 (Spring 1972).

CAWS, PETER.  The Philosophy of Science.  Princeton:  Princeton University
    Press, 1965.

CHALFEN, RICHARD & HALEY, JAY.  "Reactions to Socio-Documentary Film Research
    in a Mental Health Clinic."  American Journal of Orthopsychiatry, 41
    (January 1971), 91-100.

CIRCOUREL, AARON V.  Cognitive Sociology:  Language and Meaning in Social
    Interaction.  New York:  Free Press, 1974.

COLE, STEWART G.  The History of Fundamentalism.  Westport:  Greenwood Press
    Publishers, 1931.

COPLESTON, FREDERICK.  Contemporary Philosophy.  2d Ed.  Paramus, N.Y.:
    Newman, 1972.

CRANDELL, S. JUDSON.  "The Beginnings of a Methodology for Social Movement
    Studies in Public Address."  The Quarterly Journal of Speech, 33
    (February 1947), pp. 36-39.

CRONEN, V. & DAVIS, L.  "Alternative Approaches for the Communication Theorist:
    Problems in the Laws-Rules-Systems Trichotomy."  Human Communication
    Research, 4 (1978), 120-128.

CULLER, JONATHAN.  "Phenomenology and Structuralism."  Human Context, 5
    (1973).

----------.  Structuralist Poetics:  Structuralism, Linguistics, and the Study
    of Literature.  Ithaca, New York:  Cornell University, 1975.

CUSHMAN, DONALD P. & WHITING, G.C.  "An Approach to Communication Theory:
    Toward Consensus on Rules."  Journal of Communication, 22 (1972).

DEETZ, STANLEY. "Words Without Things: Toward a Social Phenomenology of Language." Quarterly Journal of Speech, 59 (1973), 40-51.

----------. "An Understanding of Science and a Hermeneutic Science of Understanding." Journal of Communication, 23 (1973), 139-159.

----------. "Structuralism: A Summary of Its Assumptive and Conceptual Bases." The Review of Social Theory, 2 (April 1973), 138-163.

----------. "Interpretive Research in Communication." Journal of Communication Inquiry, 3 (Summer 1977), 53-59.

----------. "Conceptualizing Human Understanding: Gadamer's Hermeneutics and American Communication Research." Communication Quarterly, 26 (1978), 12-23.

DEMOS, R., ed. Plato: Selections. New York: Scribner's Sons, 1927.

DeGEORGE, RICHARD T. & DeGEORGE, FERNANDE M., eds. The Structuralists: From Marx to Levi-Strauss. Garden City, New York: Anchor-Doubleday, 1972.

DELIA, JESSE G. "The Development of Communicative Behavior." Handbook of Rhetorical and Communication Theory, eds. Carroll C. Arnold & John Waite Bowers. Boston: Allyn and Bacon, forthcoming.

----------, & GROSSBERG, L. "Interpretation and Evidence." Western Journal of Speech Communication, 41 (1977), 32-42.

DENZIN, N. The Research Act: A Theoretical Introduction to Sociological Methods. Chicago: Aldine Publishing, 1970.

DERRIDA, JACQUES. Speech and Phenomena: And Other Essays on Husserl's Theory of Signs, trans. David B. Allison. Evanston: Northwestern University Press, 1973.

----------. Positions. Paris, 1972.

----------. Of Grammatology, trans. Gayatri Chakrovorty Spivak. Baltimore: The Johns Hopkins University Press, 1976.

DE SAUSSURE, FERDINAND. Course in General Linguistics (1916), ed. Charles Bally & Albert Sechehaye, trans. Wade Baskin. New York: Philosophical Library, 1959.

DEUTSCH, RICHARD. Mairead Corrigan Betty Williams. Woodbury, New York: Barron's, 1977.

DIXON, AMZI CLARENCE & TORREY, REUBEN A. The Fundamentals: A Testimony to the Truth. Chicago: Testimony Publishing Company, 1909-1912.

DORFMAN, ARIEL & MATTELART, ARMAND. How To Read Donald Duck: Imperialist Ideology in the Disney Comic, trans. David Kunzel. New York: International General, 1975.

DOUGLAS, JACK D. & JOHNSON, JOHN M., eds. Existential Sociology. Cambridge: Cambridge University Press, 1977.

ECO, UMBERTO. A Theory of Semiotics. Bloomington: Indiana University, 1976.

EDELMAN, MURRAY. Politics as Symbolic Action: Mass Arousal and Quiescence. New York: Academic Press, 1971.

EDIE, JAMES M. Speaking and Meaning: The Phenomenology of Language. Bloomington: Indiana University Press, 1976.

EVANS, DONALD D. The Logic of Self-Involvement. London: SCM Press Ltd., 1963.

FABRIZIO, RAY, EDITH KARAS, & RUTH MENMUIR, eds. The Rhetoric of No. New York: Holt, Rinehart, and Winston, 1974.

FARRELL, THOMAS & AUNE, JAMES. "Critical Theory and Communication: A Selective Literature Review." Quarterly Journal of Speech, 65 (1979), 93-120.

FEUER, L., ed. Marx and Engels: Basic Writings on Politics and Philosophy. Garden City, New York: Doubleday and Company, 1959.

FILMER, PAUL. "On Harold Garfinkel's Ethnomethodology." New Directions in Sociological Theory, ed. Paul Filmer, Michael Phillipson, David Silverman, and David Walsh. Cambridge: The M.I.T. Press, 1972.

FINCH, CHRISTOPHER. The Art of Walt Disney: From Mickey Mouse to the Magic Kingdoms. New York: Harry N. Abrams, Inc., 1973.

FISHER, B. AUBREY. "Decision Emergence: Phases in Group Decision-Making." Speech Monographs, 37 (1970).

----------. Perspectives on Human Communication. New York: Macmillan, 1978.

FISHER, WALTER R. "A Motive View of Communication." The Quarterly Journal of Speech (April 1970).

FRENTZ, THOMAS S. & FARRELL, THOMAS B. "Language-Action: A Paradigm for Communication." Quarterly Journal of Speech 62, 4 (1976), 333-349.

FURNISS, NORMAN F. The Fundamentalist Controversy, 1918-1931. New Haven: Hale University Press.

GADAMER, HANS-GEORG. "Practical Philosophy as a Model of the Human Sciences." Research in Phenomenology, 9 (1979), 74-86.

----------. Wahrheit und Methode. 2d Ed. Tubingen: J.C.B. Mohr, 1965.

----------. Truth and Method, ed. and trans. Garrett Barden and John Cummings. New York: Seabury Press, 1975.

GARFINKEL, HAROLD. Studies in Ethnomethodology. Englewood Cliffs, New Jersey: Prentice-Hall, 1967.

----------, & SACKS, HARVEY. "On Formal Structures of Practical Actions." Theoretical Sociology: Perspectives and Developments, ed. J.C. McKinney and E.A. Tiryakian. New York: Appleton-Century-Crofts, 1970.

GEBSER, JEAN. "The Four Mutations of Consciousness." Origin and Presence, trans. Algis Mickunas and Noel Barnstad. Athens, Ohio: Ohio University Press.

GERGEN, K. "Social Psychology as History." Journal of Personality and Social Psychology, 26 (1973), 304-320.

GIDDENS, ANTHONY. Central Problems in Social Theory. Berkeley: University of California Press, 1979.

GIORGI, A. "Toward Phenomenologically Based Research in Psychology." Journal of Phenomenological Psychology, 1 (1970), 75-98.

----------, William F. Fischer, and Rolf Von Eckartsberg, eds. Duquesne Studies in Phenomenological Psychology: Vol. I. Pittsburgh: Duquesne University Press, 1971.

----------. "Convergences and Differences Between Phenomenological Psychology and Behaviorism: A Beginning Dialog." Behaviorism, 3 (1975), 200-212.

GOFFMAN, ERVING. The Presentation of Self in Everyday Life. Garden City, New Jersey: Anchor Books, 1959.

----------. Encounters: Two Studies in the Sociology of Interaction. Indianapolis: Bobbs-Merrill Co., 1961.

----------. Interaction Ritual: Essays on Face-to-Face Behavior. Garden City, New Jersey: Anchor Books, 1967.

----------. Relations in Public: Microstudies of the Public Order. New York: Harper Colophon Books, 1971.

----------. Strategic Interaction. Philadelphia: University of Pennsylvania Press, 1969.

GOLDBERG, HERMAN D. "The Role of 'Cutting' in the Perception of the Motion Picture." Journal of Applied Psychology, 35 (1951).

GOODHEART, EUGENE. "The Rhetoric of Violence." World Politics: Essays on Language and Politics, ed. Max J. Skidmore. Palo Alto: Freel, 1972.

GOULDNER, ALVIN. The Dialectic and Ideology and Technology. New York: Seabury, 1976.

GOURAN, DENNIS S. "Variables Related to Consensus in Group Discussions of Questions of Policy." Speech Monographs, 36 (1969), 387-391.

GREENWAY, JOHN. "Introduction." The Anthropologist Looks at Myth. Austin: University of Texas Press, 1966.

GREGG, RICHARD B. "A Phenomenologically Oriented Approach to Rhetorical Criticism." Central States Speech Journal, (May 1966).

GRICE, H.P. "Meaning." Philosophical Review, LXVI (1957), 377-388.

GRIFFIN, LELAND M. "The Rhetoric of Historical Movements." The Quarterly Journal of Speech, 38 (April 1952), 184-188.

GRIFFIN, LELAND M.  "The Rhetorical Structure of the New Left Movement:  Part I."  The Quarterly Journal of Speech, 50 (April 1964), 131-135.

GRONBECK, BRUCE E.  "Rhetorical History and Rhetorical Criticism:  A Distinction."  Speech Teacher, 24 (1975).

GROSSBERG, LAWRENCE.  "Language and Theorizing."  Studies in Symbolic Interaction, Vol. 2, ed. Norman K. Denzin.  Greenwich, Connecticut:  J.A.I. Press, forthcoming.

GUSDORF, GEORGES.  Speaking (La Parole).  Evanston:  Northwestern University Press, 1965.

HABERMAS, JURGEN.  "Toward a Theory of Communicative Competence."  Inquiry, 13 (1970), 360-375.

----------.  "On Systematically Distorted Communication."  Inquiry, 13 (1970), 205-218.

----------.  Toward a Rational Society, trans. J. Shapiro.  Boston:  Beacon Press, 1970.

----------.  Theory and Practice.  London:  Heinemann, 1974.

----------.  "Some Distinctions in Universal Pragmatics:  A Working Paper."  Theory and Society, 3 (1976), 155-167.

----------.  "Hannah Arendt's Communications Concept of Power," trans. Thomas McCarthy.  Social Research, 44 (1977), 4.

HAHN, DAN F. & GONCHAR, RUTH M.  "Studying Social Movements:  A Rhetorical Methodology."  The Speech Teacher, 20 (1971).

HANS, JAMES S.  "Hans-Georg Gadamer and Hermeneutic Phenomenology."  Philosophy Today, 22 (1978), 3-19.

----------.  "Hermeneutics, Play, Deconstruction."  Philosophy Today, 24 (1980), 299-317.

HARRE, R.  The Philosophy of Science.  London:  Oxford University Press, 1972.

----------, & SECORD, P.F.  The Explanation of Social Behavior.  Totowa, New Jersey:  Littlefield, Adams & Co., 1973.

HARRELL, JACKSON & LINKUGEL, WIL A.  "On Rhetorical Genre:  An Organizing Perspective."  Philosophy and Rhetoric, 12 (1978), 262-270.

HAWES, LEONARD C.  "The Effects of Interviewer Style on Patterns of Dyadic Communication."  Speech Monographs, 39 (1972), 114-123.

----------.  "Elements of a Model for Communication Processes."  Quarterly Journal of Speech, 59 (1973), 11-21.

----------.  "How Writing is Used in Talk:  A Study of Communicative Logic-in-Use."  Quarterly Journal of Speech, 62 (December, 1976), 350-360.

HEATH, G. LOUIS, ed. Mutiny Does Not Happen Lightly: The Literature of the American Resistence to the War. Metuchen: Scarecrow Press, 1976.

HEAP, JAMES L. & ROTH, PHILLIP A. "On Phenomenological Sociology." American Sociological Review, 38 (1973).

HEIDEGGER, MARTIN. Being and Time, trans. John Macquarrie and Edward Robinson. New York: Harper and Row, Publishers, 1962.

----------. "The Origin of the Work of Art." Philosophies of Art and Beauty, ed. Albert Hofstadter and Richard Kuhn. New York: Modern Library, 1964.

----------. On the Way to Language, trans. Peter Hertz. New York: Harper and Row, 1971.

HEINTEL, ERICH. Einfuhrung in die Sprachphilosophie. Darmstadt: Wissenschaftliche Buchgesellschaft, 1972.

HEWES, DEAN. "The Sequential Analysis of Social Interaction." Quarterly Journal of Speech, 65 (1970), 56-73.

HOPKINS, MARY FRANCES. "Structuralism: Its Implications for Performance of Prose Fiction." Communication Monographs, 44 (1977), 93-105.

HOLENSTEIN, ELMAR. Roman Jakobson's Approach to Language: Phenomenological Structuralism, trans. Catherine and Tarcisius Schelbert. Bloomington: Indiana University Press, 1974.

HOW, ALAN R. "Dialogue as Productive Limitation in Social Theory: The Habermas-Gadamer Debate." Journal of the British Society for Phenomenology, 11 (1980), 144-162.

HOWARD, DICK. The Marxian Legacy. New York: Urizen Books, 1977.

HOY, DAVID COUZENS. The Critical Circle: Literature and History in Contemporary Hermeneutics. Berkeley: University of California Press, 1968.

HUSSERL, EDMUND. Experience and Judgment: Investigations in a Geneology of Logic. Ed. Ludwig Landgrebe. Evanston: Northwestern University Press, 1973.

----------. The Idea of Phenomenology, trans. William P. Alston and George Nakhnikian. The Hague: Martinos Nijhoff, 1973.

HUTCHESON, PETER. "Husserl's Problem of Intersubjectivity." Journal of the British Society for Phenomenology, 11 (1980), 144-162.

HYDE, MICHAEL & SMITH, CRAIG. "Hermeneutics and Rhetoric: A Seen but Unobserved Relationship." Quarterly Journal of Speech, 65 (1979), 347-363.

----------. "Philosophical Hermeneutics and the Communicative Experience: the Paradigm of Oral History." Man and World, 13 (1980), 81-98.

IDHE, DON. Experimental Phenomenology: An Introduction. New York: Capricorn, 1977.

IJSSELING, SAMUEL. "Hermeneutics and Textuality." Research in Phenomenology, 9 (1979), 1-16.

ISENHOUR, JOHN PRESTON. "The Effects of Context and Order in Film Editing." AV Communication Review, 23 (Spring 1975), 69-80.

JAMESON, F. Marxism and Form. Princeton: Princeton University Press, 1971.

JONES, W.T. A History of Western Philosophy. New York: Harcourt, Brace, Jovanovich, 1975.

KERLINGER, F. Foundations Of Behavioral Research. 2d Ed. New York: Holt, Rinehart and Winston, 1973.

KLUCKHOHN, CLYDE. Culture and Behavior: Collected Essays of Clyde Kluckhohn, ed. Richard Kluckhohn. New York: Free Press, 1962.

KOCKELMANS, JOSEPH H. "What is Phenomenology?" Phenomenology: The Philosophy of Edmund Husserl and Its Interpretation, ed. Joseph Kockelmans. Garden City, New York: Anchor Books, 1967.

KRISTEVA, JULIA. The Systems and The Speaking Subject. Atlantic Highlands, New Jersey: Humanities, 1976.

LABOV, W. & FANSELL, D. Therapeutic Discourse. New York: Academic Press, 1977.

LANDGREBE, LUDWIG. "The Phenomenological Concept of Experience." Philosophy and Phenomenological Research, 34 (1973).

LANIGAN, RICHARD L. Speaking and Semiology: Maurice Merleau-Ponty's Phenomenological Theory of Existential Communication. The Hague: Mouton, 1972.

----------. Speech Act Phenomenology. The Hague: Martinus Nijhoff, 1977.

----------. "A Semiotic Metatheory of Human Communication." Semiotica, 27 (1979), 293-305.

----------. "Phenomenology of Human Communication." Philosophy Today, 23 (Spring 1979), 3-15.

LANGAN, THOMAS. Merleau-Ponty's Critique of Reason. New Haven: Yale University Press, 1966.

LANGER, S. Philosophy in a New Key: A Study in the Symbolism of Reason, Rite, and Art. 3d Ed. Cambridge: Harvard University Press, 1960.

LASCH, C. Haven in a Heartless World. New York: Basic Books, 1975.

LAUER, J. QUENTIN. The Triumph of Subjectivity: An Introduction to Transcendental Phenomenology. New York: Fordham University Press, 1958.

LAWRENCE, NATHANIEL & O'CONNOR, DANIEL, eds. Readings in Existential Phenomenology. Englewood Cliffs, New Jersey: Prentice-Hall, 1967.

LEFEVRE, HENRI. The Sociology of Marx. London: Penguin, 1972.

LEMERT, CHARLES C. Sociology and the Twilight of Man: Homocentrism and Discourse in Sociological Theory. Carbondale: Southern Illinois University Press, 1979.

LEVI-STRAUSS, CLAUDE. The Savage Mind. Chicago: University of Chicago Press, 1966.

LEVINAS, E. Totality and Infinity. Pittsburgh: Duquesne University Press, 1969.

LUIJPEN, WILLIAM. Phenomenology and Humanism: A Primer in Existential Phenomenology. Pittsburgh: Duquesne University Press, 1966.

LYNCH, DENNIS F. "Clozentropy: A New Technique for Analyzing Audience Response to Film." Speech Monographs, 41 (1974), 245-252.

MARCUSE, HERBERT. Reason and Revolution. 2d Ed. Boston: Beacon Press, 1960.

----------. One-Dimensional Man. Boston: Beacon Press, 1964.

MARX, KARL. Capital, Vol. 1, trans. S. Moore and E. Aveling. New York: International Publishers, 1967.

MARX, WERNER. Heidegger and the Tradition. Evanston: Northwestern University Press, 1971.

MASLOW, ABRAHAM. Motivation and Personality. New York: Harper, 1954.

MATHEWS, SHAILER. "Fundamentalism and Modernism." American Review, 2 (1924).

McCARTHY, THOMAS A. "A Theory of Communicative Competence." Critical Sociology, ed. Paul Connerton. London: Penguin Press, 1976.

McGUIGAN, F. Experimental Psychology: A Methodological Approach. 2d Ed. Englewood Cliffs, New Jersey: Prentice-Hall, 1968.

McHOUL, ALEXANDER. "Ethnomethodology and Literature: Preliminaries to a Sociology of Reading." Poetics, 7 (1978), 113-120.

MEHAN, HUGH & WOOD, HUSTON. The Reality of Ethnomethodology. New York: Wiley-Interscience, 1975.

METZ, CHRISTIAN. Film Language: A Semiotics of the Cinema, trans. Michael Taylor. New York: Oxford University Press, 1974.

MERLEAU-PONTY, MAURICE. Phenomenology of Perception, trans. Colin Smith, ed. Ted Honderich. London: Routledge and Kegan Paul, 1962.

----------. In Praise of Philosophy, trans. John Wild and James M. Edie. Evanston: Northwestern University Press, 1964.

----------. "On the Phenomenology of Language," trans. Richard C. Cleary. Signs. Evanston: Northwestern University Press, 1964.

----------. "The Child's Relations with Others." The Primacy of Perception and Other Essays, ed. James M. Edie. Evanston: Northwestern University Press, 1964.

MERLEAU-PONTY, MAURICE.  The Prose of the World, trans. John O'Neill.  Evan-
    ston:  Northwestern University Press, 1973.

----------.  Consciousness and the Acquisition of Language, trans. Hugh Silver-
    man.  Evanston:  Northwestern University Press, 1973.

MILLER, G. & NICHOLSON, H.  Communication Inquiry:  A Perspective on a
    Process.  Reading, Massachusetts:  Addison-Wesley, 1976.

----------.  "The Current Status of Theory and Research in Interpersonal
    Communication."  Human Communication Research, 4 (1978), 164-178.

MISHLER, ELLIOT.  "Meaning in Context:  Is There Any Other Kind?"  Harvard
    Educational Review, 49 (1979).

MORRISON, JAMES C.  "Husserl and Bretano On Intentionality."  Philosophy and
    Phenomenological Research, 31 (1970).

MORTON, A.Q. & WINSPEAR, A.D.  "The Computer and Plato's Seventh Letter."
    Computer and the Humanities, 1 (1966).

MOULTON, RICHARD G.  The Bible at a Single View.  New York:  MacMillan Co.,
    1918.

MUELLER, CLAUS.  The Politics of Communication:  A Study in the Political
    Sociology of Language, Socialization, and Legitimation.  New York:
    Oxford University Press, 1975.

NATANSON, MAURICE.  Literature, Philosophy, and the Social Sciences.  The
    Hague:  Martinus Nijhoff, 1962.

----------, & JOHNSTONE, HENRY W., eds.  Philosophy, Rhetoric and Argumentation.
    University Park:  Pennsylvania State University Press, 1965.

----------.  Phenomenology, Role, and Reason.  Springfield, Illinois:  Charles
    C. Thomas Publishers, 1974.

NELSON, HAROLD E.  "The Relative Contribution to Learning of Video and Audio
    Elements in Films."  Speech Monographs, 18 (1951), 70-73.

NICHOLS, MARIE HOCHMUTH.  Rhetoric and Criticism.  Baton Rouge:  Louisiana
    State University Press, 1963.

----------.  "Lincoln's First Inaugural."  Methods of Rhetorical Criticism,
    ed. Robert L. Scott and Bernard L. Brock.  New York:  Harper and Row, 1972.

NOFSINGER, ROBERT E., JR.  "The Demand Ticket:  A Conversational Device for
    Getting the Floor."  Speech Monographs, 42 (1975), 1-9.

----------.  "On Answering Questions Indirectly:  Some Rules in the Grammar of
    Doing Conversation."  Human Communication Research, 2 (1976), 172-181.

NORRIS, J. FRANK.  Voices of American Fundamentalism, ed. C. Allyn Russell.
    Philadelphia:  Westminister Press, 1976.

O'NEILL, JOHN, ed.  On Critical Theory.  New York:  Seabury, 1976.

OLSON, D. & CROMWELL, R., eds. <u>Power in Families</u>. New York:  Sage, 1975.

----------. "Insiders' and Outsiders' Views of Relationship:  Research Studies." <u>Close Relationships:  Perspectives on the Meaning of Intimacy</u>, ed. G. Levinger and H. Raush. Amherst, Massachusetts:  University of Massachusetts Press, 1977.

ONG, WALTER. "World as View and World as Event." <u>Intercommunication Among Nations and Peoples</u>, ed. Michael H. Prosser. New York:  Harper and Row, 1973.

----------. <u>The Presence of the Word</u>. New Haven:  Yale University Press, 1973.

----------. <u>The Barbarian Within</u>. New York:  Macmillan, 1962.

PALMER, RICHARD. "Hermeneutics." <u>Chronicles 1966-1978</u>, Institute Internationale de Philosophie, Paris, Vol. 2: <u>Philosophy of Science</u>, ed. Guttorm Fløistad. The Hague:  Martinus Nijhoff, 1980.

----------. "What are We Doing When We Interpret a Text?" <u>Eros:  A Journal of Philosophy and the Literary Arts</u>, 1980.

PEARCE, W.B. "Metatheoretical Concerns in Communication." <u>Communication Quarterly</u>, 25 (1977), 3-6.

PERELMAN, CHAIM & OLBRECHTS-TYTECA, L. <u>The New Rhetoric:  A Treatise on Argumentation</u>, trans. John Wilkinson and Purcell Weaver. Notre Dame:  University of Notre Dame Press, 1969.

POCOCK, J.G.A. <u>Politics, Language and Time:  Essays on Thought and History</u>. New York:  Atheneum, 1971.

----------. "Verbalizing a Political Act:  Toward a Politics of Speech." <u>Political Theory</u>, 1 (1973), 30.

PSATHAS, GEORGE, ed. <u>Phenomenological Sociology:  Issues and Applications</u>. New York:  John Wiley and Sons, 1973.

RABINOW, PAUL & SULLIVAN, WILLIAM, eds. <u>Interpretive Social Science</u>. Berkeley:  University of California Press, 1979.

RAVAL, R.K. "An Essay on Phenomenology." <u>Philosophy and Phenomenological Research</u>, 33 (December 1972), 219-221.

RICHARDS, I.A. <u>Practical Criticism:  A Study of Literary Judgment</u>. New York:  Harcourt, Brace and World, Inc., 1929.

RICKMAN, H.P. "Rhetoric and Hermeneutics." <u>Philosophy and Rhetoric</u>, 14 (1981), 100-111.

ROCHE, MAURICE. <u>Phenomenology, Language, and the Social Sciences</u>. London:  Routledge and Kegan Paul, 1973.

ROMANYSHYN, R. "Metaphors and Human Behavior." <u>Journal of Phenomenological Psychology</u>, 5 (1975), 441-460.

ROSENFIELD, LAWRENCE W. "The Anatomy of Critical Discourse." Speech Monographs, 15 (March 1968), 50-69.

----------. "The Experience of Criticism." Quarterly Journal of Speech, 60 (1974).

ROSENTHAL, R. & ROSNOW, R., eds. Artifact in Behavioral Research. New York: Academic Press, 1969.

ROSZAK, THEODORE. The Making of a Counter Culture. New York: Anchor Books, 1968.

RUBIN, JERRY. Do It: Scenarios of the Revolution. New York: Simon and Schuster, 1970.

RUSSELL, C. ALLYN. "Conclusion." Voices of American Fundamentalism. Philadelphia: Westminister Press, 1976.

SACKS, HARVEY, EMMANUEL SCHEGLOFF, GAIL JEFFERSON. "A Simplest Systematics for the Organization of Turn Taking for Conversation." Language, 50 (1974), 695-735.

SAGER, ALLAN H. "Modernists and Fundamentalists Debate Restraints on Freedom, 1910-1930." America in Controversy: History of American Public Address, ed. Dewitte Holland. Dubuque: Wm. C. Brown Publishers, 1973.

SARTRE, JEAN-PAUL. Being and Nothingness, trans. Hazel E. Barnes. New York: Simon and Schuster, 1978.

SCHEGLOFF, EMMANUEL, GAIL JEFFERSON, HARVEY SACKS. "The Preference for Self-Correction in the Organization of Repair in Conversation." Language, 53 (1977), 361-382.

SCHENKEIN, JIM. "Sketch of an Analytic Mentality for the Study of Conversational Interaction." Studies in the Organization of Conversational Interaction, ed. Jim Schenkein. New York: Academic Press, 1978.

SCHICKEL, RICHARD. The Disney Version: The Life, Times, Art, and Commerce of Walt Disney. New York: Simon and Schuster, 1968.

SCHMITT, RICHARD. "Phenomenology." Encyclopedia of Philosophy, ed. Paul Edwards. New York: Macmillan, 1977.

SCHRAG, CALVIN O. Experience and Being: Prolegomena to a Future Ontology. Evanston: Northwestern University, 1969.

----------. Radical Reflection and the Origin of the Human Sciences. West Lafayette, Indiana: Purdue University Press, 1980.

SCHUTZ, ALFRED. "Concepts and Theory Formation in the Social Sciences." Journal of Philosophy, 51 (1954), 257-273.

----------. The Phenomenology of the Social World, trans. George Walsh and Frederick Lehnert. Evanston: Northwestern University Press, 1967.

----------. Collected Papers I: The Problem of Social Reality, ed. Maurice Natanson. The Hague: Martinus Nijhoff, 1973.

SCHUTZ, ALFRED & LUCKMANN, THOMAS. The Structures of the Everyday Life-World, trans. Richard M. Zaner and H. Tristam Engelhardt, Jr. Evanston: Northwestern University Press, 1973.

SCHWARTZ, GARY & MERTEN, DON. "Participant Observation and the Discovery of Meaning." Philosophy of the Social Sciences, 1 (1971), 279-298.

SEARLE, JOHN R. Speech Acts: An Essay in the Philosophy of Language. London: Cambridge University Press, 1969.

SEEBOHM, THOMAS. "The Problem of Hermeneutics in Recent Anglo-American Literature." Philosophy and Rhetoric, "Part I" 10 (1977), 180-198, and "Part II" 10 (1977), 263-275.

SHAW, M. & CONSTANZO, P. Theories of Social Psychology. New York: McGraw-Hill, 1970.

SHERMAN, HOWARD. "Dialectics as Method." Insurgent Sociologist, iv (1976), 57-64.

SIEBERT, RUDOLPH J. From Critical Theory of Society to Theology of Communicative Praxis. Washington, D.C.: University Press of America, 1979.

SILVERMAN, HUGH J. "For a Hermeneutic Semiology of the Self." Philosophy Today, 23 (1979), 199-204.

----------. "Self-Decentering: Derrida Incorporated." Research in Phenomenology, 8 (1978), 45-65.

SIMONS, HERBERT W. "Requirements, Problems, and Strategies: A Theory of Persuasion for Social Movements." The Quarterly Journal of Speech, 56 (February 1970).

SLATER, PHIL. The Origin and Significance of the Frankfurt School. London: Routledge and Kegan Paul, 1977.

SMART, BARRY. Sociology, Phenomenology, and Marxian Analysis: A Critical Discussion of the Theory and Practice of a Science of Society. London: Routledge and Kegan Paul, 1976.

SMITH, P. CHRISTOPHER. "Gadamer's Hermeneutics and Ordinary Language Philosophy." The Thomist, 43 (1979), 296-321.

SMITH, DAVID H. "Communication Research and the Idea of Process." Speech Monographs, 29 (August 1972).

SMITH, HUSTON. Condemned to Meaning. New York: Harper and Row, 1965.

SMITH, RALPH R. & WINDES, RUSSEL R. "The Rhetoric of Mobilization: Implications for the Study of Social Movements." Southern Speech Journal, 42 (Fall 1976).

SPEIER, MATTHEW. How to Observe Face-To-Face Communication: A Sociological Introduction. Pacific Palisades, California: Goodyear Publishing Co., 1973.

SPIELEBURG, HERBERT. The Phenomenological Movement:  A Historical Introduction, Vo Vol. I.  2d Ed.  The Hague:  Martinus Nijhoff, 1969.

STECH, ERNEST L.  "An Analysis of Interaction Structure in the Discussion of a Ranking Task."  Speech Monographs, 37 (1970), 249-256.

STEWART, JOHN.  "Foundations of Dialogic Communication."  Quarterly Journal of Speech, 64 (1978), 183-201.

SUNDOW, DAVID, ed.  Studies in Social Interaction.  New York:  Free Press, 1967.

SULLIVAN, WILLIAM M.  "Communication and the Recovery of Meaning:  An Interpretation of Habermas."  International Philosophical Quarterly, 18 (1978), 69-86.

TALLENTIRE, D.R.  "Towards an Archive of Lexical Norms.  A Proposal."  The Computer and Literary Studies, ed. A.J. Aitken, R.W. Bailey, and N. Hamilton-Smith.  Chicago:  Aldne Atherton Inc., 1973.

TEJERA, V.  "Cultural Analysis and Interpretation in the Human Sciences."  Man and World, 12 (1979), 192-204.

THAYER, LEE.  "Knowledge, Order, and Communication."  General Systems Theory and Human Communication, ed. Brent Rubin and John Kim.  Rochelle Park, New Jersey:  Hayden Book Co., 1975.

TOLHURST, WILLIAM E. "On Textual Individuation."  Philosophical Studies, 35 (1979), 187-197.

----------.  "On What a Text Is and How It Means."  British Journal of Aesthetics, 19 (1979), 3-14.

TONELLI, FRANCO & HUBERT, JUDD.  "Theatricality:  The Burden of the Text."  Sub-Stance, 21 (1979), 79-102.

TRIANDIS, HARRY C.  The Analysis of Subjective Culture.  New York:  Wiley, 1972.

TRIMBLE, JOSEPH.  "The Sojourner in the American Indian Community:  Methodological Issues and Concerns."  Journal of Social Issues, 33 (1977), 159-174.

UNGER, IRWIN.  The Movement:  A History of the American New Left:  1959-1972.  New York:  Harper and Row, 1974.

VALLE, RONALD S. & KING, MARK, eds.  Existential-Phenomenological Alternatives for Psychology.  New York:  Oxford University Press, 1978.

VAN VALIN, ROBERT D., JR.  "Meaning and Interpretation."  Journal of Pragmatics, 4 (1980), 213-231.

WARWICK, D. & LININGER, C.  The Sample Survey:  Theory and Practice.  New York:  McGraw-Hill, 1973.

WEBER, MAX.  Wirtschaft and Gesellschaft.  Tubingen:  J.C.B. Mohr, 1925.

WELLMER, ALBRECHT. "Communication and Emancipation: Reflections on the Linguistic Turn in Critical Theory." On Critical Theory, ed. John O'Neill. New York: Seabury, 1976.

WHITEHEAD, ALFRED NORTH. Process and Reality. New York: Macmillan, 1929.

WIATR, J.J. "Sociology--Marxism--Reality." Marxism and Sociology, ed. Peter Berger. New York: Appleton-Century-Crofts, 1969.

WILDEN, ANTHONY. System and Structure: Essays in Communication and Exchange. London: Tavistock, 1972.

WILLIAMS, BERNARD. "Tertullian's Paradox." New Essays in Philosophical Theology, ed. Anthony Flew and Alasdair MacIntyre. London: Cambridge University Press, 1965.

WILLIAMS, ROBERT C. "Film Shots and Expressed Interest Levels." Speech Monographs, 35 (1968), 166-169.

WINDT, THEODORE OTTO, JR. "The Diatribe: Last Resort for Protest." The Quarterly Journal of Speech, 58 (1972), 1-14.

WOODWARD, GARY C. "Mystifications in the Rhetoric of Cultural Dominance and Colonial Control." Central States Speech Journal, 26 (1975).

WORTH, SOL. "Cognitive Aspects of Sequence in Visual Communication." AV Communication Review, 16 (1968), 121-145.

WORTH, SOL & ADAIR, JOHN. Through Navajo Eyes: An Exploration In Film Communication and Anthropology. Bloomington: Indiana University Press, 1972.

ZIMMERMAN, DON H. "Ethnomethodology." The American Sociologist, 13 (1978), 6-15.

# INDEX OF NAMES

# INDEX OF TOPICS